THE SEA WAS
IN THEIR BLOOD

The Disappearance of the
Miss Ally's Five-Man Crew

Quentin Casey

NIMBUS
PUBLISHING

Nimbus Publishing Limited
3731 Mackintosh St, Halifax, NS B3K 5A5
(902) 455-4286 nimbus.ca

Printed and bound in Canada
NB1230
Design: Jenn Embree
Cover art: Werner Wirth

Library and Archives Canada Cataloguing in Publication

Casey, Quentin, 1980-, author
The sea was in their blood : the disappearance of the
Miss Ally's five-man crew / Quentin Casey.

Issued in print and electronic formats.
ISBN 978-1-77108-479-6 (softcover).—ISBN 978-1-77108-480-2
(HTML)

1. Miss Ally (Fishing boat). 2. Marine accidents—Nova Scotia.
3. Fishers—Nova Scotia. I. Title.

VK199 C37 2017   363.12'36509716   C2016-908008-0
                                      C2016-908009-9

Nimbus Publishing acknowledges the financial support for its publishing activities from the Government of Canada through the Canada Book Fund (CBF) and the Canada Council for the Arts, and from the Province of Nova Scotia. We are pleased to work in partnership with the Province of Nova Scotia to develop and promote our creative industries for the benefit of all Nova Scotians.

"THE OCEAN WAS LIKE AN UNCARING GOD, ENDLESSLY DANGEROUS, POWER BEYOND MEASURE."

—William Finnegan, *Barbarian Days*

CONTENTS

PROLOGUE

GEORGE HOPKINS IS CONCERNED. THE WIND IS BLOWING HARD IN THE darkness outside his house in Woods Harbour, a fishing community on Nova Scotia's south shore. And the weather is getting worse. The gusts are increasing in power, and snow will soon blow in off the cold dark Atlantic Ocean, reducing visibility and making conditions treacherous.

George's son Joel is far from Woods Harbour on this brutal Sunday night in February 2013, offshore on a boat called the *Miss Ally*. Joel, twenty-seven, is aboard with four other men: Billy Jack Hatfield, thirty-three; Cole Nickerson, twenty-eight; Tyson Townsend, twenty-five; and the boat's twenty-one-year-old owner and captain, Katlin Nickerson. They've been longlining for halibut south of LaHave Bank, nearly 200 kilometres from Halifax, in an area called "the Edge," where the continental shelf falls off to deeper water.

February is a risky time of year to fish offshore, particularly in a twelve-metre (40-foot) open-stern Cape Islander. But this is when the price of halibut is best, because fewer fishermen want to go to sea to get it.

Two days earlier, on Friday, February 15, weather forecasts from Environment Canada predicted winds of 50 knots (90 kilometres an hour) would hit by Sunday afternoon. Shortly after midnight yesterday—Saturday—Environment Canada meteorologists warned that gale- and storm-force winds were approaching. A low-pressure system, churning toward eastern Canada from Cape Hatteras, North Carolina, was intensifying and expected to lie over Nova Scotia on Sunday night. By Sunday evening, as George Hopkins sits worrying in Woods Harbour, a storm warning has been in effect for most Nova Scotia waters for nearly forty-eight hours.

The worsening forecast has prompted other local boats to haul in their longlining gear and steam for shore. Aboard the *Miss Ally*, technical troubles prevented the crew from securing their gear the night before. Katlin, the young captain, decided to stay offshore until this morning, haul the gear in the morning light, and then dart for home. But even that straightforward plan failed. The gear had been difficult to find, and so Katlin wasn't able to start steering for shore until late this afternoon. He's beating a very late retreat. Though the five men are now making for home, they are directly in the path of a violent storm delivering screeching winds and waves large enough to swallow boats much bigger than the *Miss Ally*.

George Hopkins is a lifelong fisherman. Although he sticks to lobstering now, he used to skipper his boats to the Grand Banks. He's been out in big storms. The weather headed toward the *Miss Ally*—toward his son, Joel—is bad. Very bad. Perhaps worse than anything he's ever been out in.

Joel absolutely loves fishing. And dirty weather. He's likely thrilled to be riding in on storm-force winds and tall waves. Cole, on the other hand, didn't want to go on this trip at all. A burly and strong former junior hockey player, Cole cried briefly before leaving, scared of what might happen. Last night, Cole and Tyson—also a former junior hockey player and now the father of a seven-month-old daughter—voted to abandon the longlining gear and immediately head for home, to ensure they avoided the full strength of the approaching storm. The pair was overruled. The crew stayed to retrieve the gear. Now Katlin must skipper his boat in darkness. His large overhead floodlight—essentially the boat's headlight—is dead. The lighting failure first prevented the crew from finding their gear in the water. Now it means Katlin must steer his boat blindly through wind-whipped snow and towering winter waves.

Katlin grew up just down the road from George's house in Woods Harbour; he even briefly crewed aboard George's boat. Katlin comes from a line of successful fishermen. His grandfather, Wayne, is known in Woods Harbour as "the Cod Father," a nickname he earned by landing big catches. Perhaps no one in Woods Harbour brought more fish to the wharf than Wayne. Within the industry, top fishermen are known as high liners. Wayne, before he retired, was a high liner of the first degree. Katlin's father, Todd, followed Wayne to sea and is now considered one of the area's top captains.

Katlin has also followed in the family trade and is now the youngest captain in Woods Harbour. Well-liked, good looking, and possessing a crooked grin, Katlin bought the *Miss Ally* two years ago, in 2011. He's known around the local wharves for his aggressive approach to fishing. He's "fierce," they say. That reputation has helped accelerate Katlin's career: he's only three years out of high school yet he has his own boat, a crew of men all older than him, and—most importantly—plenty of quota to chase. If he can catch the fish, he'll likely make good on what is a huge financial undertaking for a twenty-one-year-old: Katlin paid roughly $700,000 for his boat, gear, and a lobster licence. On this trip, he and the crew have caught the fish. In a call home to his grandfather Ronnie Sears, Katlin reports that there's between fifteen and twenty thousand pounds of halibut in the *Miss Ally*'s hold, worth up to $160,000. Now Katlin has to guide the fish, his crew, and the *Miss Ally* to the wharf.

Fishing is not an occupation for the skittish. It's inherently dangerous: an average of five to six fishing-related deaths occur in the province each year, according to the Fisheries Safety Association of Nova Scotia. Katlin's assertive approach has served him well so far, but it has also bled into recklessness. Joel and Billy Jack crewed for Katlin during the fall lobster season.

Just before Christmas, the trio went out to haul traps on a day so blustery that all other local crews stayed on land. At sea, a large wave hit the *Miss Ally*, covering the deck with water and nearly washing Joel and Billy Jack overboard. Earlier this month, on their first halibut trip together, the *Miss Ally* crew steamed home during a freezing gale. The experience spooked Billy Jack and Cole. For this second halibut trip, Billy Jack brought a survival suit. Cole, meanwhile, only returned out of a sense of duty and a desire to get paid for the first trip.

The recent close calls have prompted more experienced fishermen to warn Katlin: be careful. Aggressiveness is good, but it can also put you, your crew, and your boat on the bottom of the ocean.

George Hopkins knows all this. He also knows that the weather tonight is unlike anything the men aboard the *Miss Ally* have encountered before. Though young, they are all experienced fishermen. Billy Jack started fishing full-time at thirteen, after dropping out of seventh grade. But tonight he and the other men are not attempting to outrun a typical storm—these conditions are ferocious. This is not the Perfect Storm but the conditions are still violent, even "nightmarish," as Sandy Stoddard, a veteran Woods Harbour fisherman, puts it.

George picks up his phone and dials Katlin's satellite phone. George wants to know how the men are progressing. He also needs to tell Katlin that the weather in Woods Harbour has deteriorated. That means the worst of the storm has yet to hit the *Miss Ally*, which is further east.

"Katlin, it's starting to blow here," George warns.

"Oh, we had the wind and it died out," Katlin replies, his voice calm.

"No Katlin, you haven't had it yet. It was just blowing here now. It just breezed up," George says. "You haven't got this wind."

"Oh, I was hoping it was all over."

"No, no, you haven't got it," George insists.

The LaHave Bank weather buoy is located about 240 kilometres south of Halifax, slightly further offshore than the *Miss Ally*. The buoy records key weather information such as wind speed, temperature, and wave height.

Tonight the buoy is reporting winds of 45–50 knots, with gusts of more than 60 knots (110 kilometres an hour). The air temperature is below freezing and the average wave height is 8 metres. Some waves are towering as high as 15 metres.

Around 7 P.M., the LaHave Bank buoy—already heaving under the force of large rollers—is lifted up by a giant: an 18.6-metre wave. This is a rogue wave, equal in size to the largest waves recorded off Halifax during Hurricane Juan in 2003.

It's a massive, heavy, black wall of cold ocean water. And it's heading toward the *Miss Ally.*

CHAPTER ONE

THE HARD LOT OF A FISHERMAN'S LIFE

THE BANNER HEADLINE ACROSS THE TOP OF THE HALIFAX *Chronicle Herald* screamed: FIVE FEARED DROWNED.

It was Thursday, March 23, 1961. Three longliners out of Lockeport, Nova Scotia, had been caught in a vicious Atlantic storm. Searchers had spotted wreckage from one of the vessels, the 17-metre *Muriel Eileen*, and the five men aboard were presumed dead. The other two vessels, the *Jimmie & Sisters* and the *Marjorie Beryl*, were still unaccounted for. In all, seventeen fishermen were missing.

Aboard the *Marjorie Beryl* was Edward Stewart. Edward had a long history with near-death experiences: in 1942, during the Second World War, Edward was injured when his fishing boat was torpedoed. He and his crew rowed 160 kilometres to shore. Later, he nearly drowned when an anchor became tangled around his leg while he was mooring a boat. He'd also survived blood poisoning from a spider bite he received while duck hunting. Had Edward's knack for escaping sticky situations finally come to an end?

The three missing crews had been fishing on the Emerald Bank, about 200 kilometres southeast of Halifax. A fourth Lockeport boat, a dragger called the *Herbert R. Swim*, captained by Earl Benham, was nearby. Earl and his crew had been at sea for a week when the storm struck on Tuesday around 2:00 A.M. The morning winds gusted to 110 kilometres an hour. By 8 A.M. the wind had ripped off all but one of the boat's radio antennas. Earl's eleven-man crew on the *Herbert R. Swim* was able to cobble together a makeshift antenna from scavenged parts. They could hear other boats communicating but couldn't send messages of their own. Earl heard the captains of the *Jimmie & Sisters* and the *Marjorie Beryl* talking. Overpowered by the wind and waves, they were laying-to, attempting to let the storm blow over. "They didn't sound worried," Earl later recalled. Captain Benham pushed on for port and arrived in Lockeport with his boat heavily coated in ice and damaged from the storm. His fellow skippers never arrived.

Those on shore suspected that all three vessels experienced heavy icing. The combination of low temperatures, rough seas, and strong winds likely caused thick layers of ice to form on the vessels' decks. Longliners of the sixties and seventies often returned to port loaded with fish, leaving only centimetres of freeboard—the distance between the deck and the water. Heavy ice pushes a longliner lower in the water, and eventually under it.

A search party made up of Navy ships, aircraft, and a flotilla of shipping vessels combed the area, seeking any sign of the three boats. On Wednesday, March 22, a day before the *Herald*'s headline, a search boat had spotted the *Muriel Eileen*: only the boat's superstructure was above water. There was no sign of life. The next day a plane spotted an orange barrel believed to be from *the Jimmie & Sisters.* Back in Lockeport, family and friends of the missing men hovered near their marine radios, hoping desperately for good news. "We know the hard lot of a fisherman's life and its dangers," said Lockeport's mayor, Malcolm Huskilson. "We know what they have to face, and that doesn't make waiting any easier."

Between them, the seventeen missing men had more than seventy children (the captain of the *Marjorie Beryl* was married with eight kids, and a crewman on the *Jimmie & Sisters* had twelve children, including a daughter born just one month after he was lost). Fifty of the children attended school on Thursday as the search continued, unsuccessfully, out at sea. As Heather Eileen Taylor, daughter of *Muriel Eileen* captain Lawrence Taylor, summarized: "On that one night, half the children in my class lost their father."

A memorial service was held in Lockeport on Sunday, April 30, 1961, at the United Baptist Church. Afterward, the congregation gathered at a local wharf. Nine hundred mourners stood in freezing rain as an easterly gale blew along the waterfront. Floral wreaths were stacked aboard a Fisheries patrol vessel, which, once the wind subsided, took the wreaths out to sea.

The 1961 loss of the seventeen Lockeport-area fishermen is just one of the countless tragedies referenced in *Lost Mariners of Shelburne County.* It's a three-volume set of books recording the names of fishermen lost from coastal communities stretching from Sable River down to Woods Harbour. In between are dozens of fishing towns and villages, including Green Harbour, Sandy Point, Roseway, Port La Tour, Barrington Passage, Clark's Harbour, Shag Harbour, and on and on. The first volume of *Lost Mariners* was published in 1991. Combined, the three volumes provide a seemingly endless list of names, dates, storms, sinkings, flipped dories, life-ending waves, collisions, drownings, and heartbreak. Between 1856 and 1991, the year *Lost Mariners* was published, Shelburne alone lost more than 280 men to the sea.

It's unlikely that any fishing community along that stretch of coast has escaped the loss of local fishermen. Certainly not Woods Harbour. Located midway between Yarmouth and Shelburne, Woods Harbour is a one-road community completely dependent on fishing. For as long as people have lived in Woods Harbour—European settlement dates to 1770; First Nation settlement before that—residents have drawn food and, later, their livelihoods, from the sea. And when fishermen go to sea, not all come home.

The Woods Harbour Fisherman's Memorial records the names of men lost at sea back to 1847. Since then, every Woods Harbour generation has witnessed and endured the loss of local fishermen. In the worst cases, the sea swallows entire crews. Men who had walked the local wharves just days before suddenly vanish, often without a trace, without any clue as to what happened.

The morning of September 11, 1950, was peaceful. The sky was grey and the offshore water of the fishing grounds was smooth, broken only by the jumping of sunfish and whales, and the occasional slapping tail of a shark. In fact, the past week had provided beautiful fishing weather. On this Monday morning the crew of the *Emma Marie* surveyed the calm water while eating their breakfast. The *Emma Marie* was one of a handful of Woods Harbour swordfishing boats working on the bountiful fishing grounds of Georges Bank, a massive shoal located between Cape Cod and Nova Scotia, roughly 225 kilometres from Woods Harbour. The local fleet included the *Asenath*, *The Oran*, the *Debutante*, the *Nickerson*, and the *Sir Echo*—all 50-footers. For most, it was the final trip of the season. Hurricane season was upon them and the offshore waters would soon be smashed around by massive waves and extreme winds. It would soon be a place to avoid.

The crew of the *Emma Marie*—captained by Vincent Goreham—noticed the crew of a nearby dragger, the *Elaine W*, hauling in its gear. The gear usually went out at this time of day. Puzzled, Vincent steered the *Emma Marie* over to investigate. He asked Johnny Beck, captain of the *Elaine W*, why he was packing up.

"Are you fellas tired of living?" Johnny Beck hollered back. "If not, you'd better scratch for land."

A hurricane was closing in from Cape Hatteras and captains were being urged to get to shore. Vincent had a ship-to-shore radio aboard the *Emma Marie*, but it didn't carry well. He, like many of the other captains, had been unaware of the oncoming storm.

"Mister, I'm leaving right now," Vincent replied to Johnny.

Vincent began steaming for land around 9 A.M., followed closely by the crew of the *Debutante*. Within half an hour, a dense fog developed and huge waves rolled in. Soon after, heavy rain began to pour and the wind whipped up to 40 knots (75 kilometres an hour). The Woods Harbour boats were beating a hasty retreat, but they'd departed the fishing grounds too late.

By 10 A.M., the *Emma Marie* and the *Debutante* were on the northern edge of Georges Bank. The wind was now out of the northeast and "right in their teeth." In other words: the two boats had to plow straight into the hurricane-force winds. The progress was slow. Vincent had both his engines running, yet the *Emma Marie* was barely moving forward. Over his radio, Vincent heard that the other boats to the west, including *Sir Echo*, were also struggling to get home. Vincent quickly realized his crew could not reach shore by evening. The pouring rain was restricting visibility and waves were beginning to tower over the boat, rivalling the height of the *Emma Marie*'s tall spars. When darkness descended, the crew could see nothing but the white water churning all around them. By 2 A.M. the hurricane was in full force: 14-metre seas and 90-knot winds (166 kilometres an hour).

Vincent's brother, Wordlow Goreham, took the wheel while Vincent controlled the two engine throttles. When giant waves approached, Vincent slowed the engines. With each giant swell, the boat was pushed half under water before emerging on the other side of the wave.

While approaching Seal Island, Wordlow suddenly shouted: "Look out!"

Vincent looked up and saw a wall of white water.

He pulled the throttles back just as the mass of seawater crashed on the *Emma Marie*'s bow. The force of the water immediately smashed out four large windows in the wheelhouse. The onslaught filled the wheelhouse to its ceiling, completely submerging Vincent and his brother.

"I'm drowning!" Vincent yelled, his mouth just above the water.

"Me too!" shouted Wordlow.

As the boat rose on the next wave, the water began draining from the wheelhouse down to the bilge. But the pressure of the receding water then prevented the other five men from climbing out of the forward cabin. The water rushed down into the forecastle like a torrent. The men inside assumed their boat was sinking. Eventually they emerged, soaked, cold, and frightened.

"Get the dories! Get the dories!" cried crewman Lester Nickerson, wrapped in a blanket.

"Dories?" Vincent responded. "What do you think you're going to do with dories?"

In such conditions dories would be useless—they'd likely flip immediately and smash apart in the violent waves. Instead, Vincent ordered his crew to start pumping the half-sunken boat. They did so mainly in the dark, aided by only flashlights; the wave that flooded the wheelhouse had knocked out the electric power and killed the engines. The boat was nearly emptied of water and the crew outside on deck, when Vincent saw another huge comber about to land on his crippled boat.

"Hang on!" he yelled as he slammed the back door of the wheelhouse. Another wave inside the cabin would surely sink the boat.

The men were left to cling for their lives on deck. As the wave poured down, Vincent kept his hand on the cabin door. When the wave passed and the water stopped, he pulled the door open and called for each man to yell out his name. All were still onboard.

The crew managed to start the engines and board up the busted windows, leaving a small hole for Vincent to peer through. Around 3 A.M., another high wave broke over the boat and smashed off the stand—a seat that extends six metres over the bow from which fishermen hurl their harpoons at the swordfish.

As daylight appeared, crew member Everett Goreham, another of Vincent's brothers, stared out a wheelhouse window. There were foaming breakers as far as he could see. Their wooden boat, meanwhile, was smashed to pieces. "We'll never make it," he said.

The combers continued to break around and on top of the *Emma Marie*, but eventually Wordlow—exhausted and bloodied at the wheel—turned to Vincent, his brother, and said:

"I believe it's going to be all right."

"Ay'a, it's going to be all right."

Eventually, the crew spotted Duck Island, one of the many islands dotting the southwest Nova Scotia coast, roughly 7 kilometres from Woods Harbour. The other men started shouting, but Vincent cautioned: "We're not in yet." Still, he was clearly relieved. He turned away from the crew to conceal his tears.

Vincent and the crew of the *Emma Marie* arrived at the dock in Woods Harbour around 6 p.m. on Tuesday. A trip that usually took nine hours had taken thirty-six. The men were finally safe, as were the crews of the *Asenath*, *The Oran*, and the *Debutante*. Yet all were troubled to hear that the *Nickerson* and the *Sir Echo*—captained by Sheldon Goreham, a lifelong Woods Harbour resident—had not yet emerged from the hurricane. Sheldon was aboard the *Sir Echo* with a crew of four, including two of his three sons: Aubrey, twenty, and Crowell, sixteen.

It wasn't until the next day—Wednesday—that the *Nickerson* arrived in Yarmouth, towed in by a much larger vessel. During the first day and night of the storm, the *Nickerson* had steamed near the *Sir Echo*, but the boats eventually separated. By Thursday the *Sir Echo* was still missing, so Vincent called government officials in Halifax to request a search boat. (The Canadian Coast Guard was not formed until 1962—twelve years later.) He boarded the naval minesweeper provided for the search, but the minesweeper's radar and modern equipment detected no sign of the *Sir Echo*. Eventually, a clue emerged: a fisherman, one of many who had joined the search, found two hatch covers floating at sea. One had two names written on it: Libby and Belle. These were the names of Sheldon Goreham's nieces. They had written their names on the hatch just days before the *Sir Echo* left port.

A few days after the hurricane, mainlanders spotted smoke rising from a little island off Woods Harbour. Could the crew of the *Sir Echo* have beached there and started a fire? Searchers went to investigate as locals gathered at the wharf, waiting for news. So many cars lined the road near the wharf that one resident said Woods Harbour looked like New York City. Searchers, however, only found an unattended fire, likely left by men collecting Irish moss, a popular type of seaweed.

On September 20, 1950—eight days after the hurricane—a Grand Manan fisherman found the *Sir Echo* floating on its side. It was towed to Meteghan, an Acadian fishing village north of Yarmouth. Vincent Goreham travelled to Meteghan and found the *Sir Echo* tied up at a wharf. Through the skylight he could see the body of Captain Sheldon Goreham floating in the cud—the area where the crew eats and sleeps. Sheldon's Bible was floating nearby. After the boat was pumped free of water, Sheldon's body lay chest-down on the top bunk. It looked like he was trying to speak to someone on the lower bunk.

The *Sir Echo* normally contained many rocks, for ballast, stowed under the cud floor. To Vincent, it looked like something had happened very quickly during the hurricane because the rocks were piled on the stove. It was determined the men aboard the *Sir Echo* likely perished on September 12, though it was unclear exactly what happened. Some surmised Sheldon suffered a heart attack; one captain held that the *Sir Echo* drifted onto a shoal.

After inspecting the boat, Vincent started back to the wharf. He stepped on something hard and looked down. There was a bare foot sticking out from the pile of ballast rocks. It was one of Sheldon's sons, Aubrey. Perhaps Aubrey was fetching some food from the locker when the *Sir Echo* capsized. Whatever happened, it left the twenty-year-old buried under the rocks. The other three crewmen, including Sheldon's son Crowell, were never found.

The bodies of Sheldon and his son Aubrey were taken to a funeral parlour in Meteghan, where Vincent officially identified them. The undertaker placed two jackknives on a table. A knife had been found in a pocket of both men, the handle of each carved with their initials. Vincent took Aubrey's knife and agreed to eventually give it to the remaining Goreham brother, Purney. Twenty years later, Vincent met Purney—then twenty-five—after the young man returned from a lobstering trip. Vincent explained the significance of the knife and handed it to the young man. Purney accepted his brother's knife with tears in his eyes.

CHAPTER TWO

THE YOUNGEST CAPTAIN AT THE WHARF

KATLIN NICKERSON WAS ONLY THREE YEARS OLD—TUCKED INTO A SMALL coat and wearing a toque—when his father, Todd, first took him lobstering. Katlin threw up most of the day, and was green by the time he returned home to his mom, Della. Todd was partially relieved. Perhaps Katlin wouldn't take to fishing. Todd's father and grandfather fished. Maybe Katlin would tread another path. Todd couldn't know for sure, however, so Katlin continued to join him for one day of lobstering each year. Todd always checked to make sure he chose a day when the weather would be fine, and eventually Katlin's seasickness passed.

Todd had also started fishing with his father as a young boy. He first stepped on a boat around age four, and was only ten or eleven the first time he joined his father, Wayne, on a swordfishing trip. In a community of skilled and experienced fishermen, Wayne was considered the very best. In the local phone book, he was listed as Captain Wayne Nickerson. The book was full of fishermen and captains, yet he was among the few actually listed with the "captain" designation.

Todd estimates his dad covered more area than just about any other local fisherman. As mate, Todd fished with his dad on the Grand Banks, in Bermuda, off the Bahamas, off Labrador, in Hudson Bay, and on the Flemish Cap, about 650 kilometres east of St. John's, Newfoundland. Other than dragging, Wayne took part in just about every segment of the fishery: he went lobstering, crabbing, caught groundfish of all varieties, and longlined for swordfish and tuna. If it swam in the sea, Wayne probably caught it. After his retirement, when asked why he went fishing, Wayne responded with a shrug: "I don't know. It's just in ya. You just love it."

For most of his career Wayne skippered boats for large companies, including Clearwater. "He always had one of the bigger boats," Todd remembers. "He was one of the first guys to take those hundred-foot longliners." From 1987 until 1993, Wayne helmed the *Atlantic Horizon*, a 130-foot steel boat he often loaded with more than two hundred thousand pounds of fish on the Grand Banks. There's a video on YouTube capturing the activity of the *Atlantic Horizon* crew while fishing on the Grand Banks in 1987. Wayne is in the wheelhouse. Down below, Todd, then about eighteen, and the rest of the crew can be seen baiting trawl and, later, hauling in the catch of cod and halibut. Todd—with a thick mop of red-blonde hair and wearing green rain pants and black gloves—is pulling fish off the trawl line. At one point he loses his balance and slips backward into a pile of fish. The man closest to Todd turns to the camera operator with a big smile and asks: "Did you get that?"

"Yeah, I got 'im," the cameraman replies.

The crew laugh. Todd stands up and, rubbing his tailbone, moans: "Ah, fuck."

In another scene, Todd is reclining on deck, smoking a cigarette. Behind him the sun is just below the horizon. The water is calm. He smiles.

In high school, Todd fished with his dad during summer vacations. He quit school in grade twelve and shortly after, in 1987, joined his father full-time, crewing for Wayne for four years aboard the *Atlantic Horizon*.

At sea, Wayne was militaristic. "He was a hard fella to fish with," Todd says with a laugh. "He was pretty set in his ways." As another Woods Harbour fisherman puts it: "You had to dance when Wayne told you to dance, or you wasn't going to be aboard the boat."

"He went at it hard," Todd adds. Wayne worked his crews, but they also caught plenty of fish and made money.

Wayne's knack for packing his hold with fish was matched only by his ability to pack his belly with food. The Cod Father was only one of Wayne's nicknames. He was also known as "Big Wayne." For much of his life he weighed more than 350 pounds, and in his later years topped 400, despite being no more than five-foot-ten. Wayne's physique was partially the result of more than twenty years spent sitting in the wheelhouse of big boats for weeks at a time, getting little exercise. "And he loved to eat," Todd says. "He enjoyed his food."

Fishing can encourage bad eating habits: erratic meal times, big dinners, barbecues, junk-food snacks, and a tendency toward deep-fried fare. Each season Wayne gained a few more pounds. Todd laughs as he recalls one particular story about his father. Wayne was skippering the 90-foot *Eastpack II* in sloppy conditions. The boat rolled to port and the arm of Wayne's captain's chair broke off. Falling over, he grabbed for the wheel and tore it clean off. Wayne landed on the other side of the wheelhouse with the wheel still in his hand. When he retired from fishing, Wayne bought the long-standing greasy spoon diner in Woods Harbour. He renamed it Captain Wayne's Café.

Todd's longest stretch at sea with his father was in 1988. The trip involved two boats; the other skippered by Adelbert "Dellie" MacKinnon, another well-known local captain who had fished from Greenland to the Caribbean. Wayne and Dellie steered their boats for nine days to Hudson Bay "looking for fish that weren't there" as Todd puts it. Reports of good fishing turned out to be false. They eventually turned back and headed for the dependable Grand Banks. The trip lasted thirty-nine days.

Todd got his captain's papers in 1989 and skippered the *Atlantic Horizon* for a trip while Big Wayne was moose hunting. It was his first significant stint as a captain. Todd eventually realized he wanted to skipper full-time. Wayne wasn't surprised. "All young ducks like to try their wings," he told his son. Todd made his final trip with his father in 1990. It lasted thirty-one days and the crew returned to shore with one day of shopping left before Christmas. "It was a real old salt trip," Todd recalls of the weeks spent splitting and salting fish at sea. "I said, 'that's enough.'"

Todd met Della Sears, the daughter of a local fisherman, when they were both just kids. She was a friend of his younger sister, and lived up the road. The pair started dating in 1988. Their son, Katlin, was born on March 15, 1991, and Todd and Della married that August. He was twenty-three, she was nineteen. That same year Todd started fishing boats for other fishermen. Though he and Della broke up after a year of marriage, they reconciled and their second child, a daughter, Falon, was born in 1993.

Around this time, Big Wayne put up the cash for Todd to get a lobster licence, enabling him to truly fish for himself. A boat, gear, and lobster licence cost Todd roughly $150,000.

"We thought it was a lot of money at the time, but not compared to today," he says, noting a similar package now costs $800,000 to $1 million, depending on the value of the boat. "A good lobster season back then [made you] $30,000 or $40,000. Now most people catch that in the first two weeks."

Todd later added a swordfish licence and, in 2002, bought the Cape Islander he still fishes on today: the *Cock-a-Wit Lady*. Woods Harbour was named for Reverend Samuel Wood, an early settler. The original name of the area was "Cockouquit," from the Mi'kmaw word for a species of duck. Today "Cockawit" is a slang term for Woods Harbour. A "Cockawitter" is someone from Woods Harbour. Thus, Della was Todd's "Cock-a-Wit Lady."

*Todd Nickerson, Katlin's father. Todd started fishing with his father—
Katlin's grandfather—Big Wayne.*

Life as a fisherman's wife meant Della was often alone at home with Katlin and Falon for long stretches. In Woods Harbour, it was the norm for many families. Della knew her father-in-law, Big Wayne, was often gone to sea for weeks at a time. Todd was merely following his example. "It's how we grew up," Della says. "That's what we always knew." Often, the hardest task was integrating Todd into the routines she'd established while he was gone.

Katlin had a typical Cockawit childhood: much of it was spent in the woods building camps, hunting, setting rabbit snares, fishing for trout, and getting on a four-wheeler as early as his parents would allow (and likely before that, in secret). Katlin could often be found with his best friend, Sherman Crowell, on the abandoned rail bed that runs through Woods Harbour. And, like many of the local boys, Katlin played baseball and hockey. Like Todd, though, Katlin was small. To Della, he seemed especially tiny when fully dressed in his gear for Timbits hockey practice. Katlin didn't take to the sport initially but he eventually played forward in minor hockey and, briefly, for the Barrington Ice Dogs, the local junior team.

From the beginning, Katlin's name caused confusion. Correctly pronounced "Cat-lynn," it was often pronounced "Kate-lynn." Della remembers her son's name often being mangled over the public-address system after he scored goals in hockey. He'd look up at her in the stands and she'd mouth back to him: *Sorry*. Normally, Della called her son "Kat." Only when she was mad would she address him by his full name. But those moments were rare. Della and Falon could descend into shouting matches, but Della and Kat never fought, and he never swore—at least not around her. "Of course it's going to sound like I'm building him up, but he was a good kid," she says. "All kids go a little awry when they become teenagers but Kat never really did that either."

Still, Della often worried about Katlin. Perhaps it was because he was born on March 15—the Ides of March. Or maybe it was just a mother's sixth sense. "Every time he would leave I would always have a bad feeling," she recalls. "I always had this weird feeling."

Tina Crowell, mother of Katlin's best friend, Sherman, had the same fear. One day, when Katlin was a teenager, Tina told Della so. "She was worried that something was going to happen to [Katlin]. I never forgot the day," Della says. "I cried and I cried and I cried." And though she didn't initially admit it to Della, it was a feeling Tina never shook off.

Throughout his teen years, Katlin's interests involved either being outside or fixing things. Todd says his son was sixteen before he displayed any interest in girls.

"He never had time for that. He was too busy hunting or fishing or checking snares or building camps or four-wheeling or something," Todd says.

Katlin wired his camps, built go-karts, taught himself to weld, learned to scuba dive, and spent a year fixing up an old Camaro that he and some friends stored in his family's barn. "He could build anything," Della says. "I called him an old soul. Most anything, he could figure it out."

Devin Smith, a childhood friend who played hockey with Katlin and went through junior high and high school with him, says Katlin's childhood ingenuity was best revealed in the series of pulleys he set up in his bedroom.

Katlin, age seventeen, and Della.

The pulleys enabled him to lie on his bed and, when he heard his sister approaching, pull a string to slam his door shut. "He was always thinking," Devin says. "He was a smart guy."

Della's cousin Troy Sears recalls it slightly differently. Katlin loved to take things apart to see how they worked, but "nine times out of ten it didn't go back together the way it started," Troy says. In his late teens and early twenties, Katlin lost or broke at least six iPhones. One day Della found him outside, behind his truck, using a pick to search for his lost phone in a snowbank. Concludes Steven d'Entremont, another cousin: "He destroyed everything he touched."

❦

Fishing permeates Woods Harbour. It dominates the local chatter and the economy. There are stacks of lobster traps in many yards, and boats are constantly in sight, whether at the two local wharves—Lower Wharf and Falls Point Wharf (known locally as Upper Wharf)—or in cradles on land. If your father is not a fisherman, then your uncle or best friend probably is. As one Woods Harbour fisherman puts it: "If we don't make any money fishing, this place would be a ghost town."

Katlin started fishing seriously with his father in his mid-teens. Starting at fourteen or fifteen, he regularly secured a work permit that allowed him to miss school in December—prime lobster season. He'd spend the month lobstering with Todd on the *Cock-a-Wit Lady*, and join his father for swordfishing trips during his summer holidays. Despite his early immersion in the industry and culture, it appeared—for a time—that Katlin wouldn't follow his father and grandfather to sea. At Barrington Municipal High School, he displayed an interest in carpentry. It appealed to the builder in him. "He always liked to build stuff, ever since he was old enough to swing a hammer," Todd says.

Katlin enrolled in the Options and Opportunities program. Commonly called O2, the program provides high school students "more hands-on learning experiences," including work placements at local businesses. The goal is to improve the transition from high school to professional life or a post-secondary program for students "who may not be fully engaged with [...] school." Katlin's focus in the O2 program was carpentry. As part of a co-op he did some roofing work, helped construct new houses, and changed windows and doors. Near the end of grade twelve, Katlin's plan for the upcoming fall was set: he'd study carpentry at the Nova Scotia Community College in nearby Yarmouth. During the summer he'd earn money fishing.

John Symonds first met Katlin around this time at Dixon's Marine Group in Woods Harbour. A bear of a man, John stopped in because he needed some welding work done before the start of scallop season. He also needed another crew member. Katlin, then eighteen, was working in Dixon's welding shop, earning extra credits for the O2 program. Once he had his hours, he could join John's crew. But could John wait? To John, Katlin seemed like a good kid. "He looked like somebody I wanted to take with me," he recalls.

Katlin joined John on his boat, the *Hit N' Miss*, in June of 2009 and spent the summer scalloping. After just a few trips with Katlin, John came home and told his wife, Gina, he wanted to adopt the boy. "I can't say enough good about him," John adds. "He was just number one. He was a go-getter."

Something changed during the summer Katlin spent scalloping with John Symonds. The experience steered him away from carpentry. It wasn't for him—at least not as a career. The lure of fishing was impossible to avoid.

Katlin came of age during some very profitable years in the lobster industry. He saw young men not much older than him driving brand-new trucks during the week, and mud-splattered four-wheelers on weekends. Like most of his friends, Katlin wanted the same toys. Graydon Mood says it's a common frustration among local high school students: you're stuck in school while your older buddy—with no more education than you—is making $80,000 a year. "It's hard. You see the money," says Graydon, who fished his own boat before working at his family's company, James L. Mood Fisheries Ltd. "Your buddy has a truck and a wheeler. And you're stuck riding a bike to school. It's quite tempting."

Adds Katlin's mom, Della: "You can make so much money so fast with fishing. There's a lot of bills and a lot of debt, but there's a lot of money too."

When catches and prices are good, fishing can put money in a fisherman's pocket quicker than most land-based options. Katlin saw this reflected in the shiny vehicles parked at the wharf and in driveways and garages throughout Woods Harbour. Seven days before his carpentry course was due to start—in September 2009—Katlin suddenly announced to Della: "Mom, I don't want to go." He wanted his captain's papers instead. "I was kind of shocked because he didn't want to go on the water and then everything just reversed," she recalls. Her response to Katlin: "If you don't want to go, then don't go." She figured there was no point in studying a subject if you were likely to abandon it later.

His father had a different approach. "I tried to talk him out of it," Todd admits. "I guess everybody always wanted their kid to be a doctor or lawyer or something that was going to be higher paying and less work. I wanted to see him get his schooling first."

But it was an unwinnable argument. Like his father and grandfather, Katlin was going to be a fisherman.

꽃

Katlin stayed on with John Symonds after the 2009 scallop season, joining him for the 2009–10 lobster season and another scallop season during the summer of 2010.

John grew up on Cape Sable Island. Fishing—particularly for cod, pollack, and haddock—was a matter of survival. It kept his family alive. It also affected John like a drug: he couldn't get enough.

The first day of lobster season is known as Dumping Day. For fishermen in ports from Halifax down to Brier Island, Dumping Day occurs annually on the last Monday in November (there are different seasons across the Maritimes, depending on location). In Woods Harbour, an armada of Cape Islanders departs from the wharves each Dumping Day. The boats steam away in the early morning darkness, each one fully loaded with traps that will be regularly baited, set, and hauled during the six-month season. Dumping Day is like a race, and plenty of preparation is required. It can be very stressful.

But not for John Symonds.

"We will have 375 traps on the boat. And I'm going to have a grin on my face—you're going to be able to see every one of my teeth," he says excitedly, looking anxious to pop from his living room chair and head straight to his boat. "I can't wait to go. This is what I'm programmed to do. I love it. I love it. I love it. It is not a job for me. And I'm good at it. I'm not number one, but I'm striving for it." For John, nothing tops the feeling of steaming back to the wharf with a big haul. "I get such an adrenalin rush out of it. I love hauling that next pot to see what's going to be in it," he says. "I wouldn't trade my life for nothin'."

During lobster season, little else matters to John. The southwest Nova Scotia lobster season runs through Christmas and New Year's Day to late May. For John, Christmas is now just another dinner. He eats as quickly as possible to get back on the water. His focus is solely on ensuring a successful season. "When I come home, I want something in my crates. A lot of these fellas want to get in at dinnertime so they can watch Oprah. I got all summer to watch Oprah. I don't care about her," he says. "I'm here to make money."

In Katlin, John found someone who shared his passion for fishing and his willingness to work.

Katlin and a fellow crew member, J. P. LeBlanc, aboard John Symonds's boat during lobster season in April 2010.

In late December 2009, a screeching gale rolled along the coast. By New Year's Eve the weather had slackened and John was heading out to haul his traps. The trip was voluntary for his crew; he knew they might be celebrating long into the evening. Katlin was eager to help John haul traps, though he noted his girlfriend, Jenna Jones, hoped he'd be in at a decent time for a party that night.

"I'll do what I can," John replied.

On the way home, however, they had to slog through a strong breeze. The *Hit N' Miss* didn't reach the wharf until 11:30 P.M.

"Just tie the boat up and you go," John told Katlin.

Katlin secured the boat and scurried up the wharf to his truck, waiting girlfriend, and the New Year's Eve party. John stayed behind in the dark. He drained water from the live well—the onboard tank that holds live lobsters—and started picking the crustaceans out. Around 1 A.M. he considered heading home. Then he saw Katlin strolling back down the wharf.

"Why are you here?" John asked him.

"Ah, Jenna wasn't happy and the party wasn't much fun, so I'm back to help you pick out the lobsters."

The pair plucked lobsters out of the live well until finally John decided it was time for bed. John appreciated the help. "But I don't think his girlfriend was overly impressed," he says, grinning.

During Katlin's year-long stint aboard the *Hit N' Miss*, John often relied on the younger man's ability to fix things. When John dented the tailboard of his new truck with a trailer, Katlin responded with his typical refrain: "That ain't nothin'! I can fix that." Katlin patched the tailboard flawlessly with body fill, and the repair went unnoticed when John later traded the truck in. Katlin was also a proficient welder and often worked on John's scallop gear. "The scallop rig I had was probably the fanciest one in southwest Nova by the time he got done with it. It was in perfect shape," John says. "Katlin could do anything. He was very talented."

At sea, Katlin often experimented with new rigging and gear setups, and John gave him full permission to tinker. Often, though, the items Katlin fixed or re-jigged were ones he had himself broken. In his first season scalloping with John, Katlin wanted desperately to man the main winch that hauls the scalloping rake off the ocean bottom. The scalloping rake, which plucks scallops (as well as rocks and other sea life) off the bottom, is a heavy piece of equipment that can do a lot of damage on deck if not controlled properly. Katlin eventually earned his turn at the winch. Bringing the rake on deck, he let it drop too quickly. The rake smashed the dump table—a big table that sits across the stern of the boat, where the rake is usually stored. But John didn't mind, knowing Katlin could probably fix it. Katlin's tendency for clumsy destruction prompted John to give him a nickname: Cletus.

Despite his lowbrow nickname, Katlin took fishing seriously. While sipping on a bottle of orange juice or nibbling on a Reese's Peanut Butter Cup, he would ask John countless questions on topics ranging from tides to the intricacies of setting gear. "You only had to show him once," John says. "He caught on so quick. He was just like a big sponge."

Though separated in age by twenty years, the two became close friends. (John is closer in age to Todd, Katlin's dad, and Katlin was only three years older than John's son, Nolan.) The pair talked almost every day and Katlin often joined John and his family for dinner. Katlin joked he'd like to return in another life as one of the cats pampered by John's wife, Gina.

Katlin's presence in John and Gina's house increased following Todd and Della's separation in 2010 after nearly twenty years of marriage. Della and Falon moved to Cape Sable Island, twenty kilometres away, while Katlin remained home with Todd in Woods Harbour. "It was a hard time for him, watching his mom and dad go separate ways," John recalls. "It always is when your parents are breaking up. I had the same problem growing up. You ask yourself: 'Was it something I did?' You always put the blame on yourself. He needed someone he could talk to."

Often, over dinner or a cup of tea, it was John and Gina who reassured Katlin. John told Katlin what he'd already told Todd: Todd was very lucky to have a son like Katlin. "I couldn't find a fault in him," John says.

When Katlin was expected for dinner, John's teenage daughter, Paige, would often alert her friends. Katlin wasn't tall—only about five-foot-nine—but he had charm and, as John puts it, a smile that could "melt butter." "He was a ladies' man. He had the girls. A lot of 'em," John says with a laugh. "But work come first." Adds Katlin's long-time friend Devin Smith: "There was always a girl trying to talk to him, trying to get around him."

Katlin's charm did not only affect the opposite sex; he also charmed John Symonds. "I thought of him as my son almost. I wanted him to be mine. He was just awesome," John says. "He had everybody's heart."

For John, working with Katlin didn't feel like work. Katlin was always chipper, calm, polite, and quiet—at least until he got to know you. Then he'd gab your ear off. And he didn't panic in stressful situations. "Katlin was calm. He did not freak out. He would just relax and just deal with the situation," John says.

Katlin also adhered to John's zero-tolerance policy for drugs and alcohol at sea. John says it's a growing problem: crews going to sea with stashes of drugs, such as marijuana, cocaine, and ecstasy. He's seen swordfish boats headed out for two-week trips to the 200-mile limit stocked with boxes of sixty-sixers of Captain Morgan. "They take it to kill the pain," he says. "[But] if you can't go out there and stay sober for two weeks, you've got a problem."

John keeps his boat at the Falls Point wharf in Woods Harbour. He estimates there are about one hundred boats in the local area, and his is one of maybe five with no drugs aboard. "It's a big problem," he says. "And it's getting worse. People are getting killed. People are getting hurt. People ain't coming home." John offers no flexibility on the issue. At sea he is a teetotaller.

Katlin followed John's rules. He also took on any task and was often the first out of his bunk when there was work to do. "He was always on time. He was always happy and always ready to go," John says. "When I asked him to do something, I didn't have to go back and make sure that he did it. He did it and he did it right. And he did it with pride. That's how I knew that he was going to be a captain one day."

John thoroughly enjoyed having Katlin aboard, but he knew his young friend wouldn't be with him for long. Katlin didn't want to crew for a living. He wanted to be a captain. "That boy was determined to go to the wheel of a boat. That's what he was programmed to do," John concludes. "It was born in him."

It was around this time that Katlin secured his Fishing Master Class IV certification—his captain's papers. A class IV certification is comparable to a driver's licence: you learn the right-of-way rules, and about lights, buoys, charting, and other navigational basics. Katlin took courses at the Nova Scotia Community College in Shelburne and later passed a series of exams. The process took about three months and cost roughly $3,500.

On a fall evening in 2010, Katlin called John to say he wouldn't be crewing for him anymore. Todd wanted Katlin to fish with him. John sensed that Katlin would be happy staying aboard the *Hit N' Miss*, but his father was giving him an opportunity to skipper the *Cock-a-Wit Lady*.

"Dad's gonna let me run his boat," Katlin told John.

The news crushed John, but he knew it was probably good for Katlin to fish with his father, particularly in the wake of his parents' break up.

"You do what you have to do," John told Katlin.

John, sadly and somewhat reluctantly, hired a man to take Katlin's spot.

Katlin worked for his father aboard the *Cock-a-Wit Lady* during the 2010–11 lobster season, skippering the boat on days Todd stayed on shore. After many years at sea, Todd was beginning to tire of fishing in the winter. "I wouldn't just give any eighteen-year-old my boat, but I knew [Katlin] knew what he was doing," Todd says. "Sometimes he'd ask me questions I couldn't even answer, and I had a lot more experience than he did."

Katlin was asked to skipper for other boat owners looking to stay on shore. "People are actually asking him to take boats. And I'm thinking, 'He's just a kid,'" Della recalls. "It freaked me right out."

Katlin's first freelance gig arrived in the fall of 2010—shortly after leaving John Symonds's boat—when he skippered the *Manola S.* The *Manola S.* was, in the words of one fisherman, a "hard-looking boat" that appeared to be homemade. Its orange, weathered, banged-up hull showed visible signs of repair. Around the wharf, the *Manola S.* was sometimes referred to as the "Wounded Cheesy." Katlin called it the "Limp Cheesy," in part because it required a number of repairs while he was skipper. Della recalls a story about Katlin's crew cleaning the boat's oven and finding an old pork chop inside that was hairier than a person.

The condition of the *Manola S.* didn't deter Colby Smith from jumping aboard. Colby met Katlin in minor hockey and the two became close friends. He appreciated that Katlin was an "adrenalin junkie" who wanted to go "full tilt" on four-wheelers, in trucks, and on boats—on anything with an engine.

Not surprisingly, Katlin's favourite TV show was *The Dukes of Hazzard*. Like the Duke boys, Colby and Katlin loved ripping around in their trucks. Katlin's white truck could be immaculately clean and, an hour later, splattered with mud and grit. "If he saw a big muck hole or a swamp, he couldn't pass by it," says cousin Troy Sears. "He had to go in it."

Colby was also drawn to Katlin's easygoing way. If something broke, a situation turned sour, or plans fell through, Katlin's response was always the same: "Ah, that ain't nothin'!" When Katlin was asked to skipper the *Manola S.*, Colby had one thought: *I want to be aboard*. He wanted to know what Katlin would be like as a captain.

Colby crewed for Katlin aboard the *Manola S.* during the summer of 2011, fishing for tuna and swordfish. Colby made three full trips with Katlin that season. A couple other trips ended early because of mechanical troubles. Katlin was handy but when you require parts there's only one option: head back to shore. Despite the breakdowns, Katlin's crew did reasonably well. They caught some fish and Colby ended the summer with a decent settlement. And he decided he'd go back to sea with Katlin if the opportunity arose.

"He was a pretty good leader. Confident. He wasn't really scared of nothing," Colby recalls. "He could handle it." Did he feel safe with his friend at the wheel? "There's always the chance of something happening but I didn't feel like my life was put at risk," Colby says. "He had a good head on his shoulders. He was pretty safe about everything. I've been with worse captains—I'll put it that way."

By the fall of 2011 Katlin was twenty years old, and Todd noticed his son had lost some of his boyishness. Though still trim, Katlin had started to fill out. Todd told him to watch out because he might balloon up like his grandfather. Todd also realized Katlin was not content being at the wheel of the *Cock-a-Wit Lady* or freelancing for the other captains in the area. "He wanted to have his own boat," Todd says. "He had the drive, I'll give him that. Maybe I pushed him too hard. I don't know. Sometimes I feel that way."

Todd suggested Katlin just get a lobster licence and double up with him on the *Cock-a-Wit Lady*. That would give them twice the haul and only one boat to worry about. But that plan didn't interest Katlin. "He wanted to do it all on his own."

Katlin started hunting for a boat that fall and heard that Shawn Sears was selling his rig: the *Miss Ally*. Shawn was born in Pugwash, Nova Scotia, but moved to Cape Sable Island at age twelve to live with his grandparents. "I think I was supposed to be a farmer but I turned out a fisherman," he says.

Like many locals, Shawn started in the fishery by harvesting Irish moss. He later crewed on lobster boats and bought his first rig at age twenty-two. Shawn owned a few boats before he had the *Miss Ally* built in 2006. It was a typical Cape Islander: 41 feet (12.5 metres) long, made of molded reinforced plastic, and powered by a 480-horsepower Volvo diesel engine. Built by Malone's Boat Repair in Woods Harbour, it had a yellow hull, a white wheelhouse, and red trim. Shawn named his new boat after his only granddaughter, Ally Symonds.

Shawn went lobstering and fishing on the *Miss Ally* from 2006 until 2011. It was a seaworthy boat, easily pulling him through a number of stiff breezes. But after decades on the water, he decided it was time to sell his boat, gear, and lobster licence. It was precisely the package Katlin required to launch his career. Shawn knew Katlin—he lived just down the road. "He was kind of young and he was quite sure of himself," Shawn recalls. "But he was smart."

Shawn wasn't surprised this twenty-year-old was interested in his boat. He was aware of Katlin's fishing pedigree and knew he'd been skippering boats for other captains. "I knew he was capable of going fishing. There was no doubt about that," Shawn says. "He was young and inexperienced, but we all are when we start out, right? We're all learning as we go along."

The two men talked several times and Katlin inspected the *Miss Ally* at the Falls Point wharf. Shawn was hoping to get $1 million for his boat, gear, and licence, but prices had dropped in recent years and he was satisfied with Katlin's offer of $700,000. Katlin submitted an application to the Nova Scotia Vessel Loan Program, which provides loans to fishermen building, buying, or upgrading their vessels. His application approved, and with the help of a down payment from his maternal grandparents, Ronnie and Bonnie Sears, Katlin bought the *Miss Ally* in the fall of 2011. "My parents helped him," Della recalls. "It costs a good fortune to get into [the industry]."

Shawn Sears recalls it as a straightforward deal settled between him and Katlin. "No lawyers or nothing," he says. "He just bought the rig and that was it. There was no fooling around." His fishing career over and his rig sold, Shawn headed to Fox Creek, Alberta, to drive a rig of a very different type: a vacuum truck used to transfer liquids and clean up spills in the oilfield.

Katlin's career, meanwhile, was just beginning. He was now the youngest captain at the wharf, perhaps by a decade; few twenty-year-olds helm their own boats. Typically, a fisherman with aspirations of skippering his own rig has to put in many years at the back of other boats, working up to the wheelhouse, and saving enough money to do so. Katlin had jumped from the deck to the wheelhouse quicker than most.

It's late November 2011 and Katlin is preparing for his first Dumping Day as captain of his own boat. He's set up on his grandparents' front lawn, patching holes in the lobster pots that came with the *Miss Ally*. John Symonds, Katlin's friend and former captain, pulls up. A meticulous fisherman who prides himself on the quality of his equipment, John is appalled by the state of the gear Katlin is planning to go lobstering with. The pots are weathered and in need of extensive repair. John tells Katlin to put the worst of the pots away.

"I've got fifty pots sitting in the field up there," John says, pointing. "They're in a lot better shape than these. If you're going to go lobstering, you're going to have something that's actually going to catch lobsters. Come on."

"I can't afford it," Katlin responds.

"Did I tell you I was going to charge you anything?" John replies. "Put them aboard your boat."

John uses lobster pots that are smaller than the typical traps. Katlin often teased John about his "Bambi pots" when he crewed aboard the *Hit N' Miss*. He makes no such jokes now; he's just happy to have some decent traps. John also helps Katlin equip the *Miss Ally* with proper safety gear. The pair mounts a new life raft and John goes with Katlin to Dixon's Marine to pick up survival suits. The suits are critical but Katlin's boat didn't come with them. At sea, John was taught to use his survival suit as a pillow, to ensure he always knew where it was. "Katlin had a survival suit for every man," John says.

Katlin makes a number of other upgrades to his boat. Shawn Sears, the previous owner, had an admittedly "plain Jane" approach to his gear and setup. Katlin wants more sophisticated systems. The *Miss Ally* does have a live well for storing lobsters at sea, but Shawn, who didn't go lobstering overnight, hadn't hooked it up. Katlin sets up the piping for the live well, changes some hydraulics, and installs new electronics and software for mapping the ocean floor. John is happy to help his former crew member get ready for the season. They splice lines, install a new trawl chute, and add a rack for storing high flyers. "I done everything I could to help Katlin. I wanted him to succeed," John says.

Despite his keenness, Katlin's initial attempt at running his own boat proves difficult. For one, the *Miss Ally* suffers a few breakdowns during Katlin's first lobster season, forcing him to use his father's boat just to haul his traps. Then there's the price of lobster: just $3–4 a pound at the start of the season. It's a terrible price, especially for a skipper with a new boat and a giant loan, and there's no guarantee the price will rise later in the season. Katlin has entered the fishery during a rough stretch.

In the summer of 2012, Katlin uses his boat to fish for halibut on Middle Bank, about 100 kilometres off Canso, Nova Scotia. Later that summer, he gets a call from Reg LeBlanc, owner of Wedgeport Lobsters Limited. Reg runs nearly a dozen companies. He holds fishing quota, lobster licences, and runs a trucking business. Among his holdings: fifty thousand pounds of swordfish quota.

But Reg is not a fisherman (he gets seasick). Instead, Reg hires local captains to fish his quota for him on his boat, the *Row Row*. The *Row Row*'s usual captain is unavailable so Reg must find another skipper. Katlin has been recommended. Reg doesn't know Katlin but he's willing to give a younger captain a shot at pulling in his fish. Reg will take 30 percent off the top, and Katlin will get a 5 percent cut for serving as captain. Then the cost of fuel, gear, bait, ice, food, and other expenses will be sliced off. What's left will be divided equally amongst Katlin and the crew.

With Katlin at the wheel, the *Row Row* crew heads out in search of swordfish and tuna. Their first trip spans from late July to early August and yields a good haul: more than twenty-five thousand pounds of fish.

In mid-September, Katlin takes the *Row Row* to the Grand Banks. After two weeks at sea, he and the crew have twenty-eight thousand pounds of swordfish on ice in the hold. There's some tuna in there as well, along with what fishermen call "junk fish": shark and mahi-mahi (also known as dolphinfish). On his way home, Katlin calls John Symonds, his former captain.

"I got 'em John!" Katlin blurts over the satellite phone.

"You did?"

"Oh yes, I got 'em. I found the big ones: the 400-pounders. We stuffed the last one in there and I'm on my way in."

At the wharf, however, Katlin discovers the market is flooded with fish. His catch fetches just $78,000—half what it might have netted in a seller's market. Price aside, Katlin did catch the fish. Reg LeBlanc has only known Katlin for a few months, and has only talked with him briefly at the wharf while the *Row Row* has been unloaded. Yet Reg is impressed: Katlin is young, but he is also aggressive and has delivered. "Katlin was very calm and cool," Reg recalls. "I liked that about him. Nothing would excite him. He'd try anything."

Reg wants Katlin to fish for him aboard the *Row Row* again next summer. That's still a way off, however. Katlin will fish for lobster starting in late November, but then he'll need some fish to catch during the winter of 2013 to tide him over until summertime. Reg is pretty sure his business partner has halibut quota Katlin could fish for during the winter—he'll make a call.

On a fall day in 2012, Katlin drives to West Head on Cape Sable Island to talk with Terry Zinck. Terry owns Xsealent Seafood Company, a fish-processing company that deals in groundfish and lobster. A former fisherman, Terry has been in the processing side of the industry for three decades. Xsealent's facilities, made up of blue steel buildings, span five acres near the West Head wharf. Katlin knows Terry well: he played hockey with Terry's son, Brock, and Terry has done business with Katlin's dad, Todd. Katlin now has a boat but needs fish to catch; Terry's company holds a large amount of quota.

The quota system is complicated, confusing, contentious, and, among many fishermen, a source of great frustration. For halibut, like most ground-fish, the federal government sets an annual total allowable catch—T. A. C.—an overall pie that is divided and doled out to a variety of players, including individual fishermen and companies. The amount of halibut any one player can catch depends mainly on the history of their past catches. In Shelburne County, many fishermen lament that the pieces of the pie are bigger than they once were, but fewer people hold those pieces. In other words: there's been a consolidation of halibut quota into fewer hands.

In the 1990s, the federal government regularly reduced the total halibut quota, down to a low of 850 metric tons. That meant everyone's individual quota shrunk proportionally. Some fishermen found they couldn't make a living on their shrunken quota, so they sold it to other fishermen, thus pooling quota amongst fewer people. The result: large quota portions held by fewer players. Terry Zinck is one of those players.

Terry buys fish from fishermen who hold quota, but his company also has its own quota. That quota only exists on paper, though. Terry needs fishermen to pull the fish from the water and turn the numbers into actual product. Local captains seeking quota to fish often approach him. This is the first time he's been approached by Katlin—and perhaps the first time he's been contacted by a twenty-one-year-old captain. But Terry doesn't care about Katlin's age.

"Katlin was an aggressive young man and he was the kind of fisherman you wanted to have come on board with you because you knew he was going to fish hard," Terry says. "You're looking for the stars that are out there. Those are the guys you want. And he qualified." Katlin also comes with a personal recommendation from Reg LeBlanc.

Katlin has a longline groundfish licence, but he doesn't hold any halibut quota, so he'll pay a fee to fish for Terry's. They make a handshake deal, and it's open-ended—there's no fixed limit to what Katlin can catch. Katlin will likely be able to make a number of trips pursuing Terry's quota. He'll be paid by the pound for the fish he catches, and a portion of that payment will go right back to Terry as compensation for the quota access.

Come February, Katlin will take the *Miss Ally* offshore and into winter waters in search of halibut. First, though, he must secure a crew.

琵

Halibut are shape-shifters. Like most fish species, a halibut larva swims with its belly facing the ocean bottom, an eye on each side of its head. But by the time a halibut is between 16–20 millimetres in length, something weird happens: its left eye begins to migrate over the top of the head toward the right side. The migration continues for several months until both eyes are on the right side.

The colour of the fish also makes an odd change during this period: pigment is restricted to the right side of the body. A juvenile halibut then starts to swim like an adult—with its non-pigmented, eyeless side facing the bottom, and its coloured, two-eyed right side facing up. In the case of the Atlantic halibut, the top (technically right) side varies in colour from greenish-brown to dark chestnut brown, while the bottom (left) side is white in young fish and usually mottled with grey or even cherry red in older, larger fish.

Physically, halibut are recognizable by their flat bodies, odd eyes, and large mouths that are filled with very sharp, curved teeth. Strong swimmers, halibut can evade potential predators such as sharks and seals. Atlantic halibut grow quickly—approximately 10 centimetres per year—until they reach maturity. They grow to a length of 2.5 metres and weigh in excess of 650 pounds. The typical lifespan of an Atlantic halibut is twenty-five to thirty years, though they can live up to fifty provided they don't bite any baited hooks.

The Atlantic halibut is the largest of all flatfish and is present on both sides of the Atlantic Ocean. In the northwest Atlantic, halibut are found from the coast of Virginia all the way up to northern Greenland. Atlantic halibut are widely distributed across Canada's east coast. They live on or near the ocean bottom and are most commonly found at depths of 200–500 metres, in the deep-water channels running between ocean banks, as well as along the edge of the continental shelf. Atlantic halibut prefer water temperatures between 3 °C and 9 °C and, when not feeding—on redfish, cod, haddock, smaller halibut, or lumpfish—often bury themselves in sand on soft sections of the ocean bottom. Although they generally remain in the area of their birth, halibut have been shown to migrate extremely long distances. In 1946, a halibut was tagged near Anticosti Island, off Quebec. Seven years later the same fish was caught on the west coast of Iceland, having travelled more than 2,500 kilometres.

According to Fisheries and Oceans Canada, Atlantic halibut stock has often been overfished. In fact, the fishery was completely unregulated until 1988. That year a total allowable catch was set for the first time: 3,200 metric tons. The figure, however, was cut down significantly in 1995—to 850 metric tons—in direct response to an eight-year decline in landings. Since 1999, the total allowable catch has been raised several times.

Katlin is entering the halibut fishery at what is, historically, a good time. The quota has tripled from the low of the 1990s—to 2,400 metric tons in 2013—and the price is up, especially in winter when fewer fishermen are willing to go offshore.

Gary Dedrick—president of the Shelburne County Quota Group, which allots and tracks quota held by Terry Zinck and others—tells a reporter it's an "explosion" in the halibut fishery: "They're going anywhere from $7 to $10 a pound," Gary says. "That's a big incentive to go try to catch some."

Atlantic halibut is now a widely sought-after fish, known for its firm and tasty flesh, but it wasn't always in demand. In fact, the fish was long considered undesirable and even a nuisance. It wasn't until 1820 that halibut gained popularity in the northeast United States. Demand in Boston quickly depleted local stocks in that area, so fishermen pursued halibut stocks further offshore, including on the shoals off Nantucket and on Georges Bank, which stretches for 250 kilometres between Cape Cod and Nova Scotia. During the 1850s catches declined again, pushing American halibut crews into Canadian waters, particularly around Browns Bank, located about halfway between Georges Bank and the Nova Scotia coast. From about 1860, Canadian and American fishermen started pursuing halibut on fishing grounds off Nova Scotia and Newfoundland, in the Gulf of St. Lawrence, and even up to western Greenland. Back then halibut were caught with handlines. At the end of each line was a hook baited with fish scraps, and a lead weight to ensure the hook sunk to the bottom. Today, handlining is a quaint technique from a bygone era; longlining now dominates the sector.

The current method involves placing long lines of baited hooks on or just above the ocean bottom. A longline is set by first placing an 80-pound anchor on the bottom. The boat will then steam ahead at 7 or 8 knots (15 kilometres an hour) as the line, with a baited hook every five metres, shoots out the back. This is considered the most dangerous aspect of longlining and with halibut fishing it usually occurs in the middle of the night. The goal is to set the lines before dawn, because halibut usually bite in the morning.

The baited line flows from coiled tubs that sit on deck. Each tub consists of 300 fathoms (550 metres) of rope and about a hundred hooks. A typical longline "string" consists of as many as twelve tubs of line, or "gear," meaning a single string can stretch along the bottom for 5 or 6 kilometres. The tail end of the line is again weighed to the bottom with an anchor. Each anchor is tethered to a buoy, or "balloon," that floats on the surface. Tethered to the balloon is a high flyer, which is a tall buoy with a radar reflector at the top. The high flyers help captains locate their gear and signal to other boats that a line is on the bottom. Thus there is a balloon and high flyer at each end of a string, sometimes separated by many kilometres.

It's typical to set a number of strings—say, five strings of ten tubs each—and it usually takes three or four hours for a crew to get all its gear on the ocean bottom. After a short break, the crew starts hauling in the first line they set, perhaps around 10 A.M. First, the high flyer is brought on deck. Then the line is hauled up on a roller on the starboard (right) side. This is known as "tending the rail." Another crew member coils the line back into tubs as it comes on deck. Old stale bait still on the line (typically herring, squid, or mackerel) is tossed overboard. Any halibut hanging on the line are snagged with a gaff (a stick with a large hook on one end), brought aboard, dressed, lowered into the hold, and packed with ice. Most are later shipped to the United States. The fish are consumed across the country, shipped from two main distribution points: Boston and New York City.

Halibut aren't dangerous, but as one fisherman notes: "If you put the gaff to them, they come to life." An average of one or two fish caught per tub of gear is considered a good haul for a halibut trip. After being hauled aboard, the lines are re-baited and set aside on deck for the next "set." It usually takes about ten hours to haul up all the gear. After a three- or four-hour nap, the crew begins the process again in the middle of the night.

Longlining is a labour-intensive occupation. To do well, Katlin will need a strong, experienced crew. Crew members often jump between boats and there's always someone looking to hop aboard. Katlin has a mental list of guys he can approach about crewing this winter. The first two names are obvious: Joel Hopkins and Billy Jack Hatfield. Joel and Billy Jack are Katlin's main lobster crewmen; they are also good friends. They camp together, hunt together, and are both known for their wild behaviour. When it comes to fishing, however, Joel and Billy Jack are very different. Both grew up on boats and have fished for years, but Billy Jack views fishing more as a means of securing a good, quick paycheque. Joel, meanwhile, genuinely loves being at sea—fishing is his passion. For Joel, rough conditions only add to the fun. You can't make it wet enough or cold enough or sloppy enough to deter Joel.

CHAPTER 3

DEFINITION OF A BADASS

JOEL HOPKINS STOOD OUT IN WOODS HARBOUR. EVERYONE KNEW JOEL. Mainly it was because of his outgoing personality and daredevil antics, including his habit of roaring down the main road on his four-wheeler or dirt bike. "He always lived on the edge, no matter what he done," says Joel's father, George Hopkins. "He was just wide open, Joel. Everything he did was that way—even his fishing."

Joel also stood out in a very white area of a predominantly white province.

"You know Joel is adopted, right?" asks his mother, Mary, on our first meeting. "Maybe you don't know."

"Joel is black," George interjects, cutting to the point.

George and Mary met as teenagers. He was a local boy from a fishing family; she was an American "city girl" who visited Woods Harbour in summertime. Mary grew up in Lynn, a community just north of Boston, where her father worked for General Electric. The family of one of Mary's friends was originally from Nova Scotia. As a teenager Mary joined the family during their return vacations to Woods Harbour. One summer she met George.

"I had a motorcycle. I think she was in love with the motorcycle more than me," he says, laughing.

George and Mary were married in 1976 and adopted four children. First came Nathan, then Hollie. When they applied to adopt their third child, George and Mary were given different options, including a biracial child or a child with Down's syndrome. Mary didn't care if the child was green. They got Joel.

Joel was born in Antigonish, Nova Scotia, on July 14, 1985. Both his biological parents were black. He was three months old when Mary and George took him to live in Woods Harbour. Their fourth child, Jesse, also black, joined the family thanks to Joel: Jesse's birth mother wanted him to join a family that already had a black child. Mary and George attempted to nurture Joel and Jesse's shared heritage. They bought books about historical black figures like Jackie Robinson, and took the family to Halifax to visit the former site of Africville—an African-Canadian village that was demolished by the city in the 1960s. Joel and Jesse found it all very boring. "How long do we have to stay here?" Joel would ask his parents. Joel and Jesse begged to be taken go-karting instead. "They didn't want no part of it," George recalls with a laugh.

Woods Harbour is a white town, but Joel and Jesse—aside from a couple small incidents—were treated no differently than any of the other children. They were the sons of a fisherman, just like the rest of the boys. "They was treated so well here," George says.

"We didn't see skin colour with them," adds Jennie Huskilson, a friend of Joel's from the time they were both toddlers. "They were from Woods Harbour and that was it."

Mary and George Hopkins.

Joel and George shared no genetic connection, but Joel took to his father's occupation like a fifth-generation fisherman. "His birth parents, neither one of them had anything to do with fishing," Mary says. "But it seemed like from the time he was little that's all he wanted to do. That's all he would talk about."

George had started fishing on weekends when he was ten or eleven, but he wasn't sure he'd be a fisherman. His father owned a fish plant but George definitely didn't want to work there. At twenty he got his captain's papers. He has been fishing ever since. For a time he owned a 65-footer called the *Mary and Nathan* (named for his wife and their first son). He took the boat offshore longlining for hake, cod, and haddock. "We used to go down to the Grand Banks. We'd load that boat every trip," he recalls. "It took three days to get there and sometimes four days to come back because she was loaded. We made good money at the time."

Joel joined George on fishing trips as a boy. At age eight Joel was aboard for a swordfishing trip. The ride to the fishing grounds was rough, the boat heaving the whole way. George was in the wheelhouse when Joel emerged from down in the galley and bunk area looking pale.

"You feel all right?" George asked.

"Oh yeah, I'm all right," Joel responded unconvincingly.

Joel then promptly vomited on the deck. He was terribly seasick but didn't want his dad to know. Joel feared George would turn the boat around.

"I imagine you're wishing you'd never come," George suggested when Joel returned to the wheelhouse.

"Oh no! I'm so glad I come," Joel responded earnestly.

"You didn't throw up in my bunk, did you?"

"No, no, no," Joel insisted.

George later found his bunk full of barf and half wished he'd left Joel on shore.

It was apparent early on that Joel relished the aspects of fishing that kept many others on land: rough seas, bad weather, and the potential for injury.

Another time, Joel—perhaps nine or ten—joined George and a cousin, Kent Devine, for a tuna trip off Sambro, Nova Scotia. Joel was casting a line to catch mackerel to use as bait. The hook pierced one of Joel's fingers, yet he didn't even peep as George pushed the hook fully through Joel's finger, removed the barb, and reversed the hook back out. Kent was astounded that Joel failed to flinch, but George knew why: Joel didn't want to go home. "He just loved it. I never seen anybody love fishing so much," George adds. "I never loved it like him."

There's one particular childhood photo of Joel seated with his arms around a swordfish. Mary says she can see love in her son's eyes. "I don't think I've ever had a man look at me like that!" she says before laughing.

So what was it about fishing that hooked Joel?

"Fishing is a little bit wild and he's certainly wild," George says.

"It just seems like from the time we got him he was wild," Mary adds. "He was wild but he was the most loving of all the kids. He was one of the quickest to say 'I love you' and the quickest to hug you." She smiles. "But also the quickest to make you really mad."

When he was twelve or thirteen, Joel went tuna fishing with George off Grand Manan, New Brunswick. In port on the island, Joel disappeared. George searched frantically but couldn't find his son anywhere. He checked the entire boat, around the wharf, in the water, and paced the town. But there was no Joel. Around 2:30 A.M. George returned to the boat and found Joel asleep in his bunk. The next morning George asked Joel where he went. Joel's answer was simple: he'd made some friends.

One night at home in Woods Harbour, Joel's sister, Hollie, woke Mary to report that Joel was missing. Like George on Grand Manan, they launched a panicked search. Eventually Joel sauntered home. He'd heard some music outside, crawled out his window, and trekked through the woods to find the source: a nearby party. Everybody there was older than Joel. "But he had to go have a yarn with them," Mary says, shaking her head. "And when he was done he came home."

"Mom, I was fine," Joel insisted.

From an early age Joel could talk to nearly anyone. In the early '90s, the Hopkins family travelled to Sunday River, Maine, for a skiing vacation. They were only on the hill a half hour when a man skied up alongside Joel.

"Hello, Joel," he said.

"'Hello Joel?'" George repeated, incredulous. "How would you possibly know who Joel is? We just got here."

"There's nobody on this mountain who doesn't know Joel," the man replied.

"He could meet people anywhere," George concludes.

And he fit into most social situations. George's older sister, Ethel, is part of a local women's bi-weekly social club. One day Joel stopped in to see his "Aunt Ettie," not knowing the meeting was in progress. "It's all old women and they're all in their seventies," George says. "So Joel goes in there and sees all these women and instead of just leaving like most teenagers would, he sits right down amongst them and stays there all night. And has a yarn with them. They all got a big kick out of it—Joel telling his stories."

"He was friendly," Ethel adds. "It didn't bother him who was there."

Joel's sweet side meant he could sit and gab with Ethel's white-haired friends, but he was also a scrapper. "He loved to fist fight," Mary says.

George drove Joel to his hockey games—which were sometimes as far away as Halifax or the Annapolis Valley—and despite having driven three hours to the rink, Joel would get kicked out of the game in the first period. He was only five-foot-five and 140 pounds but he'd skate right out to the biggest guy on the ice—even if he was a foot taller—and start a fight. Five or ten minutes into the game and Joel was done.

George shakes his head. "Mary wouldn't even take him to hockey by the end of it." For Joel, fighting was entertaining. After a game, he could easily befriend the same guy he'd tried to deck.

Jessica Mood, a cousin and childhood friend, was at a hockey game with Joel in Shelburne when word spread that Joel liked to fight and was good at it. When Joel exited the rink there was a group outside waiting for him. A challenger wanted to test Joel's reputation. Joel walked into a circle of strangers. He had no backup. Joel took a number of shots but, according to Jessica, also delivered a couple head-butts. He won and walked away. "He wasn't scared of nothing. He had no fear," Jessica says. "He wasn't scared of nobody."

At parties, Joel could bail friends out of tense situations with ease. If one of his friends seemed on the verge of a fight, Joel would step in between the two men. At the beginning of high school, Joel heard that an older student was bullying Jennie Huskilson, who lived just down the road from him in Woods Harbour.

"Don't worry about it," he told her.

"What do you mean?" she asked.

"You'll never have to worry about it again. I can promise you that," was all Joel said.

Jennie later saw Joel talking to the guy who was pestering her. She never learned what was said, but the bullying stopped immediately. For Jennie, Joel was like a protective older brother. "If he was your friend, he would do anything in the world for you," she said. "Anything."

Joel's performance in the classroom, however, was far less commanding. Joel was extremely sociable and a scrapper, but he was not a scholar. "He hated school," Mary says. Part of Joel's problem was the wildness in him. He'd also been diagnosed with ADHD; he just couldn't sit still. "Unless he was sitting on a wheeler or a dirt bike," George quips.

Joel quit school a month shy of finishing grade eleven. At seventeen, he was fishing full-time. And he was content. "That's all he wanted to do," Mary says. "Either that or he was on his dirt bike or his four-wheeler or he was hunting."

Joel was short but he was quick, agile, lean, strong, and had barely any body fat. He had six-pack abs but they weren't earned from hours of crunches. As George puts it: "Joel had muscles and he didn't do anything to deserve it." Earned or not, Joel's physique meant he was well suited to crewing on fishing boats. But Joel didn't apply his athleticism just to hauling traps and gaffing swordfish: he could scamper through rigging, climb ropes, and do backflips on deck. He snatched seagulls out of the air—cat-like, with his bare hands—then tied ribbons to their feet and let them go. Later, George would hear puzzled fishermen declare: "I seen this gull go by with a ribbon on his foot!"

When fishing as a boy with George, Joel would beg his dad to steam alongside other boats. Joel would then grab the boom on George's boat and swing out over the water, his feet dangling just above the waves. It was a trick he never abandoned. Ivan Cameron crewed alongside Joel for five lobster seasons, hauling, baiting, and moving traps. One rough day the pair was bringing gear back on deck when Joel briefly disappeared. Ivan suddenly heard Joel shout his name. Ivan looked up to see Joel hanging from the boom, suspended over the water. It was a dangerous move, especially on a windy day. But Joel just laughed and easily swung back on deck.

"He was just like a monkey," Ivan says.

Ivan was much older than Joel—a career fisherman in his late fifties—but the two got along well. Joel often complimented Ivan—"Iv" as he called him—on his strength, saying it was impressive a man his age could still handle the physical deck work. "That was kind of encouraging to me," Ivan says.

Joel also looked out for Ivan. One night Ivan was walking up from the wharf when three guys in a truck—clearly drinking—started hassling him. One of the guys reached out and grabbed Ivan by the neck. Joel, still on the boat, bolted to the truck to protect his deck mate.

The age difference between Joel and Ivan was only apparent in terms of their sleeping patterns. Joel preferred to sleep in, but that's not possible when lobstering. Ivan would often pick Joel up around 5 A.M. and many mornings had to honk the horn to wake Joel up. "He liked to sleep in, but when you got him aboard the boat he was always there to work," Ivan says. "He was the best kind of a fella. He was a hard worker."

One day, Joel and Ivan were hauling lobster pots offshore, outside of German Bank, when the wind started to build. The captain, Tim Malone, asked Joel and Ivan their thoughts on going further offshore to retrieve the last hundred traps. It would involve steaming out another 15 kilometres to the boundary of Canadian and American waters.

"Yes! Yes! Go get 'em!" Joel yelled without hesitation.

Ivan said nothing. With Tim out of earshot in the wheelhouse, Ivan turned to Joel.

"You think this is a good idea, with it breezing up like this?"

"Yes! I'm all for it," Joel replied. "That don't bother me, Iv."

Ivan wanted to head in but was stuck plowing into the waves to fetch the final traps. They got most of them aboard but had to leave the final twenty behind because it was impossible to find the buoys in the large waves. The return trip to port took nine hours because of the rough seas—three more than usual. But Joel was smiling. "That was Joel. He was young and fierce," Ivan concludes. "The harder it blew, the more he liked it."

At one point, Joel went out west to work in the oil patch. He'd taken the necessary courses but didn't last one month in Alberta.

"The sea is in my blood!" he told Mary.

At sea, toughness, fearlessness, and daring can be assets. As long-time Woods Harbour fisherman Sandy Stoddard notes, fishing is a physically demanding job that requires grit. "You can't just take a guy off the streets in Halifax or take a fella out of an office job and put him out there," Sandy says. "No, it ain't gonna work for that fella."

On land, however, the traits that made Joel a desirable crewman sometimes rubbed up against social norms—and laws. Joel's friends recall stories with equal parts amazement and amusement. One example: Joel riding his four-wheeler alongside a deer, jumping on the deer's back, and unsuccessfully attempting to cut its throat with a knife. Jacking deer out of season wasn't uncommon, nor was speeding.

"He lost his [driver's] licence I don't know how many times," Mary says.

When lacking a licence, Joel usually got around town on a four-wheeler. At one point he owned a Honda racing wheeler that could go well over 100 kilometres an hour. He eventually agreed to sell the wheeler to Graydon Mood, a good friend. Graydon passed Joel $2,500 in cash and mounted the wheeler, expecting to leave. Joel looked at the money, looked at Graydon, then looked at the wheeler. He was torn.

"Ah, you gotta let me go for one last ride," Joel said.

"Go ahead, whatever," Graydon said.

Joel hopped on and tore down the road, likely passing cars as he went.

In Woods Harbour, Halloween night was a time of guaranteed troublemaking. A gang of guys would always wander around, pulling pranks and perhaps worse. "They wouldn't do terrible, terrible stuff," George explains, "but they might push a car in the ditch. One time we put a boat on top of a fella's house."

One Halloween, Joel—then about fourteen—was part of a roving gang of twenty. They were maintaining the tradition. Eventually the police arrived to snuff out the troublemaking, and Joel ran to hide in a ditch. After a while all seemed quiet. Joel emerged from the ditch and saw someone nearby; he walked up to the guy, tapped him on the shoulder, and offered a warning: "You oughtta be careful. The police are around." The man turned around. He was a cop. Joel finished his night at the police station.

George was at a baseball tournament in the Annapolis Valley around the time cellphones were becoming popular. Another father at the tournament walked up to George and said: "I just love these cellphones. I know where my kids are all the time. I can keep track of them."

"Well, I got a cellphone but I don't really need it for that reason," George responded. "The police are at my door all the time telling me where Joel is."

George and Mary both laugh. "They all knew his name, put it that way," George says of the cops. "It's funny now. It wasn't funny then."

"I don't know how you'd describe Joel," Mary adds. "He was really bad. He did a lot of bad things. You'd either love him or hate him. But most people really, really loved him."

"He didn't rob any banks or anything like that," George concludes. "But he was no angel."

Before her retirement, Brenda MacAdams Crowell worked in the credit office at the Wilson's Shopping Centre in Barrington Passage. It was common for fishermen to stop in on Fridays to cash cheques at the office. For several years Joel arrived regularly on Fridays with a cheque linked to George's company account.

Joel believed he was fooling Brenda, but she knew Joel was writing the cheques to himself. She also figured George and Mary probably didn't care. They'd call over if they did. "You could tell, just by his eyes, that he knew better," Brenda says. "He just needed some spending money for the weekend. He was kind of a bad little guy," she adds with a smile. Bad in a very likeable way. "I always called him my little boyfriend." Joel was always quick with a hug and some sweet talk. "He definitely was a character. A likeable character."

It's a sentiment echoed by Jessica Mood, Joel's friend and cousin. "You never knew what he was going to say or do. He was bad," she says. "But he was one of those guys you couldn't help but love."

George sums up his son's mischievous charm like this: "He'd give you the shirt off his back and then you'd realize it wasn't his shirt, it was mine. That's Joel."

Elaine, Joel, and their son Tate, who was born in October 2012.

Joel first hooked up with Elaine Atwood in high school. They dated for a few months but broke up. "He was charming," Elaine recalls. "He had a good heart. And he was a good friend."

One night in 2005 they ran into each other at the Dooly's pool hall in Barrington Passage. Joel was drunk and needed a ride home. "I think he got thrown out," Elaine says. She gave Joel a lift. "And that was that," she says with a smile.

Three months later Elaine, then twenty-one, was pregnant.

But not even the prospect of family life could tame Joel, who was also twenty-one. During the time Elaine was pregnant, Joel smashed his truck into an electrical power box in a driving rainstorm. He had been drinking. The crash knocked out power in the surrounding area and left Joel's truck completely torched. Joel was dragged from his truck and a member of the fire department told George and Mary it wasn't looking good: Joel's condition was critical. He was taken to hospital in an ambulance and the family rushed to see him. They found him in a hospital bed with a brace around his neck. "When I found out he wasn't dying, I was going to strangle him," George recalls. "Then he looked up at me with those big brown eyes and said, 'I love you, Dad. I'm sorry.'"

"You couldn't stay mad at him," Mary concludes. "Joel was a loveable bad. He'd get away with it because of his personality. He knew he was good-looking. And he would smile. He could talk his way out of anything."

After the crash, Elaine warned Joel: "Don't you dare do it again." In the years after—especially following the birth of their first son, Julius, in 2006—Elaine sensed Joel was calming, if only slightly. "Yes, he still rode around with his friends and did crazy things with them, but he did settle down a bit," she says. He often bought her flowers and used part of every fishing paycheque to buy something for Julius. "He wanted Julius to have wheelers and he wanted Julius to have everything fast, just like him," she says. A second son, Tate, was born in October 2012. "[Joel] was a good dad. He always wanted to show the kids about his life—fishing and that kind of stuff."

Fishing and lobstering kept Joel away from home for regular stretches, so he got a guard dog to protect his little family. "Even though he wasn't around very much he always made sure we were fine—money-wise, house-wise, everything," Elaine says. Joel and Elaine talked about getting married but neither thought a piece of paper mattered much. As Elaine put it: "We're a family, we're together."

In his mid-twenties Joel told his dad he wanted a dirt bike.

"Joel, you don't want a dirt bike," George responded, unsuccessfully.

George went with Joel to buy the bike. "Take the front tire off because he ain't going to need that," George told the seller.

He was right: if Joel knew someone was watching, he'd tear down the road with the bike up on just the rear tire. "He wore his back tire out long before the front," George says.

Joel's cousin Jessica remembers looking out her grandmother's window and seeing Joel ripping down the road on the back wheel of his bike. Jessica just shook her head. *That's Joel*, she thought. "He was your definition of a badass."

Tyler Goreham recalls the night Joel, likely not sober, tore down the road on the bike. Joel went down into a ditch and flipped over the handlebar. Before anyone could help, though, Joel was up and shaking off his bike. He exited the ditch, popped up on his back tire, and continued tearing down the road. And Joel wasn't scared to pass cars on the main road by gunning full-throttle along the dirt shoulder, either.

"Fear wasn't something he had anywhere," George concludes. "He just didn't have it."

Thus, Katlin is fairly certain of Joel's answer when he calls to explain the plan to fish for halibut more than 160 kilometres offshore in February. Joel is part of Katlin's regular lobstering crew, a position he clearly enjoys. "LETS GET ON," he wrote on Facebook on November 27, 2012, the start of the season. His enthusiasm was unaffected by low lobster prices: "can't express the adrenaline going threw [sic] [my] body can't wait."

Joel had also crewed for Katlin aboard Reg LeBlanc's boat, the *Row Row*, the previous summer. In early August, Joel badly jammed his thumb while racing to get the swordfish gear back aboard the boat. The Coast Guard had to evacuate him to shore for medical treatment and he ended up in hospital in Halifax. The injury forced Joel to take a short break from fishing. It was torture—he couldn't wait to get back on the *Row Row*. "Don't worrie [sic] boys swords and tuna haven't seen the last of me this summer I will be back on the grind and ready to load the row row," he wrote on Facebook on August 10, 2012, in his unique grammatical style. On August 26 he added: "I enjoy the ocean more than land…I'm Gona grind till I die that's what I love to do."

Katlin knows snow and cold isn't enough to keep Joel on shore, either. In fact, it's just the opposite: winter fishing will be a thrill.

"We got some fish quota," Katlin tells Joel. "Let's rig up and go fishing."

Joel, now twenty-seven and the father of two young sons, is pumped.

"We're going winter fishing!" he tells Elaine after talking to Katlin. "We ain't going lobstering. We're gonna catch the big ones!"

CHAPTER 4

BAD BOY BILL

CAPE SABLE ISLAND LIES JUST OFF THE SOUTHWESTERN TIP OF NOVA
Scotia. Known locally as "Cape Island," it's a wooded, often fog-draped patch
of land connected to the mainland via a causeway at Barrington Passage,
the local commercial hub. The island, roughly a fifteen-minute drive from
Woods Harbour, has also been long connected to the fishery. Cod and haddock helped fuel the industry until the ground fishery collapse of the early
1990s. Today lobster is king. The local municipality—Barrington—calls
itself "The Lobster Capital of Canada."

Cape Sable Island is also synonymous with the Cape Islander fishing
boat. A staple of the Atlantic inshore fishery, the first Cape Islander was
launched in 1905. The boats, typically 12–15 metres long, are known for

their distinctive high bows and long, broad, open workspaces, which are low to the sea. The design makes it easy to set and haul lobster traps, as well as longlines for halibut, tuna, swordfish, and shark.

Billy Jack Hatfield grew up in Clam Point, one of the small communities on Cape Sable Island. Born on November 29, 1979, Billy Jack displayed an early proclivity to go his own way. One day when he was very young, Billy Jack attempted to follow his Aunt Phyllis home after she stopped by for a visit. Billy Jack, dressed in a blue knit sweater and a white hat and pushing a kid's shopping cart ahead of him, followed his aunt up the shoulder of a busy road. "I hollered my lungs out and I ran and I caught him," recalls Billy Jack's father, Jack. "But he was that kind of kid from the beginning. He was going to go and do what he wanted to do and that was it."

Billy Jack grew up on the water and in the woods. His mom, Janet Reynolds, pulls out a photo of her son at about age four. He is wearing boots nearly up to his knees, camouflage pants, a plaid shirt, and a red ball cap. He is looking down, intently hacking at a log with a Bowie knife that is more than half the length of his arm. The photo was taken on an Easter Sunday in the early '80s. The family was making breakfast outside and Billy Jack was gathering kindling for a fire.

"He's only little there," Janet says before laughing. "He chopped his wood. He could start a fire with sticks. He could do anything. It didn't matter what it was."

Billy Jack liked skating and played some baseball (in grade three he took a ball to the face that broke his nose) but it was the outdoors that held his attention. "He loved to go up around the shore with his father," Janet says. "I'd make him a lunch in the morning and they'd go." After rabbit-hunting trips with his father, Billy Jack would keep the rabbits' feet and dry them behind the woodstove. "He was like a real old Indian," Janet says. "He worked with leather. He made belts and wallets. This was before he was even in school. I kid you not."

As a boy, Billy Jack roamed the woods around Clam Point with his friend B. J. Sears. They were both only about thirteen when they took chainsaws into the woods, cut down some trees, and constructed a small log cabin to serve as their camp. They whittled wooden knives and daggers, and in winter hooked their family Labrador retrievers to sleds to go dogsledding. Billy Jack had many dogs throughout his life and most were named Buck. B. J. laughs. "For some reason he stuck with the same name."

Billy Jack's enthusiasm for the woods did not extend to the classroom. Just getting him to school was a serious challenge. He refused to even go near the school for the first three days of grade primary. "When I did get him to go, on the fourth day, I had to go with him," Janet remembers.

It was a harbinger of how his academic career would progress. Why didn't he enjoy school? Janet doesn't hesitate with her answer: "He can't sit still. He's got to be busy. He'd rather be home collecting hens eggs or plucking geese or going up around the shore with his father with a picnic," she says. "School didn't move fast enough for him."

Hunting, on the other hand, was exciting. When Billy Jack was eight or nine, he and Jack went out to test a new deer caller. Out in the woods, father and son climbed a tall pine tree. Raising the caller to his lips, Jack blew a couple quick grunts. He waited three or four minutes before blowing a couple more. Out of the woods, as if by command, sauntered a six-point buck. Jack, perched in the tree, raised his rifle and fired. The deer went down and Billy Jack turned quickly to his dad.

"Call out another one!" he said.

Jack laughs. It was a fluke that a buck emerged so quickly after the call. Billy Jack had assumed there was a line of deer just beyond the trees, waiting to be lured out.

The pair's most memorable hunting trip took place when Billy Jack was thirteen. It was the first day of deer season, and father and son headed into the woods, walking side by side up an old logging road. Billy Jack was armed with a shotgun, while Jack carried a rifle. Suddenly, up ahead, they heard a loud crashing. The pair hustled up the road and into the woods to find the source of the peculiar noise: two bucks in heated battle, their antlers locked together. Father and son watched awestruck as the two animals separated and took turns charging one other, their antlers cracking like a clap of thunder each time. Both Billy Jack and Jack were struck by the violence of the exchange but eventually remembered why they were standing in the woods with two guns. Jack unloaded all but one of his bullets. Billy Jack, meanwhile, blasted his shotgun. The two bucks darted in opposite directions. One disappeared into the woods. Jack had one bullet left.

"Billy! Shoot him if you can!" Jack shouted in the direction of the remaining buck.

"I ain't got no shells left," Billy Jack called back.

Jack squeezed the trigger, firing his last bullet. Down went the buck.

Later, while skinning it, Jack noticed the deer had two holes in its body: one in the back, one in the shoulder. Hauling back the skin, they noticed there were no bullet holes. They were shotgun holes. Though he initially thought he bagged the buck, Jack realized he had missed—numerous times. "I never touched him! It was Billy. He hit him with both shots," Jack says with obvious pride. "My bullet holes was way up here in the trees," he adds, gesturing up with his hand, laughing. Billy Jack mounted the antlers. His first deer: an eight-point buck.

It was around this time that Billy Jack dropped out of school. During grade seven he often cut classes and spent his days at a camp in the woods behind the school. Before the school year ended he quit for good. "There wasn't much I could do about it," Janet insists. "I told him he had to get a job."

Billy Jack's first position was deckhand on a boat owned by Wayne Smith, a family friend, helping to longline for cod and haddock. Aboard Wayne's boat, Billy Jack started like most young men entering the fishery: doing the dirtiest work. Wayne paid him $15 for each tub of trawl he baited, a task that involved placing pieces of mackerel and squid on 360 hooks. Dressing fish—gutting them and throwing the entrails overboard—paid 3 cents per pound. If Billy Jack baited ten tubs and dressed two thousand pounds of fish in a day, he walked off the boat with $210. It beat sitting bored in a classroom. "Billy was always a hands-on fella," Wayne says. "He didn't lay back and wait to do something. If there was something to be done, and he knew how to do it, he'd being doing it."

Billy Jack learned other fishing basics, such as steering a compass course and the tricky task of hauling in a longline. You must gaff the hooked fish while also plucking the old stale bait off the incoming line. Until you master the task, it's easy to end up with a hook in your hand. "There was nothing he was afraid of. He would try most anything," Wayne adds.

With Wayne, Billy Jack also saw how to deal with emergencies at sea. One day, a fire started in the engine room. Seeing the flames, Billy Jack ran to the back of the boat and jumped up on the edge of the stern.

"We're on fire! We better jump overboard!" he yelled.

"Hold up!" Wayne responded. "Don't jump yet."

Wayne opened the engine room door and snuffed out the fire with a couple shots from a fire extinguisher. Though they had to be towed in by the Coast Guard, they were far from abandoning ship. "I don't think he even took his life jacket," Wayne recalls. "He just run for the stern."

Billy Jack didn't stay long with Wayne. He quickly moved on to better-paying gigs, hopping aboard with captains who offered the most attractive spots. In the early years, Janet often had to drive her son to the wharf. He wasn't old enough to drive, yet he was earning a grown man's wages. "Too much money, too fast, too young," Janet says. "He had four-wheelers, motorcycles, new trucks; he had whatever he wanted. He told me himself that he made too much money too fast. And it went to his head."

Billy Jack crewed for Todd Nickerson—Katlin's father—for a few years. "He was one of the best men I ever had," Todd says. Billy Jack didn't say much while aboard Todd's boat, but he worked hard. "For a small guy he probably made boarding traps look as easy as I've ever seen anybody do it," Todd recalls.

On Sandy Stoddard's boat, Billy Jack was reserved, very quiet, and worked like a machine. Sandy knew, however, that Billy Jack had another side to him. "He could get in all kinds of trouble when he drank," Sandy says. "Without the liquor, the most you'd get is a smile out of him."

Billy Jack's decision to fish wasn't surprising. His father, Jack, was fifteen years old when his own father took him fishing. It was summer and he had just finished grade eight. Jack wanted to get through grade nine before studying to be a diesel mechanic. Those plans changed at the end of the summer. "I was getting all ready to go back to school and my dad said, 'You can't go back to school. You got to stay fishing with me.' So I did," says Jack simply. Gone was his plan to be a diesel mechanic. He's been a fisherman ever since.

Jack took Billy Jack fishing as a boy but Billy Jack bored easily; he had to stay busy. "If the fish wasn't biting he'd want to give it up. He had to be doing something. He didn't want to be idle," Jack says. When steaming home, Billy Jack would volunteer to dress the fish—anything to stay busy. He'd even ask to jump aboard other boats to dress fish for the other crews. "He wasn't a lazy person, that's for sure," Jack says, laughing. Jack later discovered that Billy Jack was jumping ship mainly to sneak cigarettes. "He was getting away from me and having a little smoke."

Thinking back on his decades at sea, Jack views his connection to fishing less as a career choice and more like a physical law that couldn't be broken, neutralized, or overcome: "We was born up in this area and that's what we done and that's the only thing we knew," he says. "So I did it. And that's how Billy Jack got into fishing—through me. So probably if I'd never took to fishing he wouldn't have been fishing. Maybe that was the wrong move."

Billy Jack was often subdued and reserved. But he also possessed a wild thread—an outgoing, spontaneous side that sometimes got him into trouble: he shot deer at age twelve or thirteen without a licence; he started driving at twelve and drove without a licence until he was nearly thirty; he smashed up Janet's car more than once. Billy Jack's sister, Natasha, meanwhile, was well-behaved. "Natasha used to say Billy Jack was like my pet," Janet says. "It's not that I loved him more. It's just that he needed more guidance than she did. She was a good kid right from the get-go."

Billy Jack was quick to learn (provided it wasn't in school) and self-sufficient. He was a skilled and self-taught carpenter, and he could hunt, skin a deer, and work with leather. He even learned to quilt and sew with his grandmother, Molly, often moving fabric through her sewing machine with a cigarette hanging from his mouth. Janet believes her son could easily have survived the apocalypse. "I wanted to put that boy on a survival show," she says fondly. "The other fellas would be sent home the first day. He could have won it hands down."

Yet that rugged spirit and independent streak also caused problems. One night in his late teens, Billy Jack was staying at a campground in nearby Clyde River. He went into the woods, shot a deer, dragged it back, and dressed the carcass on a picnic table. "He was wild!" Janet says. "I shouldn't say the law didn't mean nothing to him, but he always thought if you're hungry go get it." She goes on: "He didn't follow rules in the house, or with hunting or anything. If he wanted a feed of lobsters he'd just go out and set a pot and get 'em. He abided by no rules." Janet had a licence plate made for her son's four-wheeler: "BBB" for Bad Boy Bill. "He feared nothing at all," Janet concludes.

One day, while out fishing, Todd Nickerson told Billy Jack: "You know, there's a reason God gives you fear: it's to keep you safe." Billy Jack just grinned. "He had no fear," Todd says.

Not surprisingly, Joel Hopkins was one of Billy Jack's best friends. Like Joel, Billy Jack wanted to go fast, especially on his motorcycle. The pair rode four-wheelers together and built camps. Janet was shocked the first time she saw Joel. She found him sleeping on her floor, where he'd crashed after a night out with Billy Jack. "I hauled the blanket down and he was black. I said, 'Oh my God what has Billy done? He's painted this fella!' I never seen him bring home a black boy." She soon concluded that Joel was a "good boy," and liked having him around. Whenever Joel stopped at the house Janet often asked: "Are you being a good boy, dear?"

"Yes," Joel would reply. "I haven't had a drink since..." He'd then pause and pretend to look at his watch.

Billy Jack met Theresa Goreham, a girl from Woods Harbour, when they were both about fourteen. Though never married, Billy Jack and Theresa remained together for the better part of thirteen years and had three children together: Cole, Angel, and Bronson. Billy Jack always provided for the family, even if his behaviour could be unpredictable and erratic. When Cole was a baby, Billy Jack—upset after a fight with Theresa—set the family's mobile home on fire. Neither Theresa nor Cole was home at the time, but the trailer was destroyed. Two weeks later he torched his truck. Billy Jack and Theresa separated for a while but eventually reunited.

At home, Billy Jack was often quiet. It took a while for Theresa to realize he acted "crazy" when off with friends, often fuelled by alcohol and marijuana. "When they wanted to party they called him," she says. "He'd do anything and it was usually dangerous." Theresa also believed Billy Jack was the father of a Cape Sable Island girl born five months before Angel. He wasn't listed as the father on the birth certificate, but he never denied paternity and sometimes visited her, despite not being certain the girl was his. Regardless, the possibility of a fourth child was part of a larger pattern. As Theresa concludes: "It was just a bunch of craziness for thirteen years."

Billy Jack's wild, erratic behaviour peaked during a dark period in his twenties. At one point, Janet asked Wayne Smith—the family friend who gave Billy Jack his first fishing job—to speak with her son. Wayne, a part-time deacon at the Stoney Island Baptist Church on Cape Sable Island, was also concerned about Billy Jack. He was taking hallucinogens and talking "weirdly." Among other things, Billy Jack claimed to know the location of explosives under bridges and buildings in Halifax. Wayne confronted Billy Jack at his house, challenging him on his behaviour and choices. "He said something about his relationship with God," Wayne recalls. Wayne's response was simple: "God wouldn't want you acting the way you're acting and treating your family." Wayne told Billy Jack to shape up and become a better family man. Billy Jack, visibly angry, walked out of the house. "He knew what I was saying was right, but he was trying to justify some of the things he was doing back in those days," Wayne says.

Some family members and friends believed Billy Jack suffered from bipolar disorder; others thought he simply reacted poorly to alcohol and marijuana. Wayne, meanwhile, believed Billy Jack's behaviour was linked to his drift away from the church. "He strayed a little bit," Wayne says. "He got into drugs and things, which kind of took his foundation of faith away a little bit. But the foundation is always there."

For Billy Jack, fishing was not a true calling; it was a source of fast money. A crew member working year-round for a skilled captain can easily make $75,000 to $120,000. Even six months of lobstering can net $75,000 to $90,000 depending on market prices. Carpentry, however, was Billy Jack's passion. He was self-taught but skilled. Name it and he could build it—cupboards, camps, houses, barns. As a carpenter, though, you have to pound a lot of nails to make $120,000. And there wasn't always steady work. There was, however, always a fishing boat to hop on.

In 2006, looking for a fresh start, Theresa pushed to move the family to booming Alberta. They spent a year in Grande Prairie and—after a spell back home so Theresa could give birth to Bronson—a year in the capital, Edmonton. Out west, Billy Jack found good-paying work building houses. The western oil boom meant he didn't have to fish. But the move to Alberta didn't fix the underlying domestic issues.

"He was very friendly with the women so I had to get out of there," Theresa recalls. "He done what he wanted, when he wanted, and how he wanted and that was it." In 2009, after two years out west, Theresa and the children moved back to Nova Scotia. Billy Jack remained behind. "That's where everything ended," Theresa says.

Thinking back on their time together, however, Theresa concludes Billy Jack wasn't bad all the time. "Just on the weekends," she says. "He was a good person." She laughs. "He kept things exciting. Not too many dull moments."

Theresa's brother, Sandy Goreham, thought of Billy Jack as an older brother. Billy Jack took him hunting and camping. They also spent a couple years lobstering together. "When he was good," Sandy says, "he was awesome."

Billy Jack eventually returned home to Nova Scotia and attempted to do more carpentry work. He was hired to build a maintenance shed and feed silo at a mink farm on Cape Sable Island. Needing help, Billy Jack called Wayne Smith. Wayne, who had retreated somewhat from the fishery since the days when he first took Billy Jack to sea, was happy to assist. He arrived at the mink farm to find Billy Jack with the entire project already arranged in his head. They built the four shed walls separately, and the roof in two pre-shingled pieces. Wayne thought it an odd approach, but Billy Jack had a plan. He brought in a crane and assembled the shed like a life-sized Lego set. Wayne was impressed. As usual, Billy Jack was good at whatever he put his hands to.

When the local municipality wanted a gazebo built at a small seaside park in Clam Point, Wayne—who, at the time, was also a municipal councillor—convinced Billy Jack to bid on the job. He won the contract and built a fine gazebo.

Wayne, who had previously challenged Billy Jack on his behaviour, saw changes in his former crew member. "He was thinking a little different," Wayne says. "I know his attitude was different." To Wayne, Billy Jack seemed to be heading in a better direction. "I believe he was working his way back," he says. "I think he was on the start of recovery, physically as well as spiritually."

In 2009, Billy Jack started dating Cheryl Brannen. Their relationship was a source of controversy in her family: Billy Jack was twenty-nine; Cheryl was forty-nine with grown children. Billy Jack initially told Cheryl he was older, not wanting the age gap to deter her. And to Cheryl, Billy Jack *did* seem older than his age. He was very knowledgeable for a guy not yet thirty. The couple lived together briefly in Cheryl's house on Cape Sable Island, then rented a cottage at the end of a dirt lane in Ingomar, a small peninsula roughly thirty minutes from Barrington Passage.

Billy Jack's past was unknown to Cheryl when they met, but Billy Jack did not conceal his previous behaviour and actions. "He had no problem telling me everything about his previous life and all the wild things he had done," Cheryl says. "For his thirty-three years he did a lot of living. I'll put it that way."

Among Billy Jack's admissions: he had been committed to the East Coast Forensic Hospital, a psychiatric facility in Dartmouth, Nova Scotia. He was diagnosed with a drug-induced psychotic episode and spent nine months at the hospital.

As far as Cheryl could tell, however, Billy Jack's most erratic behaviour was behind him. He seemed settled. "With any relationship there's always ups and downs, but in general our life was pretty quiet," she says. "We kept to ourselves quite a bit and just sort of did our thing." Billy Jack's problems, Cheryl determined, stemmed from alcohol. "He could be unpredictable. Drinking wasn't a good thing for him. When he drank it turned him into a different person," she says. "That was the key to changing his mood."

Though separated in age by two decades, Billy Jack and Cheryl shared creative common ground—he with carpentry, she with dress designs and home interiors. Billy Jack sometimes helped Cheryl install blinds, and together they laid a tile floor in a restaurant owned by Billy Jack's mom. "We just worked really well together," Cheryl says. "People say different things but he was a very good person. There may have been things that he had done that offended people, but overall he was a good person—a very creative person. There was nothing that he couldn't build. Whatever he put his mind to he was able to do it." With carpentry, she adds, Billy Jack's ability was "limitless."

Billy Jack returned to Edmonton in January 2011 and spent most of that year framing houses. Cheryl joined him for a time. She also brought

Billy Jack with his children: Cole, Bronson, and Angel.

his children—Cole, Bronson, and Angel—to visit during the summer. In September, Billy Jack returned home. He was homesick and missed his kids. It was also in 2011 that Billy Jack proposed to Cheryl, presenting her with a ring he had designed by a jeweller in Yarmouth. "He just sort of popped it on me one day," she says with a giggle. "Because of the age difference and some controversy I was a bit scared to say yes," she admits, "but I knew that we would be together. So eventually I accepted it." The engagement was not widely publicized. "We did our own thing and kept things fairly quiet," Cheryl says. "We tried to cause as little controversy as possible."

At their cottage in Ingomar, Billy Jack and Cheryl had cats, a German shepherd and—until the racoons ate them—chickens. One night when she got home from work, Billy Jack took Cheryl to see some sheep owned by a local breeder. Soon, the couple had five Icelandic sheep, including two rams. They kept the animals in a fenced-in patch of field just metres from the ocean. Their plan was to breed the sheep for wool and meat. Billy Jack and Cheryl also discussed a plan to fix up her house on Cape Sable Island and either rent or sell it. Then they'd rent-to-own the land in Ingomar and build a house together.

Despite his lack of enthusiasm for fishing, Billy Jack continues to go to sea for the money. For the 2012–13 lobster season he decides to crew for Katlin. It means working beside his good friend Joel.

Eventually Katlin mentions his halibut quota. He asks Billy Jack if he wants to stay on for some winter longlining trips. Billy Jack has been commissioned to build a house on Cape Sable Island in the spring. It's a project he's very excited about: it could expand his carpentry work and will definitely put to use the skills he developed in Alberta. Winter is a slow season for carpentry, however, so there won't be much work before he starts building the house. Billy Jack decides he can fit in a couple fishing trips this winter. He's not thrilled about it, but there will be some decent money at the end. Then he'll get back to carpentry, hopefully for good.

CHAPTER 5

A FAMILY HISTORY OF TRAGEDY

THE SUN WAS NOT YET UP ON OCTOBER 29, 1975 WHEN THE CREW OF THE *Sylvialynn* landed its gruesome catch.

The *Sylvialynn*, a dragger out of Saulnierville, Nova Scotia, a rural Acadian fishing village, was 50 kilometres west-northwest of Yarmouth. At about 5:15 A.M., the crew realized they'd solidly snagged their net on the bottom, 160 metres below. The net was eventually freed and hauled up, revealing a grisly sight: tangled inside was part of a human body.

On deck in the early morning darkness, the startled crew of the *Sylvialynn* no doubt wondered: *who is this and why are they on the bottom of the ocean?*

A light wind blew from the northwest and the sky was clear when the *Colville Bay* motored away from Woods Harbour on April 3, 1974. Victor Brannen, the boat's owner and captain, was in the wheelhouse. On deck, his six-man crew was preparing for what they hoped would be a profitable trip. The seven men, all from Woods Harbour, had the *Colville Bay* loaded with enough ice and bait for at least five days of fishing off the rock-strewn and treacherous southwest coast of Nova Scotia.

Built in 1960, the *Colville Bay* was originally a scallop dragger. Victor had recently remodelled the wooden 62-footer, however, with extensive alterations and additions, turning it into a longliner. Among the additions: a slaughterhouse, a trawl loader, and a gas-powered battery charger at the aft end of the wheelhouse. This was the *Colville Bay*'s maiden voyage as a longliner. The crew set a number of trawls in the Bay of Fundy, between German Bank off Woods Harbour and Lurcher Shoal off Yarmouth.

But then the *Colville Bay* disappeared.

The boat was reported missing on April 9, 1974, after failing to return to Woods Harbour, and an extensive search was launched. Two planes and a helicopter were used to search from the air, while fifteen local fishing boats and four federal vessels patrolled the water for a glimpse of the Cape Islander's green hull and white wheelhouse.

The weather had been mostly cloudy in recent days, with moderate winds and seas. On the evening of April 6, three days after the boat left shore, a moderate gale had passed over the area where the *Colville Bay* crew was thought to be fishing, bringing showers and flurries. Had the boat been roughed up in the gale?

Wreckage found by the searchers quickly supported another theory.

Near Brier Island, searchers found floating bait tubs and two unmoored high flyers used to mark fishing gear at sea. They also found pieces of the *Colville Bay* that had been scorched, including a burnt set of steps that once led to the wheelhouse. The evidence led investigators to the following conclusion: "An explosion and fire occurred which allowed the crew no chance of survival."

It was suspected that Victor Brannen's remodelling efforts might have contributed to the sinking. His alterations, including modifications to the engine housing and wheelhouse, were surveyed for insurance purposes, but certain changes did not comply with the Fishing Vessel Inspection Standards, and were not inspected by the Canadian Steamship Inspection branch. Could the new gas-powered battery charger have been at fault? The investigation report, which remained sealed from public view for thirty years, noted that fire detectors or explosive gas detectors might have prevented the incident. Also troubling was Victor's decision to ditch the boat's dory, leaving seven men with only a four-man life raft. Plus, the life raft was stowed atop the wheelhouse. A fire in the wheelhouse or engine room would have made the raft inaccessible and thus "preclude any hope of escape." Despite the efforts of investigators, the *Colville Bay*'s disappearance remained mysterious. As the official search and rescue report noted: "No trace of the seven man crew were found."

More than a year passed and the details of the *Colville Bay* sinking faded into the long list of local fishing vessels that had simply disappeared, taking their crews to the ocean bottom. Then, in October of 1975, the crew of the *Sylvialynn* pulled up human remains, specifically a right thigh that ended at the knee. The thigh was still attached to white underwear and blue jeans. A leather belt, with various designs and the word "Kodiak" emblazoned on the back, was still looped through the jeans. The soggy clump also included chest-high waders and a brown T-shirt with *Sand Point, Alaska* on it.

The crew of the *Sylvialynn* landed the remains onshore in Meteghan—the same Acadian fishing village that the Woods Harbour-based *Sir Echo* was towed to after the 1950 hurricane. A medical examiner later confirmed the identity: Berton King, one of the seven men from the *Colville Bay*. The wreckage found with Berton's remains further confirmed fire on the lost boat. A death certificate was issued, and RCMP in Barrington Passage notified Berton's family. Still, the mystery persisted—and still does—of what exactly happened to the *Colville Bay*.

The *Colville Bay* sinking maintains a lingering presence in Woods Harbour, if only among those residents old enough to remember it. For most, the loss of the *Sir Echo* in 1950 is considered ancient history. The *Colville Bay* sinking occurred recently enough to still affect memories. The macabre retrieval of Berton King's remains, draped in his last outfit, only adds to its staying power.

Cole Nickerson was born a decade after the *Colville Bay* disappeared—January 6, 1985—but he was certainly familiar with it. Andrew Nickerson, a *Colville Bay* crew member, was Cole's great-uncle. Cole's father, Stephen, was about twelve years old when the *Colville Bay* disappeared. Stephen remembers being at the wharf, watching his Uncle Andrew and the other local men prepare for their trip. Stephen was close with his uncle; he recalls Andrew coming to the house to help build lobster pots with his father, Norman (Cole's grandfather). Once, when Stephen was a boy, Andrew bet he could throw a baseball from their garage over the top of a nearby hall. Stephen recalls the ball flying over the hall and thinking it was a throw not even a major-league outfielder could match. After the *Colville Bay* disappeared, Stephen cried himself to sleep at night, wondering what happened to his uncle. A packed memorial service was held at the local wharf, and it was the first time Stephen saw his father, Norman, cry.

Yet the *Colville Bay* sinking didn't deter Stephen from going to sea. If you're a man living in Woods Harbour, you're likely a fisherman. "If you're staying here that's what you'll be doing," Stephen says. "There's the odd one that works in Yarmouth and might become a dentist or something like that, but if you want to stay here that's pretty much what you're going to be doing—lobstering or fishing."

Cole on a halibut trip in 2008, fishing with his cousin Grant and his Uncle Tyrone.

Stephen quit school in grade eight. "I didn't like school. Nobody around here did, really," he says. "You see the guys two or three years older than you going around in cars and making money. Well, we wanted the same thing. What's the point in going to school?" Sixteen-year-old boys fresh out of school could quickly make more in a year than their former teachers.

Cole's introduction to the money fishing could put in his pocket came when he was about ten years old. He spent the summer handlining with Stephen and earned enough to buy himself a second-hand four-wheeler. "He loved it," Stephen says, referring to Cole's time on the water that summer.

Cole followed his dad into the fishery full-time but, unlike Stephen, Cole finished high school first, graduating from Barrington Municipal High School in 2003. "That was one thing I had always told him: 'You're getting your grade twelve,'" Stephen says. Cole spent three seasons lobstering with his father in the years after high school. He was an "A1" worker, Stephen says. Cole eventually jumped between a number of boats, lobstering, longlining, and harpooning swordfish. "He didn't want to do nothing else," Stephen says.

And he was good at it. Cole wasn't tall, about five-foot-nine, but he was stocky and solid with natural strength and big arms. Cole crewed for Sandy Stoddard, a veteran Woods Harbour fisherman who knew all the men aboard the *Miss Ally*, and proved himself to be laid-back and quiet, but also a dogged worker. "He was as strong as a bull moose," Sandy says. "I've never seen a kid at that age that had that much power." At one point, Sandy told Cole—only half-joking—to ease up when hauling in the lobster pots. Sandy feared the pots couldn't endure Cole's power.

Danny Crowell, who crewed alongside all five members of the *Miss Ally* crew at various points, was on a swordfishing trip with Cole when they landed a 240-pounder. Normally, a fish that size is dropped to the floor of the hold, and a couple of crew members drag it into the storage pen. Cole was down in the hold by himself and insisted he could handle the fish alone.

"Give it to me and I'll put it in the pen," he called up to Danny and another crew member, Benjamin Swaine.

Danny and Benjamin lowered the heavy fish as far as they could but there was still a gap between the fish and Cole's hands.

"Let it down to me," Cole said, stretching up his arms.

"We can't," Danny responded.

"Just drop it to me!" Cole barked.

Danny and Benjamin dropped the gigantic fish. Cole caught it, pulled it into his chest, and put it in the pen.

Ever a family business, Cole went lobstering for a couple seasons with his Uncle Tyrone. Tyrone also took Cole on longlining trips in summer. Cole, then in his early twenties, was generally happy and often laughing. Tyrone recalls Cole asking him to steam up to other boats. When they got close, Cole would jump out wearing a wig or a costume. Another time, while fishing with his cousin Grant, Cole hooked buoys to a wharf box to make it float, then paddled the box half a kilometre to another Woods Harbour boat using a shovel. The purpose: Cole wanted to pick up some new DVDs to watch during his downtime. "He was fun to have aboard a boat," Tyrone says of his nephew. "He was always good. No issues at all."

As a kid, Cole joined Tyrone for hunting and camping trips. Tyrone thought of Cole as a son. He was laid-back, little bothered him, and he was easy to get along with. "Everybody I know loved him," Tyrone says.

Cole's mother, Marlene, left the family when Cole was twelve. Marlene and Stephen divorced, and although Cole maintained a relationship with his mother, feelings of abandonment lingered. Cole remained in Woods Harbour with his father and sister, Loghan. Stephen remarried and the family eventually consisted of Stephen, Cole, Loghan, Cole's stepmother, Karen,

Karen's son from a previous relationship, Shale, and Shanobie—the daughter Stephen and Karen had together. Stephen laughs when explaining the mix of family members: "It's a little bit confusing."

Cole's interests were typical of a Woods Harbour kid. He played competitive baseball and hockey, including for his high school team and, later, the Barrington Ice Dogs—the local junior team. He owned a dirt bike and a four-wheeler. Cole was well-liked, sociable, and had many friends. That fact became obvious if Stephen and Karen ever went away for a weekend. Forty vehicles would soon be parked along the road near the house: Cole was having a party. And he'd park cars himself to fit everyone in. Inside, Cole ensured his friends were well fed. Like a grandparent, he often led his guests directly to the table. Among his party specialties: baked hot dogs. "He always figured that everybody had to have something to eat. He'd feed everybody up," Stephen says. Cole also cooked for his grandfather and other members of the family. "He'd bring it right to you, too. Every time. Right to the table," recalls Grant Nickerson, a cousin. "Toast with butter and jam on it. Milk in the glass. You wouldn't even have to get up from your seat." Even at sea in rough weather Cole prepared meals. It might only be Kraft Dinner but Cole was determined to eat. "We're gonna have something," he'd say.

"Cole was a pleaser: he wanted to please people," says his stepmother, Karen. "He didn't want to disappoint you. You could get mad at him and five minutes later it was all over. He'd say, 'Yeah I'm sorry.'"

Cole didn't often have to apologize for his parties. The evidence was usually difficult to find; he was a meticulous cleaner and concealer of clues. There was, however, the time Karen noticed a shoeprint on the ceiling. "I never had no trouble with him," Stephen concludes. "He always listened to me and never talked back. He was always 'Yes, Dad. Yes, Dad.' If I told him something he'd done wrong, he'd say, 'I know, Dad. I know, Dad.' He always agreed with ya." Stephen pauses, then laughs. "But then he'd go do it again."

Among the warnings Cole left unheeded: the dangers of speeding. One night, in the summer of 2011, Cole was headed to a baseball game at the local field. Showing off for the crowd, he gunned his truck to about 70 or 80 kilometres an hour, then pulled the emergency brake in an attempt spin the truck. Cole lost control and the truck rolled.

Grant Nickerson was coming up behind Cole. Seeing the truck on its side, he figured his cousin had swerved to avoid a deer. Then he saw Cole pulling himself from the cab. Cole waved his hat in the air and hollered: "I'm all right! Let's play ball!" Some of the onlookers hurried over to help. Others shook their heads.

Another time, Cole—likely speeding—smashed his truck into a telephone pole in nearby Shag Harbour. The truck looked like it had been put in a crusher, but Cole walked away with only a scratch on his back. The next morning the police came looking for an explanation. "I don't know if you got kryptonite or what but you shouldn't have walked away from [that crash]," the cop told him.

Despite the danger of his son's occupation, Stephen worried more about Cole being in a deadly car accident. Similarly, Karen was relieved when Cole went fishing, because she worried so much when her stepson got behind the wheel of a truck. "It was bad. That's where he scared me—driving," she says. "He liked to go fast. He just didn't have the luck of keeping them on four wheels."

"He had a four-leaf clover in his pocket, that's for sure," adds Cole's Uncle Tyrone. "He was a little bit destructive. He was just a Good Old Boy, as they say." It wasn't surprising, then, that Cole was a close friend of Joel Hopkins, the ultimate Woods Harbour speed demon.

In January 2012, Cole followed a route travelled by plenty of fishermen before him: he left the east coast to work in western Canada. His cousin Grant was already out there and the money was good—even if it meant leaving home and the ocean behind. With the price of lobster down near $3 per pound, there was little money to be made at home. Alberta offered a lucrative alternative.

Cole and Grant had been through adventures before. Growing up, they experienced all the typical Woods Harbour activities together: hunting, four-wheeling, harpooning swordfish, drinking, partying. In February 2004,

Cole, Grant, and a bunch of their friends were at a cabin in the woods during the "White Juan" blizzard. Around midnight, after drinking all night, Cole and Grant jumped on their four-wheelers for a ride. They ventured too far and got caught in the massive snowstorm. The snow fell so quickly that they had to abandon their wheelers. The snow rose to their waists. At one point Cole said he couldn't go on. He crawled under a nearby cabin for shelter. Grant soldiered on. "That was the night I thought I wasn't going to make it," Grant recalls. "I was pretty scared. I prayed in the middle of the road." When he finally arrived back at the cabin, his feet felt like they were frozen solid. Cole arrived shortly after, following a nap under the cover of the cabin. They had been out in the storm for nearly twelve hours.

Cole followed Grant out west, joining his cousin in Red Deer, Alberta. They were part of a pile-driving crew, sometimes working on the same truck. For a time, Cole, Grant, another of their cousins—Taylor—and a bunch of other local guys lived together in an old barracks. The rooms were small with mattresses strewn across the floor. Getting up in the middle of the night meant navigating between mattresses, being careful not to step on someone. Cole didn't much enjoy being out west. He was often homesick. He was only there for the money. Like Grant, Cole only stayed as long as he did—six months—because of the camaraderie of the guys from back home. "The only thing that kept us out there was being together," Grant explains.

Cole's short stint out west ended after he got into an argument with his boss. He likely could have apologized and kept his job, but he refused. Cole was fired and headed back east. "He told me he couldn't stand it anymore," Grant says. "He didn't like it out there. He wanted to be out there, on the water," he says pointing at the ocean behind him. "That's where all us from here wants to be."

Cole's thoughts on fishing were summed up in one of his many Facebook posts from 2012: "Gotta love the life of a fishermen [sic]!!..wet,tired,cold and broke but oh sooo very happy...lol."

Cole landed back in Nova Scotia in the summer of 2012 with his cousin Taylor. Taylor's friend Shelby Peters picked them up at the airport. Shelby didn't really know Cole. He was twenty-seven and she was only twenty.

During the drive from Halifax to Woods Harbour she mainly talked to Taylor. In early July, Shelby drove to Moncton, New Brunswick, with friends to see Nickelback play at Magnetic Hill. No one in the group really liked Nickelback, but a large group of people from the Woods Harbour area was going to hang out and party. Cole was among the group. "We shared a campsite and I woke up and he was in my sleeping bag," Shelby recalls. "No funny business but he said that he just really wanted to cuddle me. I yelled at him and that was that."

After the concert Cole and Shelby exchanged texts. Cole was headed out for a fishing trip but asked if he could take her for an ice cream when he got back. "Yeah, I guess so," Shelby responded with little enthusiasm. Cole went fishing for swordfish alongside his cousin Grant, who was also home from Alberta. They did well, making money and returning sunburned. Landing Shelby was more difficult. "I kind of fought him off a bit. I wasn't really interested," she says. "But he was fairly persistent."

"One of these days I'm going to convince you," Cole would tell her.

Shelby was from Port La Tour but was soon spending most nights living with Cole, Stephen, Karen, and the rest of the Nickerson family in Woods Harbour. At home, Cole was playful, often tackling family members to the floor for a fake fight. Throughout high school and his early twenties, however, Cole had a reputation for being a rough-and-tumble jock and a partier. "He didn't know when to stop. He'd act foolish and the next thing you knew he'd be in trouble," says Grant of his cousin. "You didn't know what he was going to do, and the next thing you knew he was in the back of a cop car."

In the beginning of their relationship, Shelby found Cole lived up to his reputation. "He had a bit of an attitude in the beginning," she recalls. "He thought that his way was the only way, and that he could do and say what he wanted. We butted heads a bit." What were the issues of tension? Partying, staying out all night and not calling, and, as Shelby says with a smile, the key question of every relationship: who gets to "wear the pants."

Initially, Shelby feared Cole might be similar to many of the men she knew in Woods Harbour—men who made fast money, spent it lavishly, and seemed unwilling to settle down. "It seems sometimes Woods Harbour is the place for boys that never want to grow up," she says, "Neverland."

Quickly, however, Cole revealed he wouldn't be one of the Lost Boys. He didn't party as often and didn't take off with his friends. He and Shelby discussed getting married, started looking for a house, and talked often about having kids. "He proved to me that he was serious and that he wasn't going to be one of those boys that never grow up," Shelby says. "He was determined to prove that he could be a potential husband someday and that he could be a potential father. It showed a lot that he was committed to making me happy. And he did it."

※

In the fall of 2012, Cole goes back to lobstering, his main source of income, working for a captain from Cape Sable Island. At some point during the lobster season, Joel asks Cole if he can help land Katlin's lobster pots. Cole agrees. While out with Joel and Katlin, Cole is told about the chance to fish for halibut in February. With lobster season slowing down, Cole figures he can easily slip away for a couple side halibut trips. He and Shelby are house hunting, and a couple of solid halibut trips could certainly help financially. Cole is close with Joel and Katlin, too; they'll have a good time, despite any winter weather. Cole secures a deckhand to cover his lobstering duties. He'll fish for some halibut with Katlin, Joel, and Billy Jack. Just a couple of trips. Then he'll go back to lobstering.

CHAPTER 6

COMPETITIVE FIRE

WITH JOEL, BILLY JACK, AND COLE SIGNED ON, KATLIN ONLY NEEDS one more crew member. Katlin asks his friend Bobby Watt if he's interested. Bobby—from Shag Harbour, just down the road from Woods Harbour—crewed for Katlin on the *Miss Ally* the previous summer, fishing offshore for halibut. For Bobby, fishing with Katlin was fun. They didn't get rich that summer, but it had been a solid season. And Katlin was an easy captain to work for. "The best I ever been with, really," Bobby says. "He liked to go hard."

Many captains stay in the wheelhouse, content to control the boat and let the crew handle the actual fishing. When Bobby was aboard the *Miss Ally*, though, Katlin set up his controls on deck, allowing him to adjust the throttle and take the boat in and out of gear from outside the wheelhouse. The setup allowed him to work the boat and also gaff fish as they were hauled in on the longline. Katlin started using the setup when he was forced to fish shorthanded, but continued using it even with a full crew because he enjoyed being on deck. Katlin is now offering Bobby a repeat of last summer's experience, but during a time of better prices. Bobby would love to join Katlin for some well-paying winter halibut fishing. But it's still lobster season and Bobby is committed as crew for Billy Joe Brannen aboard the *Doris Marie*. They haven't yet landed Brannen's traps before their typical mid-winter break. Bobby tries to find someone to replace him aboard the *Doris Marie*, but can't.

Reluctantly, Bobby tells Katlin he won't be able to go halibut fishing.

With one last spot remaining, Joel approaches Tyson Townsend, another young Woods Harbour fisherman. Like the men already signed on, Tyson grew up in a fishing family. Tyson's father, Corey, is a career fisherman and known as one of the better crewmen in Woods Harbour. Corey's father, Arden—Tyson's grandfather—fished all his life, including for halibut off the west coast of Canada.

(Tyson's family declined, through numerous third-party contacts, to be interviewed for this book. Many of Tyson's friends also declined to speak, citing respect for the family. Some friends agreed to speak, but only if the conversations were off the record. Even still, their comments were usually brief and general. Said one friend, summarizing the thoughts of the others: "What scares me is that we do live in a small community. I'm scared about what they might think about me talking about it. Are they going to be mad because I said some good things about Tyson? That's what worries me. I see these people everyday. I don't want to upset anybody.")

Tyson on the golf course.

Fishing, for Tyson, was a job. He often enjoyed it, but he'd rather have been golfing. Ask anyone in Woods Harbour about Tyson and you'll get two guaranteed responses: he was a gifted, natural athlete, and extremely competitive. "Tyson was probably one of the most competitive people you'll ever meet," says Graydon Mood, a long-time friend.

Tyson was also skilled at most sports and activities he attempted, from paintball to PlayStation. Jimmy Newell, who heads the Coast Guard station on Cape Sable Island, coached Tyson in his final year of midget hockey. "People looked to him when things needed to be done," Jimmy recalls. Tyson's extreme competitiveness sometimes left him frustrated with the efforts of others. "He always gave 110 percent and he expected the same from everybody else around him," Jimmy adds. "If that wasn't the case, he let people know that they could and should be doing better."

Like Cole, Tyson played both high school and junior hockey for the Barrington Ice Dogs. Tyson's skill only increased as he got older and gained strength. "He was really a step ahead of everybody else," Graydon recalls. Tyson was also witty and quick with a comeback. "You would never want to say anything bad about him in a crowd of people because he would make you look stupid," Graydon adds.

Growing up in Woods Harbour, Tyson was close friends with Jesse Hopkins—Joel's brother. George and Mary Hopkins always enjoyed having Tyson around their house. One day, when Tyson was in grade seven, George was cutting Jesse's hair—nothing fancy, just a buzz cut done with a pair of clippers. The fad at the time was a quarter-inch buzz. George buzzed Jesse's head and Tyson asked for the same cut.

"Call your mother," George told him.

Tyson called his mother, Lori.

"Can George cut my hair?"

"If you're crazy enough to let George cut your hair, go right ahead," she replied.

George buzzed Tyson's head just as he had Jesse's. It looked good. Shortly after, though, Tyson noticed one long hair sticking up. He asked George to fix it. George grabbed the clippers and ran them again through Tyson's hair. The second pass took off a patch of Tyson's hair right to the scalp—George had removed the guard and forgot to put it back on. "He cried and cried and cried," George recalls. The only option was to shave Tyson's entire head bald. It no longer looked good. In an attempt at solidarity, Jesse told George to shave his hair off as well. "But Jesse had a black head and it still looked good," George says, laughing. "Tyson didn't go to school for a week!"

Mary, meanwhile, remembers Tyson's sweetness: "Tyson was always quite loving. People used to say, 'Yeah, he's sucking up.' Maybe he was, but it worked!"

Tyson first met Dustin Goreham when they were both about three years old. From then on, the boys were inseparable. They played sports, rambled in the woods, and spent a lot of time at Tyson's uncle's camp in Clyde River, where they went deer hunting. The boys were also Ice Dogs teammates. Tyson, a defenceman, was team captain in 2009 when the Ice Dogs won the Junior C Maritime Championship. The tournament was held at the Barrington Arena, making the win extra sweet. "He was the guy everyone looked up to," Dustin says. "And you didn't dare not give 100 percent because he was always giving 110, and he'd let you know if you weren't."

In later years, Tyson and Dustin played for the Chiefs, a men's rec hockey league team, along with Katlin and Cole.

In school, Tyson and Dustin were a grade apart. Tyson, a year older than Dustin, quit school in grade eleven. Dustin followed shortly after. Both were attracted to the money in the fishery, and neither wanted to wait until after graduation to start working; they wanted to establish themselves as early as possible. They also wanted houses, trucks—the things fishing money could provide.

"We wanted to chase the money, I guess," Dustin admits. "Everyone kinda condemned our decision, but we had the attitude that we was gonna show them that in ten years we'd have more money than the people that graduated. Education didn't do a lot for us."

Tyson and Dustin both started groundfishing. Tyson—as he was with nearly every task or activity—was extremely competitive. He and Dustin regularly compared hauls, each hoping to best the other. "He wanted to be up there with the top guys," Dustin says.

Tyson was especially skilled at coiling trawl. If the longline gear had to come up quickly, you wanted Tyson coiling it back into the trawl tubs. "He was a hard worker," says Danny Crowell, who fished with all five *Miss Ally* crew members. "He'd put his head down and just do it." Chrisjon Stoddard, a captain Tyson spent a season lobstering with, agrees: "He was A-1. Strong. Fast." And, he adds, "a gentle soul."

Tyson aspired to be a captain. He wanted to have his own rig or skipper a company boat, much like Katlin had done before buying the *Miss Ally*. Tyson would have to save a significant amount of money to get his own boat, but if anyone could do it, it would likely be him. His friends always joked that he was stingy. Tyson didn't blow his cash, but he was quick to buy a friend a beer. "He was tight with his money but he was giving," Dustin says. "If you needed something he'd be there for you."

The 2012–13 lobster season is slowing down when Tyson asks for Dustin's advice about winter fishing. Tyson has a spot on the *Miss Ally* if he wants it, but he has never gone winter fishing before. Tyson knows Dustin went fishing for halibut the previous winter with Sandy Stoddard. They ran into some bad weather and after just one trip Dustin decided winter fishing wasn't for him. Dustin tells Tyson to expect bad weather and rough, heavy seas. Tyson is undeterred by the prospect of bad weather—he's just interested in the money. He's a father now. His long-time girlfriend, Ashley Nickerson, recently gave birth to a daughter, Lilly. Tyson and Ashley also recently bought a nice house with a big barn in South Side, a community on Cape Sable Island, where Ashley is from.

Tyson's family isn't happy about his decision to go winter fishing. "A lot of people didn't want him to go. It was a little dangerous. Everyone knows that," Dustin recalls. But Tyson has decided: he's going. A crewman aboard a halibut boat can net $10,000 to $14,000 from a four- or five-day winter trip. Tyson has bills to pay and a family to support. He'll go to sea with Katlin, Joel, Billy Jack, and Cole.

Katlin's childhood friend, Colby Smith, has been studying at community college in Cape Breton. He arrives home in Barrington at Christmastime. He's decided to quit his marine engineering program and go back to fishing. But it won't be with Katlin; the *Miss Ally* crew is set. If only Colby had arrived home a month earlier, he probably could have hopped on with Katlin for some lucrative winter halibut fishing.

CHAPTER 7

WINTER WARNINGS

THE WIND IS SCREECHING THROUGH WOODS HARBOUR AS GRAYDON Mood pulls up to the Falls Point wharf. It must be blowing 50 knots (90 kilometres an hour). Not surprisingly, all the local boats are tied snuggly at the wharf. No one is lobstering today.

It's a few days before Christmas 2012 and Graydon is headed to a party at his family's company, James L. Mood Fisheries Ltd. The company exports local catches of lobster, halibut, swordfish, tuna, cod, and haddock around the world. The Mood plant is located right at the Falls Point wharf, making it easy to load local boats with supplies, and later unload them of fish.

Glancing at the wharf, Graydon notices his boat is being moved. He always ties up next to Katlin's boat, the *Miss Ally*. It looks like Katlin and his lobstering crew—Joel and Billy Jack—are moving Graydon's boat so they can leave the wharf. It's a difficult task in 50 knots of wind. Graydon, puzzled, walks down to the wharf.

"Where are you guys going?" he asks.

"We're going out to haul pots," Katlin responds.

To Graydon, it defies common sense: when every other boat is tied up, you stay in. But Katlin's decision to haul in this weather isn't startling. Everyone knows he and his crew aren't deterred by rough weather.

At the wheel, Katlin steams into the howling wind, headed for his pots near Yarmouth. The conditions, however, make it difficult to work. Joel and Billy Jack struggle to get forty pots aboard in the miserable weather.

Suddenly, a wave crashes over the stern, completely covering Joel and Billy Jack with water. Looking behind him, Katlin can't tell if they are still on deck or overboard.

Both men are still on the lurching deck, but barely. Joel has grabbed the bench used for landing the lobster pots. It's bolted to the deck and keeps him from spilling over the side. Billy Jack, meanwhile, is pushed under water and up against one side of the boat. The water eventually drains from the deck, leaving a mess of traps, two soaked men, and a busted slaughterhouse—the small shack that provides shelter for baiting trawl in poor weather. The trio quickly retreats to Yarmouth to escape the weather. If they didn't before, they now understand why the other boats are in. They take a pounding on the way to shore, but make it to the wharf.

"Not every day u almost get washed over aboard [sic]," Joel writes on Facebook on December 23, tagging Katlin in the post, "wow nasty rogue wave."

"Dislike," responds Della, Katlin's mom, adding a sad-face emoji.

"Where was ya going anyway for 3 dollars [a pound]," asks Charles Sears, "got to be something wrong with ya head."

"I think it's the sears in him Charles lol," Della responds, explaining Katlin's decision-making.

"Now now dont be like that," Charles writes back amongst the comments, "i think its that nickerson breed lol."

John Symonds, Katlin's friend and former captain, doesn't find humour in the situation. When he and Katlin meet up, John vents his concern.

"What are you doing?" he asks Katlin sternly about the decision to haul in such conditions.

Katlin looks back at him. With lobster fetching just $3.50 a pound, Katlin is barely making any money and is behind on his payments.

"John, I got some big bills coming at me and they're not getting paid," he explains.

Shortly after, Joel tells Ivan Cameron, his former crewmate, about their narrow escape at sea.

"You want to count your blessings you didn't get lost," Ivan tells Joel seriously.

Ivan has been fishing for years, and he's approaching retirement. Katlin, Joel, and Billy Jack are young and—based on what Ivan is hearing—still harbour an it's-not-going-to-happen-to-me attitude.

"I know you need to haul your pots, but when the weather is bad you need to use more judgment," Ivan tells Joel. "You gotta respect the ocean."

And they were out alone. Ivan wonders who would have helped them had Joel or Billy Jack actually been swept overboard.

"I know you're not the captain, but you got to use judgment," Ivan says again.

"They could have been lost that day," Ivan says, thinking back on his warning to Joel. "I think they kind of got scared that time, but you know young fellas—they just brush it off. They was right back at it again."

A couple weeks later, on January 6, Joel posts a photo on Facebook capturing a large wave rising off the stern of the *Miss Ally*. "On the grind all the time," he writes.

"Looks a little sloppy, Joel," notes Melodie Jane in a comment, adding a frowning emoji.

"Yup very shitty Mel that's how we like it," Joel responds, "keeps the flys [*sic*] of us lol."

"You nut...LoL...Be careful!" Melodie writes back.

Concludes George Hopkins, Joel's dad: "I think they felt like they weren't vulnerable at all. It's like war: they don't send old guys to war. They send young men because they think they're invincible."

John Symonds is driving to the Halifax airport on Saturday, February 9, 2013—headed off for a vacation in Mexico—when Katlin calls him around 1 P.M. John has been hoping for a call. He's been calling Katlin's satellite phone but there's been no answer.

Katlin is no longer crewing for John but they stay in regular contact, particularly on the water, where they use a designated VHF radio channel to have private conversations. There's a storm blowing today and John is concerned. He wants to know how Katlin, Joel, Billy Jack, Tyson, and Cole are faring. The five men are near the end of their first trip fishing halibut for Terry Zinck. Katlin and his crew are close to home—about 20 kilometres from the West Head wharf on Cape Sable Island.

"I'm okay and we're on our way in," Katlin tells John. "We're almost to the wharf."

This initial trip, cut short by the storm, also started with rough weather. On February 4, Joel posted a frightening photo on Facebook: the *Miss Ally* heeled over, with the white water of a large wave breaking nearby. Joel admitted the conditions were "pretty nautical" but noted he was "headed with a rugged crew." His confidence didn't alleviate concerns back on shore.

"Come home now pleaseee," wrote Ashley Nickerson, Tyson's girlfriend.

"[Probably] gonna have nightmares after seein this," added Cole's girlfriend, Shelby, "you guys best be careful!"

"Please be safe and careful," added Katlin's grandmother, Bonnie Sears.

But Joel insisted it wasn't enough "to scare us."

Joel's February 4 Facebook photo.

"You guys are fearless," added Jacques LeBlanc, a fellow fisherman. "Loader up!"

The trip is now nearly over, but John knows a boat and its crew are not completely safe until all are at the wharf. Katlin says it's blowing 30–35 knots (60 kilometres an hour) and the *Miss Ally* is icing up. In winter, cold ocean spray can quickly turn to ice when it lands on a boat's deck. The ice often builds up rapidly, and the weight can quickly make a vessel unstable. John tells Katlin to ensure the scuppers—holes that allow water to drain off the deck—are clear of ice. If they're clogged, the water coming on deck has nowhere to go. Katlin assures John the situation is under control. The water is freezing as soon as it comes on deck but the crew has been knocking the ice out of the scuppers. (This is not the first time Katlin has returned to the wharf in icing conditions. On January 28, while lobstering, Joel boasted on Facebook: "On are [*sic*] way in…on freezing spray that's how we roll on the miss ally.")

Talking by phone, Katlin relays details of the trip to John, but there's not much good news. The weather and tides didn't cooperate, and the result is a meagre haul: 2,500 pounds of halibut and 2,100 pounds of white hake.

Before departing on this trip Katlin borrowed some of John's longlining gear. John's gear is of good quality and, conveniently for Katlin, stored in his father's barn.

Katlin tells John he's lost two tubs of his gear.

"Don't worry about two tubs of gear, boy," John says.

They agree to discuss it further over coffee when John returns from sunny Mexico. In the meantime, Katlin plans to head back out to sea as soon as he can, probably in three days. This trip was a bust but there's supposed to be some fine weather after this storm passes. Katlin and the crew will regroup and try again. They'll also need more gear. Katlin asks if he can borrow more of John's from the barn.

"You help yourself. Take whatever you need," John responds. He wants Katlin to secure a good haul and if his gear will expedite the process, he's pleased to help. John doesn't want Katlin to stay at sea in winter any longer than necessary.

"If it means you getting home quicker and getting your fish out of the water, get it done," John tells Katlin. "Get back out there and catch those stupid fish and get in here as soon as possible. Get it over with."

Katlin tells John he's planning to head south of LaHave Bank on the next trip, nearly 200 kilometres offshore. Even in summer it's dangerous to be that far from shore—in winter it's far worse. Bobbing at the wharf, a Cape Islander looks sizeable. Offshore, it's a mere speck on a sea prone to bad mood swings. Fishermen will also tell you that cold winter water is heavier than the warm water of summer. They insist summer waves splash; winter waves drive a boat sideways. John wants Katlin to consider all this.

"Katlin, this ain't summer no more," he says into his cellphone. "Please, please be careful."

Katlin's response is typically upbeat.

"Everything is going to be okay. Don't you worry about me," he tells John. "You go to Mexico. It's been a long winter for ya. You get down there and enjoy it. You deserve it. I'll talk to you when you get home."

The two men say goodbye and John puts his phone down. He loves Katlin like a son. He's worried. But John also understands why Katlin is planning to go back out so quickly, and with little hesitation, into rough February conditions: Katlin owes a lot of money. John knows Katlin paid about $700,000 for his boat, gear, and lobster licence. John has also carried large loans during his fishing career, but never more than $500,000. It's a lot of responsibility for a twenty-one-year-old.

Katlin's financial situation has been compounded by the recent lobster season—the one in which Joel and Billy Jack were nearly swept overboard. Katlin bought his boat just before the market crashed. The 2012–13 lobster season opened with a price of just $3 per pound. By the end of December the price was up to $4 before rising to $5 at the end of January, where it has remained for most of February. A wharf price below $5 per pound makes it nearly impossible to generate a profit. Fishermen are able to pay for expenses—fuel, bait, gear, crew—but little else. There have been many weeks when Katlin hasn't been able to pay himself. Similarly, John has been paying his crew, but not taking any money home. Neither man has made any money from lobstering this year.

During these dips in the market John lives off his savings. Katlin doesn't have that luxury. Sure, he is living at home—shuffling between Della and Todd—but he still has loan payments to make. John estimates Katlin's loans are resulting in annual payments of $100,000. The insurance bill alone would be $4,000. Annual boat maintenance costs—just to keep your rig functioning—are in the $15,000 to $20,000 range. During Katlin's first lobster season with the *Miss Ally,* in February 2012, a line from a drifting high flyer snagged in his propeller. The Coast Guard had to tow the *Miss Ally* to shore, and Katlin was forced to replace the transmission. Plus, Katlin has had to replace old gear. It's all adding to his debt load.

"When you start off with a second-hand boat and garbage for gear, and you're $700,000 or $800,000 or more in the red, I'm gonna tell you what: you want to get out of bed in the morning. You don't want to be snoozing," John says, thinking back on Katlin's financial situation. "Because when you get behind, you're done." That's why Katlin is so eager to fill his boat with halibut this winter. "He's trying to pay his bills," John says bluntly.

Halibut prices rise 25–50 percent in winter because the supply is low. It's simple supply and demand: fewer fishermen are willing to go after halibut in winter so the market is hungry for product. A solid February halibut catch will likely secure a high price at the wharf. If Katlin and the crew can catch 25,000 pounds of halibut, they'll be looking at a net return of $75,000 to $100,000. But a key fact remains: they must go offshore in the middle of winter to fill Katlin's boat. "He knew he was, so to speak, playing with fire," John admits. "He knew he was pushing it to the limit. But he had to, because he had these big bills...the boy was in debt to his eyeballs, let's face it."

It's a point echoed by Katlin's father, Todd: two years of poor lobster prices were causing his son to fall behind financially. "He got himself in quite the hole," Todd says.

It's dark and there's a blizzard swirling over Cape Sable Island as Katlin finally guides the *Miss Ally* to the West Head wharf Saturday evening. In addition to a large fleet of fishing boats, West Head is home to a Coast Guard station and Terry Zinck's Xsealent Seafood buildings. "Made it home alive," Joel writes on Facebook shortly after arriving, "hard ole grind but we goter [*sic*] done just glad to be alive on land...what a storm." The *Miss Ally* crew is back home, but not for long. They'll be heading back to sea soon. Their first stab at the winter halibut fishery has failed to deliver. They need to catch a lot more to make these trips worthwhile. As long as Terry has the quota, Katlin will pursue it.

While home between trips, Katlin talks with Reg LeBlanc, owner of Wedgeport Lobsters. Katlin did well for Reg last fall, fishing on the *Row Row*, so Reg would like to settle on a long-term arrangement. His proposal: Katlin should lease the *Miss Ally* to a fisherman in need of a boat, and then fish the *Row Row* year-round—for lobster in the fall and winter, and swordfish and tuna in summer. Reg suggests they call the venture 50/50 Fisheries. Katlin would be a partner. Reg sees it as an ideal collaboration: he holds quota and is aggressive with his business moves on land, and Katlin is equally aggressive on the water. Terry Zinck, who Katlin is currently fishing for, is interested in a three-way partnership with Reg and Katlin on a long-term deal. Terry says he'll throw some of his halibut quota into the deal. As well, a new, bigger boat would be required for the partnership, with Katlin as skipper. The trio don't reach a firm deal, but make plans to talk it over when Katlin returns from his next trip. Regardless, Katlin is elated. He's going to have plenty of fish to chase.

Reg knows Katlin cut this last storm close. Like John Symonds, he feels compelled to offer some advice. Before ending their business chat, Reg tells Katlin that he's taking too many chances—don't be so aggressive.

Reg doesn't know Katlin well but he's already come to realize he's young and "very fierce." But Reg wants Katlin to acknowledge a fact of fishing: "Sometimes fierce costs you your life."

"Twenty-one years old," Reg says, thinking back. "I don't know if he knew the danger. And a lot of people feel the same way."

⁂

"It was a horrible trip," Cole tells his stepmother, Karen, during his short break on shore. It's clear he's anxious about going back out.

"I don't want to go," he tells Karen.

"Well, don't go then," she responds.

It's certainly not abnormal for a crew member to bail on a trip. He might be homesick, have some errands to deal with on shore, or just want a longer break. And few fishermen are excited to go out in winter. There are plenty of times in a fisherman's life when staying on shore is preferable. But in the end, most fishermen go back out.

"No. I gotta go," Cole explains to his stepmom.

The payout from this past trip won't be much. A second trip will require fewer expenses and, hopefully, yield more fish. There will likely be a much bigger settlement at the end. In other words: to get something out of this past awful trip, the crew has to go back to sea. But Cole doesn't want to. Karen can tell her stepson is sick to his stomach.

Cole's father, Stephen, is upset that his son returned to shore during an easterly gale. Cole and the others were fortunate: the wind hit when they were only a few hours from port, and they managed to avoid the biggest seas. But it's not a decision that can be repeated during winter. Stephen knows Cole is just part of the crew, but next time he must insist they head in earlier. Stephen sits his son down.

"You're cutting it too close," he tells Cole. "You gotta be in twelve hours ahead of time." What if the engine fails or a rope gets tangled in the propeller? There's no room for error when you're riding a gale to shore.

"You can't fool around," Stephen tells Cole. "Anything can happen."

"Yeah I know, Dad. We did. We cut it too close," Cole says. "We won't be doing that again."

Stephen doesn't know Katlin well. He took Katlin lobstering for a day when the boy was in high school and found him to be quiet and hard-working. But that was a few years ago. Katlin has since developed a reputation for aggressive and even reckless decisions—heading out when other boats are heading in. "It was typical of them to go, but not everybody acted like that," says one Woods Harbour fisherman during an off-the-record conversation. "I think he [Katlin] was a little bit too reckless, I do." In the past, Stephen has expressed his disapproval of some of the skippers Cole has fished with, but Cole often accused his father of being negative. Stephen now wants to tell Cole not to go back out with Katlin. But he refrains. Cole is old enough to make these decisions for himself.

"I really didn't want him to go with Katlin," Stephen recalls. "I didn't want him to go. But didn't want to interfere neither."

To Stephen's later regret, he doesn't push the issue any further.

⁂

At some point during the stopover Katlin visits his friend and past crew member Bobby Watt. Bobby already turned down a spot on the *Miss Ally* because he was committed to crew on a lobster boat. Katlin just wants to make sure Bobby hasn't changed his mind or his plans, because he's still welcome to come along for the next trip. Bobby isn't sure if someone has dropped out—or wants out—or if Katlin just wants an extra man aboard in the winter conditions. Regardless, he still can't go.

⁂

Tyson talks to his close friend Dustin Goreham during his brief break between trips. Dustin knows the boys on the *Miss Ally* had a rough ride in, but Tyson doesn't talk much about that. In fact, Tyson mentions the fun they had before the bad weather hit. Fishing is draining work and often dangerous. When out with a good crew, however, fishing can feel like a vacation—yes, you're working on little sleep, but you're also free from other responsibilities. With the right mix of guys, there's plenty of joking and laughs. Tyson is good friends with everyone aboard, with the exception of Billy Jack, who he doesn't know as well. Tyson has played hockey with Katlin and Cole, and is close friends with Joel's brother Jesse. This is a good group to be fishing with. Tyson had fun on the first trip, even if it was a dud financially.

Compared to the other guys aboard, Tyson isn't a thrill-seeker or adrenalin junkie. With a new house on Cape Sable Island and a seven-month-old daughter at home, Tyson just wants to get paid. Tyson's friends know he takes his new role as a father seriously. Lately, Tyson appears settled, family-focused, and content. His daughter, Lilly, is his first priority now.

"I've got a little girl home," Tyson tells Dustin. "I got to finish my trip and make my money. I'm going to go finish this trip and we'll see how it goes from there."

⁂

Sandy Stoddard pulls into the parking lot of the No Frills grocery store in Barrington Passage on Sunday, February 10. He plans to head to sea later in the day in search of halibut. First, though, he needs some final provisions.

Sandy quit school at age fifteen to go fishing. His father was an alcoholic and Sandy needed to help support his mother and siblings. He started by working on his uncle's longliner, making $100 a week and giving his mother $80, sometimes more. By nineteen he had his own boat. During a forty-year career Sandy has fished all over the east coast, including on the Grand Banks. He's escaped hurricanes and nearly lost many of his boats to storms and big waves. He's also brought a lot of fish and lobster to the wharf in his years as a captain. Sandy, short and stocky and now in his late fifties, considers himself a top-ten fisherman in the community—a high liner.

In the No Frills parking lot, Sandy spots Katlin, who is also stocking up. Katlin plans to head back out on Tuesday, a couple of days after Sandy. Sandy has known Katlin since the young skipper was a baby; he thinks of Katlin as a son. Sandy believes Katlin is quickly following men like himself and Big Wayne, Katlin's grandfather. Katlin is young but assertive, and Sandy has little doubt: Katlin will soon be a high liner himself.

Standing in the parking lot, Sandy and Katlin chat about their plans. Katlin tells Sandy he's got some halibut quota left to catch in a fishing zone that includes the LaHave Bank. After that, he'll head up closer to Cape Breton, where Sandy will be fishing.

"Call me when you leave and I'll give you some places out there," Sandy says, offering GPS coordinates of good fishing spots.

"Good. I'll call you when I get underway," Katlin says.

Like Katlin is now, Sandy used to be the youngest captain at the wharf. Now Sandy is nearly the oldest. He definitely sees some of his younger self in Katlin's aggressive and ambitious approach.

"Be careful," Sandy adds before turning away. "Don't be a hero. It's February. Watch the weather."

Later in the day, with a fair wind blowing, Sandy and his crew depart from Port La Tour on the *Logan & Morgan*. They have thirty-six hours of steaming ahead of them to reach the fishing grounds off Cape Breton. The weather, for the next four or five days at least, is expected to be perfect.

On Tuesday, February 12, Katlin is making his final preparations. He's planning to leave the wharf after supper.

Della tells Katlin she'll cook something for him before he leaves, but almost immediately regrets the offer. She's worried, as usual. She always worries when Katlin goes fishing, but winter fishing is a source of particular anxiety. She feels something bad might happen. "I was thinking, 'Oh, I don't really want to cook because suppose it's the last time I cook for him,'" she admits.

Katlin, meanwhile, is dealing with one aspect of the trip that has been causing him stress: a fisheries observer might have to join him on the voyage. Observers are randomly assigned to fishing boats throughout the province. At sea, they take detailed notes about the trip and the catch, to ensure the crew is following regulations such as not catching undersized fish or fishing in restricted areas. Observers also take biological samples. Katlin's licence number has been randomly spit out of the observer system, meaning he has to take an observer along at some point soon, though hopefully not now. Katlin doesn't think there's enough room aboard the *Miss Ally* for four crew members, himself, and an observer. His boat only has four bunks down below and he sleeps in a makeshift bunk in the wheelhouse.

Katlin calls to explain the situation. He reaches Albert Moore, the general manager of Javitech Atlantic, a Nova Scotia company contracted to provide observers, many of whom are prepared to go to sea with only a few hours notice. Based in Yarmouth, Albert is familiar with many of the fishermen in the area. He knows Katlin's dad, Todd, and has talked to Katlin before.

"I haven't got a whole lot of room," Katlin tells Albert. "I don't think it's going to be very comfortable for an observer this trip."

Katlin mentions that he has plenty of quota to pursue. There will be other trips. Could they set something up for later in the winter or in the spring? It's up to Albert to decide whether an observer goes aboard or not. He's already got an observer in mind for this trip and has the guy's phone number nearby. In situations like this Albert tries to use common sense: bumping a crew member to make room for an observer will hurt someone's income. That said, every licence holder knows they must take an observer if asked to. It's not optional.

Albert has seen the forecast. The weather isn't looking ideal. Poor weather can inhibit an observer's work, making it hard to take biological samples. Albert mulls the situation. This trip might not yield much anyway. To Katlin's relief Albert agrees to send an observer on a future trip.

"We'll do it later when the weather is better," he tells Katlin.

Albert puts down his phone. He doesn't know it now, but he's just spared a life.

As a boy, Billy Jack hung out often with his friend B. J. Sears. One evening when they were both eight years old, the pair headed down to the Cape Sable Island shore. Later, as darkness set in, Billy Jack's father, Jack, began to worry. Where were the boys?

Jack walked toward the coast and eventually came within view of a large pond near the shore, known locally as the Dyke. Though still far off, Jack could see what looked like two small figures out in the middle of the pond, floating on a plastic box cover. A dog was swimming near them, pawing to also get aboard. The makeshift raft was clearly unstable and the boys looked to be on the verge of flipping over. It was spring and the winter ice had only recently melted in the Dyke. The water was still frigid. A fall into the cold water could be deadly. Jack hustled down to the pond, stopping only to quickly grab a stick. At the water's edge he discovered it was only B. J. floating on the plastic cover—Billy Jack was on shore. Jack was livid.

"If I was your father you'd get a beating right now for that foolish stunt," he hollered at B. J. "You could get drowned."

Jack then turned to his son.

"I wasn't on it! I wasn't on it!" Billy Jack insisted.

But Jack was sure he'd seen two heads bobbing on the improvised raft. Jack put the stick to Billy Jack's ass. "You get up there and you get home."

Jack insists it was the first and only time he hit his son. And it turned out to be unjustified. Jack later learned that Billy Jack was telling the truth—he wasn't on the raft after all. At the time, Jack wanted only to be sure Billy Jack learned an important truth: cold water will kill you quickly.

Billy Jack has now been scared twice aboard the *Miss Ally* in just a few months. And Billy Jack doesn't scare easily. First there was the wave that covered the stern and nearly washed he and Joel overboard during lobster season. Being pushed under water frightened Billy Jack. This past halibut trip has also upset him. The storm they steamed through to reach the wharf was clearly a serious one: Billy Jack arrived home to Ingomar to find half a dozen trees toppled on the ground, smashed over by the strong winds.

On Sunday, the day after landing in port, Billy Jack and his fiancée, Cheryl, spent the day with his three kids. He took them to Sunday school at the Ingomar church, then skating. There was a ham dinner and, in the evening, hot chocolate. At the end of the day, Billy Jack and Cheryl drove the kids back to their mom, Theresa, in Woods Harbour. It was a fun, relaxing day.

Billy Jack doesn't have much time before the next trip and there's one task he must take care of before heading back out on the *Miss Ally*: he's decided to borrow a survival suit from a friend, Gordie Marsh, because, as far as Billy Jack knows, there are none aboard. Perhaps recalling his father's harsh lesson, Billy Jack wants to respect the lethal potential of cold water. Based on the previous trips, he wants to be prepared.

Billy Jack tells Cheryl this will be his last trip aboard the *Miss Ally*. He'll settle up after this one and then focus more on carpentry, including the house he's been commissioned to build. Leaving their cottage in Ingomar for Cape Sable Island, Billy Jack throws his gear into the trunk of Cheryl's car. He also loads his new survival suit and slams the trunk closed.

꿿

Shelby Peters, Cole's girlfriend, leaves the Nova Scotia Community College campus in Shelburne where she's studying office administration, and heads back to Woods Harbour. Cole is leaving tonight and she wants to drive him to the wharf.

Shelby arrives at the house and finds Cole in the kitchen. He's sitting on the floor, back against the dishwasher. His head is between his knees. To Shelby, her boyfriend appears devastated. Cole, who could handle a body check on the ice and once manhandled a 240-pound swordfish by himself, begins to cry. There are only a couple quick tears, but they are telling: he is scared. Cole's biggest fear is drowning and he has a bad feeling about this trip.

Shelby picked Cole up from the wharf after the last trip; she knows Katlin and the crew only just beat the weather. She could barely drive through the blizzard to fetch Cole that night. Cole hasn't told her much about that trip, only that the weather was bad and that some poor decisions were made. Cole wasn't pleased with how it was handled. It's clear Cole does not want to go back halibut fishing aboard the *Miss Ally*.

"Just don't go," Shelby says, consoling him. "If you don't want to go, don't go."

Cole's stepmother, Karen, is standing nearby and offers similar advice.

"If that's how you feel, Cole, then don't go."

"It ain't that easy," he replies.

Cole feels obligated. He and Shelby are saving for a house. Shelby also knows that Cole believes he disappointed his family by bailing from his job in Alberta. He doesn't want to be seen as someone who quits just because he's not enjoying himself. He also doesn't want to abandon the other guys, especially not this close to their departure. He said he'd go back, so he will. One more trip.

Cole and Shelby don't linger in the house. Cole collects himself, grabs his bag, and the couple walks to the car.

Della also returns home from Shelburne in the afternoon and, despite her hesitation, starts making supper for her son. Katlin is in the basement, where he's spent much of the day sorting trawl. Katlin has been living with Della and her boyfriend, Adam Newell, on Cape Sable Island for close to a year now. After his parents separated in March 2010, Katlin remained in Woods Harbour with Todd. Della longed for Katlin to move in with her. When he showed up with his TV in April 2012, Della knew he'd be staying for a while.

Katlin eventually emerges from the basement. Della has dinner ready: steak, baked potatoes, and salad. They sit down to eat and Katlin tells his mom that a fisheries observer won't have to tag along after all.

"So I don't have to worry about that," he says, clearly relieved.

They finish eating and step outside. Della doesn't even need a coat. It's warm for February. Katlin loads tubs of trawl and some other gear into the back of his white Dodge pickup. Della pulls herself up into the driver's seat. She'll pick up the crew and drop them off so they don't have to leave their vehicles at the dock. Conveniently, tonight, they're all on Cape Sable Island. They grab Billy Jack first, at Cheryl's house. She usually stays on the island when Billy Jack is fishing from West Head. He's got his gear and his survival suit. As he steps toward the truck, Della immediately notices that Billy Jack's hair is long.

"Whoa, Billy, you need a haircut," Della teases.

"I know. I never got a chance," he says. He'll get it cut when they get back.

Della then drives to Tyson's house. Earlier in the day Billy Jack was smoking fish and had mentioned it to Tyson.

"You never got over," Billy Jack says to Tyson after he climbs into the truck.

"Nah," Tyson replies. He spent his departure day with his girlfriend, Ashley, and their daughter, Lilly. "Ashley likes me to do that," he says.

The truck is packed so Della drives to the West Head wharf to let Billy Jack and Tyson out. Cole is already there when they arrive, sitting in a car with Shelby. Tyson walks over and pokes his head in the window. He eyes some beer in the car.

"Oh we'll take that with us and we'll party out there," he jokes.

Cole smiles. He's no longer visibly upset. He tells Shelby she should get back; he doesn't want her to be late for supper. Outside the car, Cole announces he fixed one of the boat's heaters. They definitely won't be cold in their bunks.

"I won't be either," Katlin says, motioning to a small heater he brought from home.

Tyson, Cole, and Billy Jack step aboard the boat and stow their bags. Della and Katlin then drive down the road to pick up Joel in Clark's Harbour, the main community on Cape Sable Island, where Joel, Elaine, and their two kids are staying with Elaine's parents. Joel and Elaine recently bought a house nearby. It has an ocean view and belonged to Elaine's great-grandmother. The deal closes soon. They'll make the move from Woods Harbour when Joel gets home from this trip. Joel jumps in the back seat, puts his head back, and exhales.

"I don't know what I'm going to do with Julius," he says of his son. Julius is six and has been trying to use snowbanks as ramps.

Della smiles. "Ah Joel, I wonder who he gets that from."

Back at West Head, Katlin and Joel pop out of the truck. Della notices a brown toque left behind in the cab.

The final photo: the Miss Ally *leaving West Head wharf on February 12, 2013.*

"You want this?" she asks Katlin.

"Nah, I probably won't need it."

Della nods. When Katlin isn't looking she shoves it in the side of his bag. Katlin and Joel then notice that another captain has moved his boat so it's easier for them to load the *Miss Ally.*

"Man, that's some nice that that fella would do that for us," Joel says.

Standing nearby, Della silently hopes that Katlin is that type of captain: considerate and willing to put others before himself.

Katlin and Joel hop aboard and within five minutes Katlin announces he's ready to depart. Della sits on the wharf and snaps some photos as the final adjustments are made. She'll send Katlin one of the photos later. He sometimes uses her shots for his profile picture on Facebook.

At 6:22 P.M., the lines are cast off and Katlin nudges his boat into gear. Della watches the yellow hull of the *Miss Ally* move away from the wharf. Long the wife of a fisherman, she knows it's bad luck to watch a boat disappear from sight. She takes a final photo—the *Miss Ally* edging around the corner of the wharf—then turns away. She gets back in the warm cab of Katlin's truck and drives home.

Della doesn't know it now, but she will never see her son again.

Back in Woods Harbour, Shelby parks her car at Cole's house and goes upstairs to their bedroom. There she finds flowers, a card, and a ring. Despite his anxiety about the trip, Cole didn't forget that he would be away for Valentine's Day. It's another sign, Shelby thinks, that Cole has softened up. She opens the card.

At the bottom, scribbled in Cole's handwriting, are three words.

Love you babe.

CHAPTER 8

A MONSTER APPROACHES

THE CAPE SABLE LIGHTHOUSE STANDS ON A SMALL PIECE OF LAND,
composed of shifting sand dunes, just off the southern tip of Cape Sable
Island. At 30 metres, it's the tallest lighthouse in Nova Scotia.

The original wooden lighthouse was built in 1861, in direct response to
the loss of the SS *Hungarian*. The *Hungarian* was one of Canada's largest
iron-hulled steamers. On February 20, 1860, the barque-rigged ship was on
route from London, England, to Portland, Maine, when it wrecked on Cape
Sable. Flares from the ship were spotted at 3 A.M. and by daybreak fishermen
on Cape Sable Island could see people clinging to the ship's masts. The water,
however, was too rough for a rescue effort.

All 205 people aboard the *Hungarian* died. Bodies washed up on shore, as did fine textiles—part of the cargo—and, according to legend, a diary whose final entry was: "Lizzie dies tonight." A year later a lighthouse was constructed on Cape Sable to warn approaching ships of the shallow water and rocks. The current lighthouse, a white octagonal concrete tower built in 1923, houses a radar-transponding beacon and projects a flashing white light. It's a key navigational aid, known to anyone who takes to the surrounding water. Says one local fisherman: "You know where that lighthouse is at all times."

By 7:40 P.M. on Tuesday, February 12—about ninety minutes after leaving West Head wharf—Katlin and the crew are south of Cape Sable Island. Katlin has the *Miss Ally* steaming east at 6 knots (11 kilometres an hour). In the distance, off the port side, is the Cape Sable Lighthouse. Its beam is likely visible to Katlin in the wheelhouse, and perhaps to Cole, Joel, Tyson, and Billy Jack if they're nearby, chatting with him. More likely the light goes unnoticed by Katlin and his crew; they've spotted the Cape Sable light plenty of times before. Tonight they're probably focused solely on the trip ahead: the weather, where they'll fish and, most importantly, getting some sleep before they start.

As promised, Katlin calls Sandy Stoddard, aboard the *Logan & Morgan*, for advice on fishing spots. Over the satellite phone, Sandy passes along some coordinates and water depths he thinks will be fruitful this time of year. Sandy is happy to offer guidance to Katlin. He also feels the need to, once again, emphasize caution.

As a young skipper Sandy felt invincible. He ventured into bad storms with little doubt that he'd emerge unscathed and with a full hold of fish. Three different times Sandy was written off in storms—everyone on shore assumed he wouldn't make it back. One day, early in his career, Sandy was at the wharf preparing to head out on the *Debbie & Jamie*. His Uncle Alfie strolled down the wharf.

"What are you doing?" Alfie asked.

"I'm going out."

Sandy Stoddard.

"Did you see that sundog today?"

Sandy paused. "What's a sundog?"

Alfie said nothing. He turned and walked back up the wharf.

Out at sea, Sandy got caught in a huge storm, with wind gusting to 75 knots (145 kilometres an hour). He lost twenty-six tubs of brand-new gear and was fortunate to get back to shore at all. Sandy was tying up at the wharf after the trip when Alfie reappeared.

"Now you know what a sundog is," his uncle said.

A sundog—when bright spots or coloured rays appear to come off the sun at certain angles—is now one of the many signs that warn Sandy of poor weather. Another adage he lives by: "A ring around the moon, bad weather's coming soon."

Now on the satellite phone with Katlin, Sandy has taken on the role of his Uncle Alfie.

"Be careful," he tells Katlin. "Don't take no unnecessary chances."

Katlin and the crew begin setting their gear on Wednesday, February 13. Katlin remains in regular contact with Sandy as their crews set and haul gear. The two men are far apart on the cold Atlantic but they share information and keep one another updated on their progress, chatting every day and night by satellite phone.

Sandy is roughly 100 kilometres east of Canso, Nova Scotia, which is up near Cape Breton. There are other boats fishing far to the east of his position. Katlin and his crew are more than 300 kilometres west-southwest of Sandy, closer to Woods Harbour but still nearly 200 kilometres offshore. They're fishing off LaHave Bank, near the edge of the continental shelf.

The first reports of bad weather arrive on Thursday afternoon, broadcast over each captain's very high frequency (VHF) radio. (Environment Canada marine forecasts are broadcast continuously over designated VHF weather channels.) Light winds on Saturday are forecasted to increase to 40 knots (75 kilometres an hour) on Sunday and last until Monday morning. By early Friday morning, however, the forecast has worsened: west winds of 50 knots (90 kilometres an hour) are coming on Sunday afternoon.

Chrisjon Stoddard, Sandy's son, arrives at the fishing grounds near his father at 3 A.M. on Saturday morning. Chrisjon, helming the *Benji & Sisters*, started fishing with his father at age six. It was Boxing Day and Chrisjon, standing next to a pile of toys, asked to go to sea with his dad. Sandy, thinking his son would be easily deterred, agreed. Chrisjon could tag along, but he couldn't bring any toys. Chrisjon ditched his new presents, packed his bag, and joined Sandy for the entire week-long trip. "That was my dream. I was going to be like Dad. I was going to go fishing no matter what," Chrisjon recalls. As a boy, Chrisjon went fishing with Sandy during every March break and Christmas vacation. "I went every summer that I can remember, from elementary school right until I graduated."

Even though he was still only in high school, Chrisjon was making $40,000 to $50,000 each summer. He graduated with $50,000 in the bank, land in his name, and a new truck in the driveway. Chrisjon estimates he put in ten thousand hours as a deckhand. But he wasn't content, as some are, with being an "average deckhand." "I knew someday I'd be up in the wheelhouse. I just didn't know how long it was going to take," he says.

At nineteen, a year after graduating high school, he became a captain. He started out skippering his father's boat and spent a summer on the Grand Banks. Though similar in age to Katlin when he took the wheel, Chrisjon estimates he had three times as much experience at sea. He credits his dad with teaching him how to handle a boat in a storm. "I learnt by him and going by his lead and learning from his actions," he says.

Chrisjon's time at sea has not been without incident. At age sixteen, while fishing far offshore with his dad, a stingray stung him. Chrisjon nearly had to be airlifted to land. Sandy was patched through to a doctor in Halifax. "If he's still breathing the worst has passed," the doctor told Sandy. Another time, an incoming hook snagged the side of the boat. The hook eventually broke free but the line was under tension. The hook shot at Chrisjon, breaking his nose and injuring his right eye. "My face was the bull's eye," he says, still bearing a scar. He points to his pupil with pride, noting it won't dilate properly.

In the early morning darkness of Saturday, February 16, Chrisjon's crew fires out their longlining gear. Shortly after they begin, Chrisjon receives the latest Environment Canada forecast. It's not good. A low-pressure system is expected to develop near Cape Hatteras, North Carolina, tonight and intensify as it tracks north. By tomorrow night—Sunday—the system will be lying directly over Nova Scotia, creating gale- to storm-force winds. A storm warning is now in effect for the waters from the Bay of Fundy to Cape Breton and beyond. Any boats still out when this storm arrives will have to face snow, whipping winds of 50 knots (more than 90 kilometres an hour), and waves up to seven metres tall. Chrisjon has just set his first string of gear, but he won't be staying long. He picks up his radio and calls his father.

"You listening to the weather?" Chrisjon asks.

"No, not really," Sandy responds, unconcerned.

"It's giving quite a bad storm."

"Is it?"

"Take a look at it."

Sandy checks the forecast. There's a vicious winter storm on the way.

"Yeah, that don't look good," Sandy tells Chrisjon.

The father-son pair decides they'll head for Cape Breton once their gear is pulled in. Chrisjon knows Katlin is also at sea, and he's fished with every guy currently aboard the *Miss Ally.*

"You better call Katlin and let him know," Chrisjon says.

"Yeah, I'll call him," Sandy assures him.

Katlin is more than 300 kilometres to the west of Sandy and Chrisjon. The storm will be thrashing through his area many hours before it hits Sandy and Chrisjon. Katlin must also retreat, and soon. Sandy calls Katlin on his satellite phone.

"Did you look at the weather forecast?" Sandy asks.

Katlin hasn't.

"It's not giving very good weather," Sandy notes.

"The weather ain't that bad here," Katlin responds.

"Not right now, because it ain't got there yet."

Sandy explains the situation: there's an approaching low-pressure system that will bring 50 knots of wind and big waves. And the storm could intensify en route. It's time to retreat.

"You gotta get your gear and get outta there," Sandy advises.

"What are you and Chrisjon doing?"

"We're gettin' our gear back and we're gone. We're going into Cape Breton."

"I'll get my gear and I'm gonna go too," Katlin says.

But it will be another thirty-six hours before Katlin finally has his gear onboard and begins steering the *Miss Ally* toward shore.

It's nearly dark on Saturday when Sandy's crew hauls in its final piece of gear. Sandy and his son, Chrisjon, promptly turn their boats toward Petit-de-Grat, an Acadian fishing village on the southern tip of Cape Breton. By 5 P.M. Environment Canada has issued a new, even worse forecast: waves on Sunday evening will now reach 8 metres. Sandy calls Katlin to confirm he's also on his way in. Aboard the *Miss Ally*, it's Joel who answers the satellite phone.

"What's going on?" Sandy asks.

"Katlin's laying down," Joel responds.

"Laying down? What's he doing laying down?"

"We couldn't find our gear."

Joel tells Sandy that the boat's inverter isn't working. Without it, they can't power the bright overhead light the crew uses when working at night. The type of light used on the *Miss Ally*—and many other fishing boats—is not designed for fishing. Such lights normally hang from telephone poles and are used for lighting baseball fields. The halogen bulbs run on 110 volts. On fishing boats, the lights—commonly called "crab lights"—require a power inverter, located in the engine room, to convert the boat's 24-volt setup to 110 volts. If the inverter fails, the lights won't work. The lighting setup is clunky but essential. High flyers—the pieces of longlining gear that stick above the water—are topped with radar reflectors, making them traceable by radar. But in rough weather it can be hard to detect them because they dip behind waves and are rolled by the wind. The hunt for your gear is made easier if you have an overhead light, typically mounted high above the wheelhouse. During bad weather, the crab lights are running constantly so you can find your gear—and see what's coming at you.

Katlin's inverter has failed, disabling his overhead light. Without it, Katlin is essentially driving the *Miss Ally* blindfolded. And with the high flyers hiding between waves, it's becoming increasingly difficult to locate the gear. Joel tells Sandy the plan: they'll stay the night, find and haul the gear at first light Sunday morning, and then gun for shore to outrun the storm.

Sandy knows no fisherman wants to leave gear behind. And Katlin borrowed about half of the gear for this trip from John Symonds. John has helped

Katlin extensively—first giving him a deckhand job and, more recently, aiding Katlin as he worked to get his own boat shipshape and profitable. The idea of returning with little or none of John's good longlining gear must be influencing Katlin's thought process, at least to some degree. But sometimes you must abandon your lines, buoys, anchors, and high flyers and simply hope to retrieve it all later.

"You fellas can't stay there," Sandy tells Joel. "You gotta get out of there. It's giving a bad breeze."

For now, though, the *Miss Ally* will stay offshore. It is not, however, a unanimous decision. Cole calls his girlfriend, Shelby, on Saturday night. She can tell he's not happy. Cole tells Shelby that he and Tyson want to come in. Fuck the gear.

"Tyson and I aren't happy. We're upset," Cole tells her. "We want to go in. We're done."

Shelby knows Cole isn't reckless like he used to be. A younger version of Cole may have voted to stay out, might have even been excited to remain at sea and ride the rough waves. But he's matured in recent years and tonight Cole wants to steam for shore. Not that votes matter—fishing boats are not run as democracies. A captain always has final say, and that decision is to be respected. Cole and Tyson have been outranked.

Cole's call with Shelby is brief, as most conversations by satellite phone are. Shelby mentions that she is going to view a house on Monday. Cole asks her to take some photos.

"If you like it, get it," he tells her.

Cole is in a better mood by the end of the call. Shelby can sense a smile on the other end. Cole tells Shelby he misses her and can't wait to come home.

"This will keep me going until I see you again," he says.

"I love you."

"I love you, too."

Later Saturday night, as Cole and the rest of the crew lie in their bunks waiting for daylight, a massive storm is building and barrelling toward them. The conditions, now tolerable, will soon deteriorate. And rapidly.

At 3 A.M. Sunday morning, Environment Canada issues another grim, worsening forecast: by tonight, the waters around LaHave Bank will be churned up by 50-knot winds (more than 90 kilometres an hour). There will also be driving rain, fog, a risk of thunderstorms, then heavy snow. The waves are now forecast to reach 10 metres.

On Sunday morning, Sandy Stoddard calls Katlin again.

"How ya making out?" he asks.

The crew has located the gear—about twenty-five tubs worth—and is starting to haul it in, Katlin reports.

"It's not bad here right now. We ain't got no wind," Katlin tells Sandy.

"You're going to have wind before nightfall. You got to get your gear and get going."

"As soon as we get it we'll be on our way," Katlin assures him calmly.

Katlin gives a similar report to Terry Zinck at Xsealent Seafood. Katlin is fishing for Terry's quota. Although he used to be a fisherman himself, Terry doesn't tell those who fish for him how to conduct their affairs at sea. It's a business arrangement and each man is free to do his own thing. Today, however, the forecast is menacing. Terry suggests Katlin abandon the gear and race for shore to ensure he and the crew beat the storm. They can always get the gear later, Terry reminds him. But Katlin is confident they can haul the gear aboard and get underway in time to outrun the approaching low-pressure system. Katlin tells Terry he'll call later to set up a time on Monday to unload the boat.

The call never comes.

Hours pass and the storm approaches from Cape Hatteras, yet the *Miss Ally* is no closer to shore. It's not until late Sunday afternoon that Katlin, Joel, Tyson, Billy Jack, and Cole finally get the gear in. The positive news is that they've made a good haul. Via satellite phone, Katlin tells his grandfather Ronnie that they have between fifteen and twenty thousand pounds of halibut in the hold, including a 250-pounder. Katlin wants his grandfather to come see the big fish when they reach land.

Terry Zinck is paying $8 per pound at the wharf. It's a good price for halibut, especially compared to the lousy lobster prices this season. Katlin can do the rough calculations in his head: if there really is twenty thousand pounds of halibut in his hold, he is sitting on $160,000 worth of fish. After paying quota charges, including $57,000 to Terry, he'll be left with about $93,000—enough to cover expenses and ensure a nice payday for himself, Joel, Tyson, Cole, and Billy Jack. And Terry has quota left. They'll be able to return for more fish.

But first they must outrun a ferocious winter storm.

Tied up in Cape Breton, Sandy Stoddard is confused. Why did it take so long to pull in twenty-five tubs of gear? By now, however, it's a moot point. With the gear stowed, Katlin is finally steaming for shore. He's headed for Sambro, Nova Scotia, a small community outside Halifax that's home to a Coast Guard station. Yet the storm Katlin was hoping to escape has descended. Between 4 P.M. and 6 P.M., the wind at the LaHave Bank weather buoy—located 250 kilometres south of Halifax—jumps in speed from 29 knots to 51, with gusts to 62 (115 kilometres an hour).

"The wind has just struck here," Katlin tells Sandy over the satellite phone. "It's blowing hard."

"Well, be very careful," Sandy warns him.

The water around the *Miss Ally* is now full of large lurking waves. As daylight disappears, Katlin—without his overhead light—can't see any of them.

Katlin's father, Todd, is in Jamaica enjoying a break from the cold when he realizes he's missed a couple calls from George Hopkins, Joel's dad. Todd sends George a text back to find out why he's calling. George texts back: the boys are still on the water and there's a gale blowing. Todd's vacation buzz quickly evaporates. He has been checking the American forecast. He knows there's bad weather headed for Nova Scotia. But Katlin and the crew should have been in long ago—yesterday, in fact. Todd calls Katlin.

"What's going on?" Todd asks his son. "I thought you were going to be in last night."

"I know, I know. We couldn't get the gear," Katlin explains.

Todd detects that Katlin is defensive about the situation. He tells his son to forget about their slow hauling and just focus on getting to land. Katlin says that's the plan: they're headed for Sambro. He also tells Todd the wind is screeching from the west at 70–80 knots (130–150 kilometres an hour).

"I've never seen it blow so hard," Katlin says.

"Oh, jeez." It's all Todd can muster.

Todd had been impressed and slightly jealous when Katlin told him the names of the four men he secured as crew for halibut fishing. When Todd started out, he was bailing guys out of jail to work on his boat. "I don't know how you rounded up such an awesome crew," Todd had told Katlin. Todd now knows his son and the crew are in a real mess: the sea is already starting to punish Katlin's boat. Katlin tells Todd he's lost the temporary tailboard that runs across the stern. Installed when longlining, it ensures gear doesn't fall off the back of the boat. They were hit by a wave and the force of the water smashed the plank out.

"The stern is gone," Katlin tells his dad.

Water from the wave also swept away some gear, including anchors. The crew has since secured the remaining gear as best they can without getting washed over themselves. The wave that hit the *Miss Ally* was clearly large: a section of the boat's bait shack has also been ripped off and swallowed by the sea. Made of plywood and equipped with a fluorescent light, the shack provides some shelter from the elements when the crew is baiting trawl at the stern. John Symonds helped Katlin install the bait shack on the *Miss Ally*. John used U-bolts to secure the shack's two-by-fours to the boat's monkey bars—a rack of metal bars on the port side. It would require an immense force to tear the bait shack away.

"And there goes the rest of the baiting house," Katlin says suddenly while updating his father. They've just been hit by another wave. Despite the conditions, Todd doesn't detect any panic in his son's voice. Katlin is calm.

The crew is also using the satellite phone to update their families. Joel calls Elaine, his long-time girlfriend and mother of his two boys, including four-month-old Tate.

"I just called to tell you I love you," Joel tells her. "We're headed into Sambro."

"Okay, call me when you get there," she says.

Around 9 P.M. Billy Jack calls his fiancée. Cheryl can tell it's Billy Jack on the other end, but she can't make out a word he's saying. The connection is poor. That afternoon, Cheryl had driven from her house on Cape Sable Island to the West Head wharf. She was expecting Billy Jack to be back by then. She sat in her car for a while but saw no sign of the *Miss Ally*, Billy Jack, or the rest of the crew. She drove back home to wait. Now on the line with Billy Jack, she's anxious to know when they'll be in. But all she hears is crackling and static. Then the line goes dead.

Della, also on Cape Sable Island, has been in regular contact with Katlin since dropping her son at the West Head wharf five days ago. Today she's talked to him via satellite phone about twenty times. She's been reading him weather updates from Maine so he can get a sense of what's headed in his direction. Katlin hasn't spared Della any details as the weather has intensified around him and his crew. She knows the bait shack has been torn off.

"Why are you telling me this?" she asks at one point. "I don't want to know that stuff."

Up to this point Della has been home with her boyfriend, Adam. Around 8 P.M., Della's best friend, Sundae Atkinson, stops by, followed shortly by Sundae's husband, Eddie. Just after 9 P.M., Katlin calls Della and asks for a favour: he needs her to drive his truck to Sambro in the morning. He'll need it to fetch lumber to fix the bait shack. Katlin also asks his mom to bring eleven anchors to replace the ones that have been swept away. It's an encouraging request: Katlin is making plans to ensure they can get back to sea as soon as this storm passes. The conditions are bad but Katlin remains upbeat. To Della, he doesn't sound afraid.

No one else shares Katlin's confidence, however. Docked in Petit-de-Grat, Cape Breton, Sandy Stoddard is growing increasingly anxious. Shortly after 9 P.M., just as Sandy is about to turn in for the night, Katlin calls with an update. He tells Sandy about the wave that smashed off the stern board and bait shack. This is serious. Sandy knows all the men aboard the *Miss Ally*. Cole and Billy Jack both crewed for him, as did Cole's father, Stephen, and Tyson's father, Corey. And then there's Joel.

One day, when Joel was a kid, Sandy was painting buoys at the wharf. George Hopkins pulled up in a new truck, Joel sitting beside him. George walked down to one of the boats and told Joel to stay in the truck. Of course, Joel went right down to Sandy and began bothering him as he painted. Joel repeatedly pestered Sandy before scurrying up the wharf when Sandy seemed ready to act.

"You little bugger! If I get my hands on you I'll fix you," Sandy barked.

Joel kept up the antics until Sandy finally sprung up and grabbed him. Sandy shoved both Joel's hands in the can of orange paint. But Sandy's attempt at discipline failed: Joel proceeded to chase Sandy around the wharf with paint-soaked hands. Sandy sprinted away and quickly darted into George's new double-cab truck, jumping in one side and then out the other. Joel followed right behind, plastering orange handprints on the door handle and all over the pristine interior.

"George, you gotta get up here and get 'em!" Sandy screamed. "He's into the paint!"

"I'll kill him! I'll kill him!" George hollered as he hurried up from the wharf.

Joel has since become a skilled, fearless fisherman. By Sandy's measure, the *Miss Ally* is crewed by strong, hard-working men. And Sandy is now very concerned about their safety. He tells Katlin to contact the Coast Guard; it's important that rescue officials know the *Miss Ally* is being battered by this storm. Katlin agrees to call. A short time later, however, Katlin calls Sandy back—he couldn't get through.

"Can you call the Coast Guard for me?" he asks Sandy.

"Yup."

Sandy, aboard the *Logan & Morgan* in Cape Breton, contacts the Coast Guard in Sydney to report that Katlin and his crew are in difficulty. Sandy tells the Coast Guard what he knows: the *Miss Ally*, approximately 150 kilometres south-southwest of Sambro, has lost its inverter and is without lights. The boat has already been hit by at least one wave, and has suffered some damage to the stern. Most concerning, Katlin is reporting winds up to 80 knots (150 kilometres an hour). As George Hopkins warned Katlin earlier in the evening, the weather has worsened. At 80 knots, wind does not howl—it screams.

The Beaufort Wind Scale, developed in 1805 by Sir Francis Beaufort of the British Royal Navy, classifies the force of wind on a scale from zero to twelve. If Katlin's measurements are correct, the *Miss Ally* is facing winds well into category twelve, which is anything over 64 knots—hurricane level. "The air is filled with foam and spray. Sea completely white with driving spray; visibility very seriously affected," states the Beaufort description of category-twelve conditions. Then there are the waves: consistently in the range of 14 metres in height. Long and lonely stretches of ocean allow wind to travel unabated for hundreds and thousands of kilometres, building waves to terrifying heights.

At the wheel of the *Miss Ally*, Katlin is trying to keep his boat upright in conditions that would trouble even the most seasoned skippers. Sandy knows these conditions must be nightmarish. In his call to the Coast Guard in Sydney, Sandy also relays Katlin's position. Despite the situation, Sandy remains optimistic. Or perhaps he's in denial. Putting down his phone, Sandy turns to his son, Chrisjon, whose boat is tied up nearby.

"Once this storm goes by we'll be able to get back out."

Chrisjon looks at his father. "We're not going back out."

"Why not?" Sandy snorts.

"We're going home to a memorial."

"Don't talk so foolish."

"Dad, they ain't gonna make it."

Around 9:20 P.M., a Coast Guard dispatcher in Sydney passes all of Sandy's concerning information on to staff at the Joint Rescue Coordination Centre (JRCC) in Halifax.

Based in the dockyard at Canadian Forces Base (CFB) Halifax, JRCC Halifax is responsible for coordinating all east coast search and rescue operations involving emergencies in the air and at sea. JRCC Halifax's coverage area is enormous: all of the Atlantic provinces, the eastern half of Quebec, the southern half of Baffin Island, and a massive area of the western North Atlantic Ocean; its total coverage spans 4.7 million square kilometres and 29,000 kilometres of shoreline. When an air or marine emergency occurs, JRCC Halifax is the focal point. It collects and distributes information, and coordinates the use and movement of "rescue assets," including Coast Guard ships and Air Force planes and helicopters. In other words, JRCC is the director in each search and rescue operation—tasking and guiding the various search players.

Though JRCC is part of the Department of National Defence, it is operated with the Canadian Coast Guard, hence *Joint* Rescue Coordination Centre. JRCC Halifax is manned twenty-four hours a day, seven days a week by three maritime coordinators—a mix of Air Force and Coast Guard officers. They work in an open room, at workstations with multiple computer monitors. On one wall is a digital clock. Its large numbers display both local time and "Zulu" time (also known as Coordinated Universal Time or Greenwich Mean Time), a universal standard used in maritime and aviation circles. The locations of active JRCC cases are displayed on a large wall-mounted monitor, each identified by an icon of a sinking ship.

On Sunday evening, Coast Guard officer Ray McFadgen is working his usual twelve-hour shift at JRCC. Designated as the lead coordinator on the new case, he begins to compile information related to the *Miss Ally*, a Cape Islander that's clearly in a tough spot. "The crew of the *Logan*

& Morgan did not like what they were hearing from the vessel and are very concerned about it," McFadgen writes in his first entry in the JRCC incident log.

Sandy Stoddard isn't the only one concerned. Jimmy Newell, the commanding officer of the Clark's Harbour Coast Guard station on Cape Sable Island, is also worried. The son of one of Jimmy's deckhands has been in contact with Katlin. Katlin told him about taking a large wave, the busted stern board, and the damaged bait shack. Jimmy has been in the Coast Guard for thirty years. "A lot of times in search and rescue it's a gut feeling that you have," he says. Tonight, he has a very bad feeling.

Jimmy immediately calls JRCC. Over the phone, he tells Ray McFadgen what he's been told: the five-man crew is struggling. And they're young—the captain is only twenty-one years old.

"It's a bunch of kids aboard there," Jimmy tells McFadgen. "They're all young fellas—not a whole lot of experience."

McFadgen has worked at JRCC since 1999. Before that he spent fifteen years at sea, conducting offshore search and rescue, fishery patrols, and tasks ranging from buoy maintenance to icebreaking. In the private sector he did subsea-cable work. His experience at sea is reflected in his grey buzz cut and matching goatee. He knows immediately that the men aboard the *Miss Ally* face a grim situation. And he's confident this case is going to end with a rescue effort. The only question is: when?

The *Miss Ally* has not yet issued a formal distress call. Katlin—preoccupied with steering his boat over watery mountains, working the satellite phone, and talking to Tyson, Joel, Billy Jack, and Cole—is perhaps unable, or unwilling, to see how this will unravel. But McFadgen and his fellow maritime coordinators have heard enough to begin "tasking resources." It's time to start assembling the pieces for a search and rescue mission. McFadgen is effectively declaring this a distress call on behalf of Katlin. In all his years at JRCC, McFadgen has never been chastised for doing too much or acting too early. Boats and planes can always be sent back to their bases, but it takes time to get them in the air and off the dock.

One of McFadgen's colleagues attempts to raise the *Sir William Alexander*, a Canadian Coast Guard ship that's already at sea. JRCC calls the high-endurance vessel using a cell number and four satellite phone numbers. Nobody answers. So JRCC asks the Coast Guard to keep calling the *Sir William Alexander* on their behalf and pass along a message: "call us [JRCC] immediately."

Another of McFadgen's colleagues, meanwhile, contacts 14 Wing Greenwood. Tucked in the Annapolis Valley, CFB Greenwood is the largest air base in Atlantic Canada. Greenwood houses Aurora long-range patrol planes as well as the two types of aircraft typically employed by JRCC for search and rescue cases: four-engine, fixed-wing Hercules airplanes, and rugged Cormorant helicopters. JRCC isn't calling for the aircraft just yet, but it's time to brief the crews and check the weather conditions at the base. Air support may be needed soon. At night, search and rescue aircraft are expected to be airborne within two hours of tasking from JRCC. (The standard during the day is thirty minutes.) Advance warning to CFB Greenwood might expedite the process.

McFadgen's next move is to contact the Canadian Mission Control Centre (CMCC), located at CFB Trenton in Ontario. The CMCC is co-located with the Canadian Beacon Registry, which has a database of Emergency Position-Indicating Radio Beacons (EPIRBs) carried by many fishermen. When an EPIRB goes off, search and rescue authorities at CMCC retrieve information about the vessel or aircraft from the database. This gives searchers access to a beacon owner's emergency contact information and identifying characteristics of the vessel or aircraft. McFadgen wants CMCC to check the database for beacons registered to the *Miss Ally*. He's told the boat does have a registered beacon and, thankfully, it hasn't gone off yet.

At 9:39 P.M., JRCC finally raises the *Sir William Alexander* and gives the crew its task: proceed to the *Miss Ally* and escort the fishing boat to port, in the direction of Sambro. The 83-metre ship should be able to shield the *Miss Ally* from some of the pounding it's receiving. Help is coming, but not anytime soon: the *Sir William Alexander* is 40 kilometres south of Peggys Cove, and there's a massive stretch of violent ocean between the two vessels. Even in good conditions the rescue ship is hours away from reaching the *Miss Ally*. In fact, Captain Rob Gray, the commanding officer of the *Sir William Alexander*, has just changed course toward land, to escape the worsening weather. Gray, a thirty-five-year veteran of the Coast Guard, had been assigned to take his ship to the Bay of Fundy, on the other side of Nova Scotia. When the *Sir William Alexander* left the Coast Guard base in Halifax Harbour, the wind was only 10–15 knots. But it's been steadily increasing—the seas are now 5–7 metres and it's blowing more than 50 knots (90 kilometres an hour). And it's getting worse.

The *Sir William Alexander* is pitching and rolling, and Rob Gray is concerned about the potential for freezing spray. He already ordered a decrease in speed, figuring he'd head down the coast and tuck into a protected bay or cove to wait out the worst of this storm. He had been aiming for Shelburne but the updated forecast convinced him to seek shelter sooner. He was headed toward LaHave when the tasking from JRCC came in. Gray now orders a new course toward the *Miss Ally*. He and his twenty-five-member crew are headed further into the storm. There will be no sheltered sleep tonight.

Back at JRCC Halifax, Ray McFadgen now has the number for Katlin's satellite phone. He dials. Katlin answers but the call is quickly dropped. McFadgen tries again and Katlin answers. Sensing he might get cut off, McFadgen wants basic information quickly.

"I understand you've had a couple of problems out there. You're making your way to Sambro, are you?" McFadgen asks.

"Yes," Katlin responds.

"What's your course and speed right now?"

"Uh, twenty-two degrees," Katlin says, before giving a slight laugh. The boat is moving so wildly it's difficult to give an exact course. "It's going back and forth so much it's really hard to [say]," he tells McFadgen. "Somewhat to the north direction."

Katlin then provides his position and says the *Miss Ally* is travelling between 5.5 and 8 knots (10–15 kilometres an hour).

"I understand you've had a little bit of damage. Are you taking on any water?" McFadgen asks.

Katlin answers but the connection is cutting in and out.

"You're badly broken," McFadgen says. "Just try again. Just give me a yes or no—are you taking on any water?"

"No."

"Okay, I understand that you're not taking on any water."

"But, uh, the wind is hauling around to the northwest and it's making it really, really hard for us to steam," Katlin adds.

"Okay. And how do you feel about how things are going right now? How are you feeling?"

McFadgen doesn't receive an answer. The line is dead.

"Hello?" McFadgen says to empty air.

McFadgen hasn't detected any panic in Katlin's voice. But it's clear his boat is being pounded. JRCC coordinators are often fed information from concerned family members that eventually turns out to be embellished, over-blown, or flat-out wrong. Worried on shore, family members sometimes misinterpret what they're told by their kin at sea. This is clearly not one of those situations. McFadgen now senses the situation aboard the *Miss Ally* is actually worse than what was presented to those on shore. "We knew immediately that we were in the weeds and it was going to be all uphill," he recalls. "I knew out of the gate that everything was stacked against them."

Over the next fifteen minutes McFadgen dials Katlin's satellite phone number three times, trying to re-establish a connection. Each time the call goes directly to voicemail. At 9:55 P.M. Katlin calls McFadgen back.

"Hello, *Miss Ally*."

"Hello."

"You've got the rescue centre."

Over a breaking, crackling connection, Katlin explains that the situation has worsened.

"The wind has changed direction, and it's making it real hard for us to make any headway at all," Katlin reports.

"Okay."

"I don't know if there is anything you can help me out with here or...."

Katlin needs assistance but there's little McFadgen can offer.

"I have the *Sir William Alexander* heading toward your position. I need you to standby on channel sixteen," McFadgen says.

Katlin concurs.

"Make sure you're listening on channel sixteen and, uh, you just steer whatever course you think you need to steer. Forget about Sambro and you steer whatever course you need to steer to keep her upright. Okay?"

"Yup. We will."

"Okay. I also need you to keep this phone clear, okay? We can't have you tying up the phone talking to family or anything else."

"Nope. Nobody's been on it," Katlin says, even though calls have been made steadily throughout the evening to many of the concerned families on shore.

"Okay. What course are you steering right now?"

"We're still going like a northerly direction. Somewhat to the north."

"Okay. Then [here's] what I want you to do: you're going to have to forget about Sambro. You're just going to have to think about keeping her comfortable."

"Yup."

"And not shipping any seas over," McFadgen adds. "So I just want you to steer whatever course you think is best. And you're probably not going to make much way anyway."

McFadgen also wants to know if Katlin is familiar with his distress beacon—his EPIRB. Yes, Katlin responds. The device is positioned on the roof of the wheelhouse.

"Okay, I understand it's probably not wise to go out there now," McFadgen says.

Katlin delivers what almost sounds like a laugh. "Uh, no," he confirms. Attempting to grab the EPIRB in these conditions would be extremely dangerous.

"And I understand that completely," McFadgen offers, "but if things really start to go sideways on you and you have no other way to get in touch, the key would be to get that beacon out of the case. If you activate that beacon, I will get that."

"Okay."

"If I see that beacon go off I'm going to assume that you're in a world of hurt."

"Okay."

"So for now I wouldn't recommend trying to send someone out on deck to get at it."

"No, I'm keeping everybody in the wheelhouse."

"All righty."

McFadgen next asks about the safety gear aboard the *Miss Ally*. Katlin tells McFadgen he has flares and an eight-person life raft. (There's also a four-person raft aboard, but Katlin doesn't mention it.) The life rafts, like the EPIRB, are mounted on top of the wheelhouse, where most fishermen keep them. When you're fishing, they're out of the way, but when you need them, the rafts are hard to get at. For Katlin and the crew, accessing the life rafts now would involve one or more of them going outside, climbing onto the roof, and maintaining a grip on the wildly pitching boat while also trying to launch a raft.

"And do you have survival suits on board?" McFadgen asks.

"No, we do not have survival suits."

"Okay."

There are five insulated survival suits aboard (perhaps six with the one Billy Jack brought) but Katlin doesn't mention them. Is he unaware they're aboard? Has he forgotten? Or does he figure the Coast Guard will move quicker if it believes the crew is without the protective suits? McFadgen is puzzled by the lack of survival suits but this is not the time to debate the merits of safety equipment.

Katlin does mention, however, that he has his Automatic Identification System (AIS) activated. AIS is a tracking system that emits a regular update of a vessel's position. It can also provide the vessel's key details, including name, heading, and size. The information is visible to the Coast Guard, other ships, and even armchair boaters back on land. With a computer and an Internet connection you can track the progress of countless vessels at sea, from fishing boats to ferries and tankers. The tracking information is updated often and allows the Coast Guard to better identify and monitor maritime traffic. AIS can help JRCC track the *Miss Ally* as it attempts to get to shore. Katlin is hoping AIS will also help guide the *Sir William Alexander* to his position.

"He might be able to pick me up on that when he gets closer," Katlin tells McFadgen. "If he can run along on my port side that would make a world of difference."

"Yep, he'll get on scene and he'll do whatever he can do to kind of ride it out. I think we're in more of a riding-it-out mode right now," McFadgen says. "The key will be just to get him there. So if you can just hang on until he gets there we'll be good."

"Yes, okay."

The call is winding to an end and McFadgen offers a final warning: "If you even suspect that things are starting to go poorly or going the wrong direction, I need to know that as soon as possible."

Katlin sounds generally positive, though as he tells McFadgen: "There was one or two weird waves that hit us and busted stuff up."

The connection starts to break up again.

"Not to worry," McFadgen says. "You do what you got to do and we'll get [the *Sir William Alexander*] down there as quickly as we can."

McFadgen asks Katlin to call JRCC in one hour with an update on his progress and position. Katlin agrees to call around 11 P.M.

"If I don't hear from you I'm going to assume that things have gone badly," McFadgen says. "So don't forget to call me."

The call ends and McFadgen types the key details into the log. After writing a couple paragraphs he enters a concluding line: "If we do not hear from him, we will assume things are going poorly. Do not forget to call!"

Down the coast on Cape Sable Island, Katlin's mom, Della, goes with her boyfriend, Adam, and her friends Sundae and Eddie to pick up a pizza. They make the short drive across the causeway to Barrington Passage in Eddie's truck. On the way home, half way across the causeway, Della gets a call from Katlin. Cellular service on the island is spotty, so Della tells Eddie to pull over. She doesn't want to risk losing the connection. Katlin tells Della the Coast Guard is en route. There's no reason to worry. He sounds calm. There's no fear in his voice. The news provides Della with some relief. Hopefully a Coast Guard ship can shield the *Miss Ally* from the worst of the wind and waves.

"We're all right, Momma," Katlin tells her before the call is dropped.

It's close to 10 P.M. and Della has heard her son's voice for the last time.

※

Shortly after 10 P.M., Ray McFadgen briefs a *Sir William Alexander* crew member on Katlin's progress: the *Miss Ally* is still upright but rescue officials are clearly assuming that may not be the case for long.

"He's on a northerly course but he's not making any headway. He's just hanging on," McFadgen says over the connection.

"Yeah I know the feeling," responds the *Sir William Alexander* crew member.

McFadgen explains it's unlikely a helicopter could reach the *Miss Ally* in this weather, thus the *Sir William Alexander* is their only option. He wants the ship's crew to establish communication with Katlin on channel sixteen, the emergency channel, as soon as possible.

"He's had some damage. It's a very young crew. We have a fairly high level of concern about this guy," McFadgen tells his colleague on the *Sir William Alexander.* "So we want to get communications right away. I don't want him disappearing off the face of the earth and us having no comms with him."

Aboard the *Sir William Alexander,* the message is understood. But as the operator notes, it's going to be a "slow go." The *Sir William Alexander* could be the crew's saviour, but the ship is still hours away. The ship's maximum speed is 16 knots (30 kilometres an hour), but in these conditions it's moving at less than half that speed. The ship's original ETA at the *Miss Ally* was 6 A.M., but McFadgen is told that estimate has been changed. The ship's speed has been cut because too much water was coming on deck. The new ETA is rough and imprecise: sometime after daybreak on Monday morning. Katlin and his crew will have to endure the waves, wind, and darkness alone.

"You do what you can," McFadgen says before signing off. "It is what it is."

Sitting at his workstation at JRCC, McFadgen senses Katlin and his crew are now truly at the mercy of the sea. McFadgen, however, keeps his thoughts to himself. "There was nothing to be gained from me telling them: 'There is a good chance that this is ending badly for you.'"

The weather on shore is also severe. McFadgen talks with Captain Colin Bond at CFB Greenwood about the possibility of deploying an Aurora. JRCC typically relies on Hercules airplanes for situations like this. A Hercules has a range of more than 7,000 kilometres, a cruising speed of 556 kilometres an hour, and is capable of short takeoffs and landings on rough runways. It's a beast of an aircraft that can weather challenging search conditions. Tonight, however, the typical standby search and rescue Hercules is grounded for maintenance. That means an Aurora is on standby. Greenwood's Auroras are typically used for maritime patrols and surveillance. For search and rescue, the Auroras are a backup option. Search and rescue workers can't jump out of the Auroras to aid people in distress, but at least the planes are good for searching. Designed to hunt submarines, the Auroras have infrared capability and strong radar systems. Captain Bond tells McFadgen there's a low-level turbulence warning for the Annapolis Valley and the wind is high. "Recommend they get some sleep," McFadgen writes in the log. "No tasking for them at this time."

At 10:52 P.M. Katlin calls JRCC for his scheduled hourly check-in. The connection is still poor.

"Is this the *Miss Ally*?" a JRCC maritime coordinator asks over the crackling connection.

"Yes, this is the *Miss Ally*," Katlin replies.

"Okay, good. Everything's good?"

Katlin responds but his voice is jumbled and inaudible.

"You're broken up. Uh, can you confirm everything is okay?"

"Everything is okay," Katlin eventually says. He asks a question but his voice is muffled.

"Um, if you are asking about the Coast Guard ship *Sir William Alexander*, they're about 50 miles away," the maritime coordinator responds.

"Okay."

The call doesn't last long. Katlin provides his current position and reads off the boat's course and speed: they are continuing to head north-northeast at about 6 knots (11 kilometres an hour).

"Okay, good. So how's everything on board? Everything good?" the coordinator asks again.

"Everything seems to be okay, like, as good as it can be, I guess."

"Okay, good. That's great."

The coordinator says he will pass the current information along to the crew of the *Sir William Alexander*, and tells Katlin to expect a call from the Coast Guard ship on channel sixteen.

"Give us a call back in an hour," the coordinator tells Katlin.

"Okay, thank you."

"All right, we'll hear from you then. Bye-bye."

"Okay, yep, bye."

Katlin puts down his satellite phone. His boat is rolling violently and shifting in ways he has not experienced before. The wind is shrieking, there's snow whizzing in the air, and he's steering into a solid wall of black. His track and position are available on the digital plotter, but outside nothing is visible. With Cole, Tyson, Joel, and Billy Jack nearby, Katlin is skippering the *Miss Ally* through a black winter hell.

Then something catastrophic happens.

CHAPTER 9

VANISHED

THE SEA WAS RELATIVELY CALM WHEN MIKE DOUCETTE WENT OVER-board. No one else aboard the *Row Row*, the lobster boat he was working on, saw him enter the water, or heard his likely screams as the boat steamed farther and farther away from him. He was alone in the frigid Atlantic Ocean in the middle of winter with no life jacket, and no way to signal for help.

It was on January 12, 2013—a month before Katlin and his crew headed to sea for their second halibut trip—that Mike, a twenty-year-old from Wedgeport, near Yarmouth, disappeared from the *Row Row*. JRCC coordinators were notified of a missing fisherman around 6:45 P.M. Shortly before, the panicked crew of the *Row Row* realized Mike was no longer aboard. They had assumed he was in his bunk. An hour had passed since he was last seen. Sixty minutes in the water. Alone.

Two Coast Guard vessels were dispatched and twenty fishing boats aided in the search. Search and rescue crews hunted for Mike from the air in a Cormorant helicopter and a Hercules plane. The Hercules crew used more than a hundred flares to illuminate the search area. Despite a fourteen-hour search in ideal conditions, Mike was never found.

Katlin had fished with Mike. The previous fall, he crewed for Katlin on the *Row Row* when Katlin was fishing for Reg LeBlanc on the Grand Banks. Mike was one of Reg's year-round deckhands, crewing on his swordfish and lobster boats, including the *Row Row*, for two years before he died.

Mike's death upset and angered Katlin.

"Fuck," he said while talking with his mom about the incident, about a week before he headed back out for halibut. It was one of the few times Della heard her son swear. He didn't understand. Couldn't more be done to find lost fishermen? How can someone simply disappear?

At 11:08 P.M. on Sunday, February 17, 2013, the Canadian Mission Control Centre at CFB Trenton calls JRCC in Halifax. The already delicate situation aboard the *Miss Ally* has deteriorated: the boat's EPIRB has been detected by satellite. It went off two minutes earlier, at 11:06 P.M. Either Katlin turned it on, or it self-activated when submerged in salt water. Perhaps the boat was hit by another large wave, or maybe they've foundered. Regardless, the vessel and its crew are now clearly in peril, and in the grip of truly treacherous conditions, roughly 165 kilometres southwest of Halifax.

The LaHave Bank weather buoy, about 90 kilometres from the *Miss Ally*'s last known position, is reporting average wave heights of 8 metres, with a maximum wave height of 15.3 metres in the past hour. These are monstrous walls of water. The wind, meanwhile, is howling from the west at up to 54 knots (100 kilometres an hour). The air temperature is sub-zero: -5 degrees Celsius.

At JRCC, the activation of an EPIRB signals an emergency. As one JRCC officer puts it: "We think, 'Oh crap—all hell has broken loose.'" The JRCC log records a flurry of activity in the minutes after Katlin's EPIRB is detected. Almost immediately JRCC pages CFB Greenwood and calls for an Aurora. McFadgen and a colleague, meanwhile, take turns desperately attempting to reach Katlin by satellite phone. There's no answer. The calls go directly to voicemail.

"NO JOY," they type into the log.

Officers on the *Sir William Alexander*, about 120 kilometres away, are also alerted to the active EPIRB. The instructions from JRCC come in: "Please make your best speed."

JRCC then contacts Halifax Coast Guard Radio to request a mayday relay, an international radio distress signal, which will indicate to marine traffic in the area that a boat is in distress.

The search has begun. But Captain Bond, aircraft commander of the standby Aurora at CFB Greenwood, cannot accept the rescue mission: there's currently severe low-level turbulence and wet snow, and his fleet is icing up. "No anti-icing capability," McFadgen types into the JRCC log. For now, nothing is taking off from Greenwood.

Two mayday messages, sent by Halifax Coast Guard Radio, fail to produce a response. There is no longer any AIS signal coming from the area of the *Miss Ally*'s last known position. Three more calls made to Katlin's satellite phone go unanswered. No one knows what's currently happening aboard the *Miss Ally*, but it's likely dire. As one of McFadgen's colleagues notes in the log, the team at JRCC is "very concerned that something went terribly wrong."

At 11:38 P.M., thirty minutes after the *Miss Ally*'s distress beacon goes off, JRCC contacts the 1st US Coast Guard District in Boston, Massachusetts.

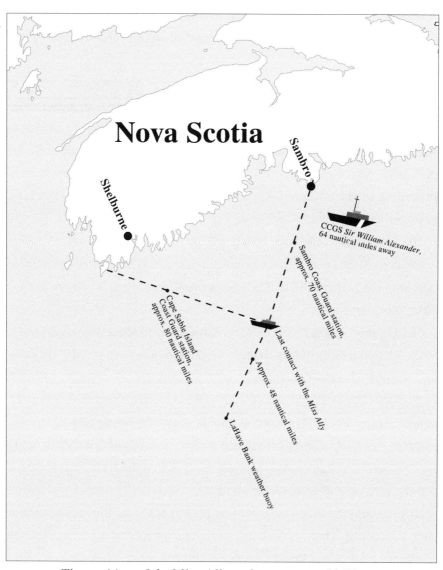

The position of the Miss Ally *at last contact: 10:52 P.M.*
on February 17, 2013.

The Canadians need air support. Canada and the United States have a reciprocal relationship when it comes to search and rescue; JRCC and its American counterparts often share information and resources. From Boston, JRCC's request is relayed to the US Coast Guard Air Station at Cape Cod.

The Cape Cod base is the only American Coast Guard aviation facility in the northeast, meaning it is responsible for the waters from New Jersey to the Canadian border. The US Coast Guard boasts that it can put a helicopter and a plane in the air—year-round, any time of day or night, in nearly all weather conditions—within thirty minutes of receiving a distress call. At 12:20 A.M. AST Monday morning, a US Coast Guard crew lifts off from the Cape Cod base aboard a HU-25 Falcon, a medium-range surveillance jet. They will aid the grounded Canadians. The main objective is to re-establish communications with Katlin. It's now been more than an hour since the distress beacon was detected, and ninety minutes since Katlin's last hourly check-in with JRCC. At sea, the crew of the *Sir William Alexander* has failed to reach Katlin by radio or satellite phone. Above Cape Cod, the Falcon pilot steers away from Massachusetts and out over the foamy Atlantic. Somewhere out there among the hurricane-force winds and snarling sea is the little yellow *Miss Ally* and its crew.

At JRCC, Ray McFadgen is attempting to determine who, exactly, is aboard this fishing boat that is causing so much anxiety on shore. McFadgen calls Jimmy Newell, the commanding officer of the Coast Guard station in Clark's Harbour, who phoned in with an initial report of trouble hours earlier. McFadgen explains that he needs to know who—other than Katlin—is aboard the Cape Islander. It's a task he can give to the RCMP if Jimmy is unable to assist.

"No," Jimmy replies. "I can take care of it."

It makes sense for Jimmy to help, especially at this hour. When it comes to issues on the water, he is considered a go-to figure in the community. Jimmy's father, Ron, was the initial commanding officer of the Clark's Harbour lifeboat station when it was established in 1966. As a boy, Jimmy often shadowed his father during watch shifts. After graduating high school Jimmy went into fishing, but it was the early 1980s and the industry was suffering a downturn. Seeking another option, he applied to the Coast Guard. He's been a full-time captain and commanding officer of the Clark's Harbour station since the late 1980s.

Jimmy leaves his house in Clark's Harbour and picks up Eric Nickerson, the Coast Guard deckhand whose son was in contact with Katlin earlier that evening. Jimmy knows Katlin and his parents, and Katlin is the same age as Jimmy's youngest son—the pair played hockey together. Jimmy and Eric will head to Della's house to see if she knows who is aboard with Katlin.

Della hasn't heard from Katlin in hours—not since around 10 P.M., when he told her everything was all right. She keeps calling his satellite phone but there's no answer. She's still at home on Cape Sable Island with her boyfriend, Adam, and her friends Sundae and Eddie. Around 12:20 A.M., Eddie goes to the window.

"Oh my God, here comes the Coast Guard," he says.

Della starts pacing, then goes to the patio door. Jimmy and Eric are standing in the dark. Della becomes completely distraught. The Coast Guard doesn't arrive at your house in the middle of the night bearing good news.

"Why are you here?" Della demands.

She turns away and continues to ask: "Why are these guys here? Why are they here in my house?"

But she already knows the answer.

Della is frantic. It's not possible to speak with her directly, so Jimmy explains to her friend Eddie that the *Miss Ally*'s EPIRB has gone off but that little else is known.

Della begins to scream.

"We can leave if it would make you more comfortable," Jimmy offers. "We'll leave and we'll come back if there's any news."

"No, do *not* leave this house!" Della snaps.

Just a few moments earlier Della couldn't bear the sight of Jimmy and Eric. Now she doesn't want them to leave: they are her direct link to the Coast Guard, and she wants to know exactly what's happening on the water.

Jimmy and Eric step further inside the house. For the next two days they'll maintain a nearly constant presence there, leaving only to briefly sleep, shower, and change their clothes.

Della now knows something serious has happened aboard her son's boat. She turns to her boyfriend, Adam, a fisherman.

"Would the boat flip over?" she asks.

"No," Adam tells her. "They don't normally flip over."

As the American Coast Guard's Falcon jet screeches through the darkness, the *Sir William Alexander* is battling 6–8-metre seas. Snow, blown around by a westerly wind of 50–55 knots (90 kilometres an hour), has reduced visibility to zero. At this rate, the *Sir William Alexander* won't be on-site until 7:30 A.M. A second Coast Guard ship, the 70-metre *Earl Grey*, is further behind. The *Earl Grey* departs the Dartmouth, Nova Scotia, Coast Guard base shortly after 1:30 A.M. The ship likely won't arrive at the *Miss Ally*'s last known position until noon. The forecast is not encouraging for either Coast Guard vessel. Hurricane-force winds are expected to dip slightly, but only to 45 knots (83 kilometres an hour). Seas up to 10 metres are still expected during the early morning before subsiding to 6–8 metres near noon.

Back in Halifax, JRCC contacts Globalstar, the satellite phone maker. Can Globalstar tell if Katlin's phone is still active on the network? They cannot, but the company says Katlin's phone was last used at 10:52 P.M. That time corresponds with his final conversation with JRCC. That means no one has spoken with Katlin since he told Halifax everything was okay. McFadgen continues to dial Katlin's number. "Number unreachable," he types into the log.

At sea, a radio operator aboard the *Sir William Alexander* is calling for the *Miss Ally* on channel sixteen: "Come in. Come in."

Silence.

With the fleet at CFB Greenwood unavailable, JRCC calls Provincial Aerospace, a private company based in St. John's, Newfoundland. Provincial Aerospace has been conducting airborne surveillance for more than thirty-five years, and has operations in Canada, the Caribbean, and the Middle East. The company's aircraft are often used for search and rescue missions. One of the company's surveillance planes, a King Air twin-engine turboprop, is housed at Halifax's Stanfield International Airport. A Provincial Aerospace dispatcher says the company can get the plane in the air, but it will take a few hours to prepare and assemble a crew.

The American Falcon crew, meanwhile, now in Canadian airspace, homes in on the signal emitting from Katlin's EPIRB. By 3 A.M., four hours after the distress beacon went off, they've tracked the signal to its origin. Down below, using infrared imagining, the crew spots what it describes as a life raft, but the visibility is too poor to determine if anyone is aboard or nearby. Their infrared technology does not pick up any heat signatures in or around the object. The crew's report on the conditions is also discouraging: westerly winds gusting to 75 knots (140 kilometres an hour) and waves towering up to 9 metres. The Falcon crew drops a self-locating datum marker buoy into the water to mark the position of what they believe to be the raft. The buoy will help searchers judge the drift of the life raft as it is knocked about in the wild sea.

After twenty minutes on the scene, the Falcon pilot guides the plane back toward Cape Cod. The weather is terrible and he needs to refuel. Anyone below is now left alone in the raging darkness.

No one knows what state the *Miss Ally* crew is in—or if they're even alive. Even so, Ray McFadgen, who's been working on the case at JRCC Halifax since the initial reports of trouble, wants to brief the families. He's sure the families must be aware of trouble on board, but McFadgen is not sure if they know about the EPIRB being deployed or that JRCC has since lost contact with the crew. No one has called yet for information, but he's anticipating they will begin soon. He taps an update into the log: "I want to get next of kin briefed asap before rumours start to circulate."

With the list of five names in hand, McFadgen begins to call the families. He's able to reach a couple of them and provides the latest—though limited— information. There's no answer at Stephen Nickerson's house, where Cole lives. The call goes to voicemail but McFadgen doesn't leave a message—this is not the kind of information that's left casually on an answering machine.

At Della's house on Cape Sable Island, Jimmy Newell—the island's head Coast Guard officer—has set up a makeshift office in her basement, near Katlin's bedroom. Jimmy is receiving hourly updates from JRCC. After each update, he walks upstairs and provides the details—scant as they are—to Della's boyfriend, Adam, or her friend Eddie. Sometimes Della is also in the room. Often, though, she retreats to her room or the bathroom and is comforted by her friend Sundae. After each update, Jimmy returns to the basement to call the other families. Jimmy hasn't been formally tasked to deal with the families, but given his standing in the community it makes sense that he acts as a point of contact between the Coast Guard and the relatives of the missing men. Plus, Jimmy knows all five men on the missing boat. While Katlin played hockey with Jimmy's youngest son, Tyson played with his oldest. Jimmy coached Tyson in his final year of midget hockey, and played on the same rec hockey team as Cole. Billy Jack shingled Jimmy's roof, and Jimmy's nephew, Jeremy Stoddard, is dating Billy Jack's sister, Natasha. And, of course, everyone knows Joel. If Joel was driving down the road on his dirt bike and Jimmy was outside, Joel would make sure to stop for a chat. The previous summer, when Joel was crewing for Katlin on a swordfishing trip and Joel injured his hand, it was Jimmy and his crew who brought Joel back to shore aboard a Coast Guard search-and-rescue life boat.

Jimmy is now calling various family members every hour with updates. He asks George Hopkins—Joel's dad—if he'd prefer a call in two hours, so he and Mary can get some sleep.

"No. Call us right away," George says. "We're not going to sleep."

While Jimmy is in Della's basement, taking hourly calls from JRCC and updating the families, his deckhand, Eric Nickerson, remains upstairs. Eric's own father was lost at sea, so he is sympathetic and knows what to say to make the situation somewhat bearable for Della. Around 4:30 A.M., Jimmy and Eric depart Della's house. They take showers and briefly nap. They return within ninety minutes of leaving.

✻

Up in Cape Breton, Sandy Stoddard and his son, Chrisjon, have their boats rafted up in Petit-de-Grat, safely out of the storm that Katlin and his crew have disappeared in. Sandy and Chrisjon's crew members are all aboard the boat Sandy is skippering, the *Logan & Morgan*. Among the two crews are Joel's brother Jesse and Tyson's brother Jeremy. They now know the EPIRB aboard the *Miss Ally* was activated. As fishermen, Jesse and Jeremy understand what that means, particularly given the current nightmare conditions. The odds of survival are slight, measured in minutes for a person not in a survival suit. Sandy approaches the two crying men and hugs them both.

"It's all in God's hands," he says. "It's whatever God deems at this point."

Search and rescue officials, however, don't factor acts of God or potential miracles into their decisions. They "task resources" and consider odds of survival in any given situation. Back at JRCC Halifax, Ray McFadgen is again attempting to get a Canadian bird in the air. At 4 A.M., Captain Bond reports that CFB Greenwood still cannot launch an Aurora because of severe turbulence and ice. The Air Force is grounded so JRCC will have to lean on Provincial Aerospace, the private surveillance company.

Around the same time, JRCC reconnects with Rob Gray, the captain of the *Sir William Alexander*. The exchange provides the most stunning evidence of just how bad the conditions are at sea. The *Sir William Alexander* is a light icebreaker.

It's 83 metres long and 16 metres wide. It's a high-endurance vessel with a range of 12,000 kilometres. It's capable of spending months at sea. It eclipses the *Miss Ally* in size, stability, and capability, yet it is struggling. In the words of Captain Gray, the ship is taking "an awful pounding" in seas exceeding 10 metres. In their effort to reach the *Miss Ally*, the Coast Guard crew must steer the ship broadside to the giant waves. As a result, the vessel is rolling constantly.

The *Sir William Alexander* is typically used as a buoy ship. The ship's crew replaces and repairs the large navigational buoys that collect weather information and help direct ship traffic—"bells and whistles" as they're called in the Coast Guard. There are five such buoys strapped to the deck of the *Sir William Alexander*. Though secured with heavy-duty chains, the buoys are working loose from their restraints and shifting on deck. For Captain Gray it's a worrying sight. The buoys are large and unwieldy. A loose buoy could puncture the ship's deck or superstructure. Then there are the cement stones that anchor the buoys to the ocean floor; they are starting to slide around on deck too, presenting another potential source of damage. In these seas, a hole on deck would quickly fill with water. If that happens, Gray will be forced to retire from this mission.

Gray orders the ship be turned directly into the waves and brought to a standstill. Members of the crew step out on deck and attempt to quickly secure the buoys and anchor blocks. The high bow of the *Sir William Alexander* protects the crew from most of the waves, but there's always the potential for water to wash over the sides. The deck of the *Sir William Alexander* is partially open and relatively low. It's a design feature that assists with buoy work, but it also means water can easily flow onto the deck from both sides. The crew, working on the heaving, wet platform, carefully secures the buoys and anchor blocks, and the ship again gets underway. Shortly after, however, the buoys start coming loose again and the whole process has to be repeated.

Communicating with JRCC, Captain Gray says his ship may have to heave-to until daylight. Heaving-to involves putting a ship in a relatively stable position, with the bow facing toward the wind to absorb most of the pounding. The boat's progress is minimal, but conditions aboard are safer and more comfortable. It's the nautical equivalent of surrendering to the conditions. JRCC is sympathetic.

"Roger, Captain. Do what you have to do for the safety of your vessel, but if possible we would like you to proceed to the raft position and then run off to the east."

"Roger, we will do our best," Grays responds.

The *Sir William Alexander* continues to pound on.

Stephen Nickerson, Cole's father, pushes himself out of bed around 5 A.M. Monday morning. He goes downstairs and notices he's missed a call from a Halifax number. It must have been Cole calling from Sambro.

The last update Stephen received came at 8 P.M. last night from Tyson's girlfriend, Ashley. She told Stephen the boys were only a couple hours from land and headed for Sambro. All seemed fine so Stephen went to bed.

Stephen now picks up the phone and calls the Halifax number back. A man answers, but it's not Cole.

"Is Cole around there?" Stephen asks.

"Cole?"

Stephen has reached JRCC. He's quickly informed about the *Miss Ally*'s distress beacon, the spotted life raft, and the continuing search. Stephen is shocked. The life raft sighting provides some hope, but not much.

Fishermen have survived in the safety of life rafts for significant stretches. On June 23, 1979, the crew of the *Cliffie Eldora* was fishing 160 kilometres south of Halifax in thick fog, when another boat rammed their 57-foot wooden dragger. The *Cliffie Eldora* sank in five minutes. The four crew members leaped into a life raft and survived twenty-six hours before a German freighter picked them up. The captain, Cyril Garland, was never found. However, the crew of the *Cliffie Eldora* benefitted from two factors that now elude the men aboard the *Miss Ally*: the *Cliffie Eldora* sunk in June, when the water is warmer, and sea conditions were, by comparison, tranquil. In this weather a raft would be tossed wildly and half-filled with water in a matter of minutes.

It's early morning and still dark outside when Bobby Watt—Katlin's friend who declined a winter spot on the *Miss Ally*—gets a call from Billy Joe Brannen, the captain he regularly crews for. Billy Joe is upset.

"What's going on?" Bobby asks groggily.

"I don't want to tell ya," Billy Joe says. "I don't want to tell ya."

Eventually he explains that a distress signal went off during the night from the *Miss Ally*. That's all he knows.

Katlin had called Bobby earlier in the evening around 10 P.M. Bobby had been at a hockey game and couldn't quite determine why the young skipper was calling. Katlin mentioned the damage to his boat's stern board and the destroyed bait shack. Why was Katlin telling Bobby this? He might have been scared and in need of someone to talk to, but Bobby didn't think Katlin sounded worried. Katlin told Bobby he'd call back when the *Miss Ally* entered cellphone range. The call never came.

Now wide awake, Bobby calls Della. There's no answer. He calls Katlin's satellite phone. No answer. Shortly after, Bobby's father, Stephen, calls. The two aren't close. The last time they spoke, Bobby mentioned trying to make arrangements so he could go fishing with Katlin on the *Miss Ally*. On the other end of the line Bobby's dad is crying. He had assumed Bobby went with Katlin. He thought his son was out there.

Bobby spends the next few days in shock. He easily could have been on the boat. He wanted to be on the boat.

"It's scary to think of," he admits. "I try not to."

By 6 A.M., all the families have been notified.

Grant Nickerson, Cole's cousin, is in a hotel room in Estevan, southern Saskatchewan, when he hears the news. He's been back out west for two weeks, again working as a pile driver like he did with Cole the year before. It's about 4 A.M.—6 A.M. back east—when, lying in bed, he picks up his phone. Posts about the *Miss Ally* are already appearing on Facebook. Squinting at his phone, Grant sees a post that says something about "praying for the boys." "As soon as I read that I knew," he recalls. "I knew exactly who it was when I read it." Grant jumps out of bed, gets in the shower, and then starts making arrangements to fly home as quickly as possible.

Sandy Stoddard, still aboard the tied-up *Logan & Morgan* in Petit-de-Grat, Cape Breton, calls JRCC just before 6 A.M. looking for an update. He gets one and is asked to tell people in Woods Harbour not to speculate about what's happened.

But the speculation has already begun.

David Hill, aboard the fishing boat *Fisherman's Provider*, calls JRCC shortly after Sandy does. He's heard the *Miss Ally* sunk. David and his crew know many of the guys aboard the *Miss Ally* and they're concerned.

"Did the guys get picked up okay?" he asks a JRCC coordinator. "We heard she went down last night."

"We can't confirm that at this time. We're still not sure," a JRCC coordinator tells him. "We're in the process of searching for her."

David's boat has just arrived at Canso after steaming into port overnight.

"It was a dirty night," he tells the JRCC coordinator.

At 6:15 A.M. the *Sir William Alexander*, after plowing through walls of water all night, is finally on scene. The crew is looking for any sign of the *Miss Ally* or its crew. The *Sir William Alexander* is sweeping electronically with radar, and searchlights are swinging from side to side. Hopefully they'll produce a glimmer of something in the early morning darkness. Mainly, though, they just illuminate the snow-filled air. There's a crew member on each side of the boat, scanning the water, one with night-vision binoculars. But even these high-tech methods are yielding nothing. In these conditions a search effort is nearly futile. It's blowing 60 knots (100 kilometres an hour) and the waves are consistently 10–12 metres high. Some are even higher, and Captain Rob Gray and the *Sir William Alexander* crew can't see them coming. Every so often they're smashed by a massive wave that sends the ship lurching. Waves are breaking on deck and it's only safe to go straight into the waves or with them. It's now unwise to go broadside to the storm.

Gray has been a commanding officer since 2000, and with the Coast Guard for more than three decades. As a commanding officer he has sailed from the Artic to the Gulf of Mexico. These aren't the worst conditions he's seen, but they're not far off. His ship is taking a pounding. In addition to the wind and waves, rain and snow have eliminated all visibility. Their search effort is fruitless. Gray doesn't want to damage his ship or endanger the crew. They'll heave-to and wait until daylight before continuing. In the meantime, they'll continue trying to raise Katlin and the crew by radio. Every call, however, goes unanswered. There is no human sound emerging from the darkness.

Ten minutes later, just before 6:30 A.M., Provincial Aerospace's King Air begins its mission. A search plane has finally lifted off from Nova Scotia, seven hours after the *Miss Ally*'s EPIRB went off. Shortly after 7 A.M., the King Air buzzes over the search area and begins homing the EPIRB signal. The pilot flies to the west but the signal weakens. The plane banks and the signal strengthens. The scene below is a mess: it's finally daylight but the weather has not improved much. The waves are still up to 9 metres tall.

Around this time the *Mount Everest*, a tanker, responds to one of the Coast Guard's mayday alerts, which have been regularly relayed since shortly after 11 P.M. The *Mount Everest* is 130 kilometres away and headed in the direction of the *Miss Ally*'s last known position. The ship could be on the scene to help search in twelve hours. JRCC's response is blunt: "If we find them in the life raft the search will be over and if they are not in the raft they will not survive another twelve hours."

At CFB Greenwood, meanwhile, the conditions have eased enough for a chopper to take off. An Air Force Cormorant lifts off at 7:40 A.M. The chopper buzzes over the interior of the province before moving off the coast to the search area.

As morning breaks, the storm that suddenly swallowed the *Miss Ally* is still making an impact. In its sweep over the Maritimes, the storm has knocked out power to thousands and left many students celebrating school closures. The weather station at Baccaro Point, not far from Cape Sable Island, records wind gusts of 80 to 90 kilometres an hour throughout much of Monday morning. Lieutenant Peter Ryan of Maritime Forces Atlantic tells reporters on Monday that searchers are still facing poor visibility and "very challenging seas." Westerly winds up to 50 knots (90 kilometres an hour) and maximum waves of 10 to 13 metres continue to thrash the waters around the *Miss Ally*'s last known position.

"There's a wide search underway and the situation is evolving," Ryan adds.

The name of the boat and its crew are not made public, but George Hopkins, who quickly becomes a spokesman for the five families, tells The Canadian Press that the lost vessel is the *Miss Ally* and its crew, including his son Joel, is experienced. "They are to a certain extent, but the captain is really young," George tells the reporter. "I don't know how experienced you can be when he's only twenty-one or so."

George has been concerned since Sunday evening. He last talked to Katlin around 10:30 P.M. but didn't get a chance to speak with Joel. To George, the situation is discouraging. Nothing has been found since the Americans spotted the life raft in the early morning. "They haven't seen anything since," he tells the CP reporter.

As the hours pass, family members grow increasingly nervous and contact JRCC seeking updates. But there's little to report: there are ships in the area and aircraft flying above. The crews are looking for the boat, the men, the raft...anything.

Then, just before 8 A.M., a Provincial Aerospace dispatcher contacts JRCC. The crew of the King Air has found the *Miss Ally*. The boat is flipped over. All that's visible is the yellow hull, being pounded by whitecapped waves.

The focus of the search is now squarely on locating the life raft, which has not been seen since 3:20 A.M. As JRCC notes in its instructions to the officers aboard the *Sir William Alexander*: "Try to find the raft as that is the only real hope for survivors." The *Miss Ally* is equipped with two life rafts: a four-person raft and an eight-person model. It's unclear which one the Americans spotted.

Around 8:30 A.M. a Cormorant helicopter arrives on the scene. An hour later the helicopter's crew spots a debris field east of the overturned vessel. There's no raft, but the Cormorant crew does spot a few survival suits floating on the surface.

They are empty.

CHAPTER 10

THE LONG WAIT

JOHN SYMONDS AND HIS WIFE, GINA, LAND BACK IN HALIFAX FROM Mexico at 10 A.M. on Monday morning. The flight, delayed in Mexico because of the storm in Nova Scotia, endures a rocky, windy landing. When the plane finally hits the runway, the passengers erupt in clapping and cheering. Safe on the tarmac, John and Gina check their phones. Gina has a message from their son, Nolan. Nolan crewed for two summers alongside Katlin. The *Miss Ally* is missing.

John is distraught and helpless to do anything. He hopes desperately that Katlin has done what John taught him to do in heavy weather: batten down every hatch, pop the boat into neutral, put the stern into the storm and let the boat be pushed by the wind and waves. In other words: let the sea break over the stern. Steering directly into such a storm—with waves crashing over the bow—is very likely to smash out your wheelhouse windows, or worse. But it's far too late for such thoughts. Katlin is no longer at the wheel of the *Miss Ally*.

As John gathers his luggage, JRCC reports that a rumour has begun circulating: the crew is safe in the life raft and the Coast Guard is alongside them. "That is untrue," the JRCC log notes. The *Sir William Alexander* is only alongside the flipped hull. For Captain Rob Gray and his crew, it's a deflating sight and an indication of just how vicious the sea has been. With twenty thousand pounds of fish in the *Miss Ally*'s hold, the boat would've had a very low centre of gravity; it would have taken a great force to flip such a weight. The capsized boat is also a reminder that the odds of finding the crew alive are deteriorating rapidly. "That kind of took the wind out of our sails, I must be honest with you," Gray recalls of seeing the hull. "You're still hopeful for a raft, some sort of survival craft. [But] it starts to look a little darker."

Yet the search continues. The crew of the *Sir William Alexander* has picked up the signal from the EPIRB and is hunting for debris. There's decent visibility, but the conditions are still complicating the effort to see anything floating in the water. There's been little reduction in the wind speed or wave heights: westerly winds are still in excess of 50 knots (90 kilometres an hour) and seas are still peaking above 10 metres. The air and sea are the same temperature: 3 degrees Celsius. The conditions are not expected to change much today. How long could the men aboard the *Miss Ally* possibly survive in such conditions? It's a question the military is now receiving from reporters. The answer, recorded in the JRCC log, is far from encouraging.

According to JRCC's cold-water survival modelling, a person immersed to the neck in a generic survival suit has a 95 percent chance of surviving eleven hours in 3-degree water. The men aboard the *Miss Ally* have been missing for more than twelve hours, and the odds of survival drop with each passing minute. In a survival suit, there's a 75 percent chance of lasting fourteen hours.

At sixteen hours the chances are 50/50. After nineteen hours the odds are down to 25 percent. And the chances of surviving twenty-four hours are bleak: 5 percent. But Katlin told JRCC he didn't have survival suits aboard (although the empty suits have since been spotted in the water).

In late February of 1967, a series of severe winter storms rolled along the Nova Scotia coast, delivering winds of more than 160 kilometres an hour and waves over 14 metres tall. The storms took out three vessels and killed thirty-five men. The *Cape Bonnie*, a 400-ton trawler owned by National Sea Products, got caught in the first storm, on February 21. The *Cape Bonnie*'s crew had been fishing for ten days on Browns Bank and LaHave Bank—the same area fished by the crew of the *Miss Ally*. While returning to Halifax in blizzard conditions, the *Cape Bonnie* veered off course. The boat hit ground on Woody Island, near Lower Prospect. The bodies of fourteen of the eighteen crew members were recovered. Most were wearing lifejackets, but there were no survival suits aboard. In February, survival time in the ocean without a survival suit is measured in minutes. If the men aboard the *Miss Ally* went into the water without survival suits, they're now long dead. The life raft remains the only hope. But even a raft can only do so much to separate one from the elements. The raft wouldn't offer much of a separation from the near-freezing water and wind.

The dire conditions have led the commanding officer of the *Earl Grey*, which arrived on scene at noon, to an easy conclusion: there's no hope for survivors. How could there be? His 70-metre ship is being pummelled. The storm has even broken one of the ship's windows. He wants his vessel to "be stood down," but the call to halt the search does not lie with the commanding officer. Orders arrive from shore: unless the *Earl Grey* is no longer able to function, the crew should continue searching.

The missing fishing boat from southwest Nova Scotia quickly becomes a major news story across the country. Among the outlets seeking updates are CTV National News, CBC National News, The Canadian Press, and, eventually, CNN in Atlanta. The search for the men aboard the *Miss Ally* has also attracted attention of Canada's top military personnel. Around noon on Monday, Chris Denko, lieutenant-colonel with the Ottawa-headquartered Canadian Joint Operations Command (CJOC) sends an email to Major Ali Laaouan, the officer in charge at JRCC Halifax. It seems Peter MacKay—the defence minister and a Nova Scotia member of parliament—is very interested in the *Miss Ally* case.

"We are trying to quell the onslaught of questions from MNDO [minister of national defence's office] regarding the *Miss Ally* SAR [search and rescue]," Denko writes. "Anticipate interest to continue on this case."

"Any specific reason?" Laaouan writes back a minute later.

"Nope," Denko replies. "Just because it's in the maritimes [*sic*] I suspect."

Across Canada, Facebook quickly becomes a hub for *Miss Ally* posts. Throughout Monday, alumni of Barrington Municipal High School, which all five men attended, use Facebook to find information on the search effort and offer prayers and messages of hope. Dozens of users replace their Facebook avatars with an image of the *Miss Ally* surrounded by candles. "The coast guard boats are on their way, boys; hang in there and keep fighting," writes one former lobster fisherman.

Some of the messages are from areas in western Canada, where many locals have moved in search of work. "Just got the most terrifying phone call…I don't even know how to handle this right now…Please just come home," writes a former Woods Harbour resident now living in northern British Columbia.

Ashley Nickerson, Tyson's girlfriend, also takes to Facebook: "Fight like you have never fought before," she writes on Monday. "I love you."

As the hours pass, friends and relatives gather at the homes of the five families. They wait nervously for a significant development that never comes. Eddie Nickerson, the warden of the Municipality of Barrington, tells outsiders that his community is consumed by the anxious wait for news from searchers. "I know all of the boys that were on the boat," he says. "It's a fragile situation."

At the Woods Harbour general store, all anyone is talking about is the *Miss Ally* and the five missing men. They're simply referred to as "the boys" or "the kids." "They're all sad," says storeowner George El-Jakl of his customers. "They're all looking for a miracle to happen. We are all praying."

Debbie Atkinson, working at the post office on Cape Sable Island, tells a Canadian Press reporter that all the men are from fishing families. "The sea was in their blood," she concludes. "I almost wish it wasn't, but it was."

Tyrone Nickerson, Cole's uncle, cannot believe this situation has again befallen his family, four decades after the loss of his Uncle Andrew on the *Colville Bay*. The boats are better built these days, and weather forecasting has improved. So how is this happening again, thirty-nine years later? It seems every generation of Woods Harbour residents endures a similar tragedy. There was the *Sir Echo* in 1950, then the *Colville Bay* in 1974. Memories fade and local residents begin to think such tragedies will never be repeated.

Until it happens again.

Rear-Admiral Dave Gardam walks into the JRCC operations room late Monday afternoon to discuss the ongoing search for the crew of the *Miss Ally*. Gardam, a thirty-five-year naval veteran, is the commander for the massive area covered by JRCC Halifax. The afternoon's search effort has delivered little. The crew of the Cormorant spotted the survival suits, but there's been no sign of Katlin, Joel, Tyson, Cole, or Billy Jack. Stephen Waller, a maritime coordinator at JRCC, tells Gardam the plan is to keep the *Sir William Alexander*, the *Earl Grey*, the Cormorant helicopter, Provincial Aerospace's King Air, and the Aurora searching overnight. (The Aurora finally gets in the air twenty-one hours after initially being called on by JRCC.)

Gardam concurs. They also discuss the fact that the window for surviving in the water in a survival suit is nearly closed. "We need to find the rafts," Waller punches into the log. "If we find the rafts then we will be at a conclusion as we will either find the people or know they are in the water and have perished." If they don't find a raft, Waller notes, two possibilities exist: either JRCC expands the search area, or assumes the rafts sank or were never launched. Gardam will return in the morning. If nothing has changed, they'll make a decision then. Waller concludes his entry: "We [will] continue to search all night [but] people need to start preparing for the possibility that there won't be a happy outcome."

Gardam, meanwhile, writes an email to Lieutenant-General Stuart Beare. Beare, the Canadian military's top operations officer, is in charge of all deployed Canadian Forces—from the Arctic to Afghanistan. "Sir, FYI [we] intend flying MPA [maritime patrol aircraft] throughout the night to see if we can find the life raft," Gardam writes. "We need to find the raft…."

Shortly before 5:30 P.M. on Monday evening, with darkness returning to the winter sky, the Cormorant crew spots a field of debris. Amongst the wreckage is the EPIRB, a life ring, and survival suits. There's still no raft and no sign of life.

A biting northwest wind is still blowing snow through Woods Harbour when the bell of the Calvary United Baptist Church rings just before 6 P.M. on Monday. Pastor Phil Williams has shovelled and salted the walkway, turned up the heat, and flicked on the lights in preparation for the evening's candle-light prayer vigil.

"God is our refuge and our strength, a very present help in time of trouble," Pastor Williams says, quoting *Psalms*, as people from Woods Harbour and beyond file sombrely into the church. There are family members of the missing men, high school friends, some old, some young. Some pray out loud, others sit quietly.

In a one-road town, you know everyone, even if just in passing.

"The community is in a very solemn mood, yet they're very hopeful," fisherman Davis Nickerson tells a *Chronicle Herald* reporter at the vigil. He's one of the roughly five hundred who attend despite the weather and power outages. "We can't give up hope. We're praying for a miracle here. We're hopeful these boys will be found."

That prospect, however, is increasingly unlikely. Late Monday, following a combined five missions to the search area by the Cormorant and King Air crews, JRCC coordinators are preparing for an eventual reduction of the search. "Facts would indicate that a catastrophic event occurred between conversation at 10:52 P.M. with JRCC Halifax and the first detection of the EPIRB at 11:06 P.M.," notes a log entry made shortly before midnight. The log also notes that a Vessel Monitoring System (VMS) position was received for the *Miss Ally* at 11:01 P.M. Sunday, meaning the boat was likely still upright with power at that time, and thus flipped in the five minutes between 11:01 P.M. and 11:06 P.M., when the distress beacon was detected.

Out at sea, the search continues late Monday night and into Tuesday morning, but conditions remain treacherous; large waves and strong winds are still hampering the effort. Both the EPIRB and the self-locating datum marker buoy dropped by the US Coast Guard are drifting east-northeast at roughly 4 kilometres an hour. The movement of both objects is helping searchers judge roughly where a life raft might have drifted. Shortly after 1 A.M. on Tuesday morning, there are four aircraft buzzing in the dark sky above the search grid: Provincial Aerospace's King Air, a Hercules, an Aurora, and a Cormorant. The Cormorant, however, after just thirty minutes on the scene, is forced back to land by the miserable conditions, which now include blowing snow. Down below, the *Sir William Alexander* and *Earl Grey* continue to plow through the North Atlantic mess. Yet, as dawn arrives on Tuesday, there is still no sign of the five men or their life raft. A line entered in the JRCC log summarizes the situation: "Time to start preparing for the fact that hope is fading."

Captain Wayne Jarvis, a search and rescue air coordinator, is far more blunt in his assessment: "We will have exceeded the point of survivability of the *Miss Ally*'s crew by mid-afternoon today," he writes in an email sent Tuesday morning to Captain Réal Brisson, the chief of Staff Operations at Maritime Forces Atlantic. "It is my recommendation that we reduce the search at sundown today." He goes on:

> The crew had no warning as there was no Mayday call. The captain did not know they had immersion suits on board, making it extremely unlikely that anyone actually got into one. With 8-10 meter seas at the time, it is believed the vessel rolled, giving the crew no chance to escape to a raft. The raft that was seen showed no signs of life when spotted, no [infrared] hotspots to indicate people were in it. The raft, that has not been seen since, is believed to have been destroyed by the weather. The survival model indicates 23.6 hours of survival for 5% of all people, well rested, in a dry immersion suit on a calm day. Even with the improved conditions of 6 meter seas, if they managed to get into a raft and remained upright, the raft would have filled with water and they would have succumbed last night at the latest.

In a separate email, Jarvis continues his frank tone: "In seas like we have, they would already be finished." Yet, because of the spotted life raft, he expects the search to continue through sundown Tuesday.

Coast Guard officer Jimmy Newell and deckhand Eric Nickerson arrive back at Della's house around 6 A.M. Tuesday. They departed the house about six hours earlier, around midnight, only after telling Katlin's mom they'd be back early in the morning. They've been in the house for most of the search, with Jimmy continuing to act as a link between the families and rescue officials at JRCC. By early Tuesday morning Jimmy has been told the search will end today.

It's time to start preparing Della for this news. Jimmy knows these missions don't continue indefinitely. Search and rescue decisions are based on survival odds, and the odds in this case are heavily weighted in the ocean's favour.

The outlook is bleak but the search hasn't been called off just yet. In fact, JRCC again contacts the American Coast Guard in Boston. Specifically, JRCC requests the services of Cape Cod's new and state-of-the-art HC-144A Ocean Sentry. The 70-foot, turboprop plane has a range of nearly 4,000 kilometres, a flight endurance of more than ten hours, and the ability to transmit and receive classified information. Most importantly, it has the latest infrared sensing technology. The Ocean Sentry will fly 500 kilometres from Cape Cod to scan the cold ocean for any sign of Katlin, Joel, Billy Jack, Tyson, or Cole. But the plane won't be available until Tuesday afternoon. The search won't end before the crew of the Ocean Sentry is able to conduct a scan of the area.

In Woods Harbour and on Cape Sable Island, the families of the missing men remain at their homes throughout Tuesday, tensely awaiting updates. Many other residents do the same. On Facebook, many people post the same photo: the *Miss Ally* with the words "Praying for a Miracle" underneath. Most of the local boats remain tied up at the Falls Point wharf, partly because of the weather, but mainly because nobody wants to be away from Woods Harbour when the news—good or bad—eventually arrives. Even Fishermen's Haven remains largely deserted. The maroon building is a popular gathering spot near the Falls Point wharf, particularly among some of the senior fishermen. George Hopkins stops in most mornings. Inside the building are some tables and chairs and a pool table. There are hockey championship banners on the wall and hockey trophies on a shelf. Today, though, it's quiet. There's no coffee in the pot, and the well-worn cribbage boards remain untouched.

This morning's search has turned up more debris. Around 9:30 A.M., the King Air crew spots a white object. Shortly after that, the Hercules crew spots two life jackets and detects a weak EPIRB signal. Just before 1 P.M., with the search clearly in its final hours, JRCC officials note that the various agencies should consider an important fact: the families, as well as the Transportation Safety Board, might still be interested in the over-turned hull. "They should think about and discuss their involvement and what other agencies [may] want our assets to do," notes a log entry. Should the *Earl Grey* stand by the hull? Should a remotely operated underwater vehicle (ROV) be deployed? The JRCC log also notes that a US Coast Guard ship is scheduled to depart Halifax later in the day. It might have useful tools aboard.

JRCC's warning appears to go unheeded. The fate and location of the hull will prove to be a major point of contention—and a sore spot with the families—in the days, weeks, and months ahead.

At 1 P.M. on Tuesday afternoon, Rear-Admiral Gardam, the regional search and rescue commander, approves a reduction of the search. Barring a new development, the search will end at 6 P.M. Provincial Aerospace's King Air crew spots the final pieces of wreckage early in the afternoon: some orange panelling, a series of orange bags tied together, and an orange floating ring that's likely tethered to the EPIRB. It's not enough to warrant further searching. The King Air crew returns to Halifax and is not re-tasked. The Cormorant crew, refuelling in Halifax shortly before 3:30 P.M., is told they won't be sent back to sea unless something urgent arises.

The weather has eased, with the west wind finally dipping below 20 knots (40 kilometres an hour) and the waves receding to less than 3 metres, but now there's little point in searching. The day's effort includes more than ten search missions by two Cormorants, the King Air, an Aurora, a Hercules, and the American Ocean Sentry. The final hours drip by before a military news release eventually confirms the decision: the search, covering 18,130 square kilometres and lasting roughly forty hours, is over. The mayday broadcasts are cancelled, the aircraft are grounded, and the *Earl Grey* and *Sir William*

Alexander both depart the search area shortly after 6 P.M. The entry in the JRCC log at 6:02 P.M. cuts to the point: "There have been no new leads and we are sending our resources back to their respective bases."

The situation in Woods Harbour is raw and Lieutenant Peter Ryan of Maritime Forces Atlantic seems obliged to offer justification for ending the search. Searches typically last only twenty-four hours, he tells a *Chronicle Herald* reporter shortly after the *Miss Ally* operation is called off. "It's always a difficult decision," he adds. "You have people who have been going out day and night in the hopes of trying to find something. We're well past thirty-six hours now. A very careful evaluation was made and it was determined it was time to stand down our resources." The partially submerged hull has been spotted at least four times since the search started, but Ryan notes there's been nothing else to inspire hope that the five men are still alive. The life raft spotted by the Americans in the early hours of the search has not been seen since. With the search called off—technically called a "search reduction"—the case becomes the responsibility of the RCMP. It's now a missing persons case.

At the Hopkins house, twenty-five people sit in silence in front of George and Mary's TV as news of the search reduction breaks. George knew this was coming—the families were told in the afternoon the search would end at 6 P.M.—but the advance warning does little to diminish the impact of the decision.

"It was like someone passing you a death certificate," George tells a reporter.

Fishermen are generally hostile to bureaucratic decisions they perceive as being made by people far away from the communities and people those decisions actually impact. Decisions concerning quotas, licences, regulations, and fish science are often scoffed at and dismissed as the work of people who don't understand the conditions at sea, or the lives of fishermen. "They don't listen to us," says Sandy Stoddard. "It's very frustrating." (Asked about fishery scientists, Sandy points at his dog: "That dog know more about the fishery than they know. They don't know nothing!")

To many in Woods Harbour and on Cape Sable Island, this situation feels similar. Except that there's more than fishermen's livelihoods at stake. Five young men could still be out there, awaiting rescue. There are parents and partners and girlfriends and children on shore with no answers. Yes, the conditions have been bad. And yes, odds of survival have eroded with every cold wave. But if there's even a sliver of a chance of survival, why is the search ending now?

Tim Nickerson, a long-time fisherman, is discussing the situation with friends at the wharf. Many residents, up and down the coast, share his opinion: the search ended too abruptly. It should have continued for at least another twelve hours, especially now that the winds have dropped and the sea has reduced its bite. Tim knows all five men. Some of them fished on his boat. A couple weeks back he was sick and Katlin offered to haul his lobster traps for him. "He went the next morning, got them, and they are now on the stern of my boat," Tim tells a reporter from The Canadian Press. He pulls out his phone and scrolls through photos of Katlin catching halibut with friends. "It shows you the integrity of these boys," Tim adds. "They were very good workers and very good men."

Tim smiles when thinking of Cole. Cole was a perfectionist, he recalls. He remembers Cole scrubbing a deck with a brush, even after the rest of the crew had left. "He was easygoing, easy to get along with, but determined to work," Tim says. "This is just devastating from the little ones right through to the grandparents."

With the search ended, Jimmy Newell and Eric Nickerson leave Della's house, having spent most of the past thirty-six hours there consoling Della and calling the other families with hourly updates. Jimmy returns home, takes a shower, changes his clothes, and immediately goes to visit his nephew, Jeremy Stoddard, and Jeremy's girlfriend, Natasha—Billy Jack's sister. Jimmy has spoken with them by phone over the past two days, but hasn't been able to visit. At the house, Billy Jack's uncle, Tom Hatfield, approaches Jimmy. He demands to know why the search has ended just as the weather has improved.

Jimmy calls JRCC to warn his rescue colleagues that concerns and questions are prevalent. The warning is unnecessary: Ray McFadgen and his colleagues at JRCC are being bombarded with calls about why the search has ended. At 7:30 P.M. on Tuesday evening, one caller is demanding to know why no effort was made to search for bodies in the overturned hull of the *Miss Ally*. "Explained to him that we are in the SAR [search and rescue] business and do not conduct any salvage," McFadgen types into the log. "He understood the explanation." Three minutes later, however, another caller is asking why the search is not continuing. It should be maintained into Wednesday, the caller insists.

The province's fisheries minister, Sterling Belliveau, feels similarly. Belliveau, a Woods Harbour resident and a former fisherman, goes on TV to argue the search should carry on. He also asks his federal counterpart, Fisheries Minister Keith Ashfield, to assist, but the case is an RCMP file now.

When Jimmy calls JRCC, around 8 P.M., McFadgen is on the phone with Todd Nickerson, Katlin's father. Todd was in Jamaica when his son's boat disappeared. Now back in Woods Harbour, he has called to argue that the search should continue into the night. "Explained to him that the events of that night suggest that whatever happened, happened quickly," McFadgen notes in the log, following their lengthy conversation.

Unsatisfied, Todd calls Global News in Halifax. He wants to go public with his plea to extend the search. He argues JRCC is ending the search just as the conditions are improving: the winds have dropped to about 15 knots (28 kilometres an hour) and the seas have subsided to less than 3 metres. It's not calm, but these are no longer hurricane conditions. "I just felt it was called off at the best possible chance to find the raft," Todd tells Global. The discovery of survival suits at sea is also encouraging, he contends. Todd argues the men must have had time to put them on, though he doesn't understand why Katlin said there were no suits on the boat. "I don't know why he would have said that."

Todd is clearly rattled by the whole situation. He claims to have last talked to Katlin at about 11:36 P.M.—a half hour after the EPIRB went off. He didn't.

George Hopkins in his dining room in Woods Harbour, pointing to the search area on a nautical chart.

It's a hopeful memory conjured by a grieving father.

Yet another call comes into McFadgen at JRCC before 9 P.M. "Explained to him that there is no evidence to recommend resuming the search and that we do not want to give the family false hope," he logs wearily. McFadgen and his colleagues at JRCC are receiving constant reminders that Katlin, Joel, Billy Jack, Tyson, and Cole are still missing. In addition to the confused and anxious callers, there are reports of planes detecting Katlin's EPIRB. At least three jetliners— including two 747s—pick up weak, intermittent signals from the EPIRB when passing over the search area late on Tuesday. Eventually, JRCC asks that beacon hits only be reported if they suddenly start appearing in a new location. Still, the lonely pings continue. Jets flying over the Atlantic Ocean continue to detect the EPIRB's dying signal into the early hours of Thursday.

George Hopkins is sitting in his living room on Wednesday morning. Photos of his smiling children and grandchildren surround him. During the search, the house was constantly filled with people offering support—sometimes thirty to forty at a time. It's quieter today. Two of his close friends are seated nearby.

On the dining room table is a chart of Nova Scotia's offshore waters. Somewhere out there is the floating hull of the *Miss Ally*. And his son, Joel, might still be in it.

George is making a desperate appeal to the Canadian government: he wants a retrieval effort launched to secure the boat and, possibly, the bodies in it. An inspection of the hull might also reveal what happened on Sunday night. Mostly, though, the families want closure. George tells a Canadian Press reporter—and anyone else who will listen—that he doesn't want to keep going to bed unsure if he's done enough to find his son and bring him home. "We need to know if there's bodies in there," he says, seated in a beige rocker. "These kids were important. They were important to me, they were important to this community," he continues, his two friends looking on. "It's five young boys in the prime of their life. We need closure. We need to know for sure that we've done everything we can."

Just down the road, Cole's father, Stephen Nickerson, has joined George in lobbying for a recovery operation before the *Miss Ally* sinks and takes its contents and clues to the bottom. "If my boy is in that boat, I want to bring him home," Stephen tells The Canadian Press reporter. "I think he's in that boat and I think attempts should be made to [salvage the vessel]."

Stephen has already asked the military for a salvage operation, but he's been redirected to the RCMP. The military's apparent ambivalence does not sit well with Stephen. "It seems like they're not going to do anything about that," he says. "They said the search is called off and it's been turned over to the RCMP. That's it. That's as far as they go. We're all mad. It should go farther."

George feels equally stonewalled. "I'm thinking if it was a movie star or some high politician, this would be looked at really quick," George tells CBC News on Wednesday.

The community's attitude regarding a possible salvage operation is best summarized by Pastor Phil Williams at the Calvary United Baptist Church: "I would venture to say that if you took a poll you would have 110 percent [support]," he says. "[We] want *Miss Ally* brought up at all costs, expense, whatever. It's essential for peace and closure."

The lack of survivors, a hull, or even bodies is also hampering the efforts of the federal Transportation Safety Board (TSB) as it attempts to determine what actually happened on Sunday night. TSB investigators arrive in Woods Harbour on Wednesday morning to review the communications between the crew and family members, friends, and search and rescue officials. They'll also examine the *Miss Ally*'s construction details, stability assessments, and inspections. Also under scrutiny is the crew's experience and training. Pierre Murray, a regional manager of operations for the TSB, says the questions are many, but answers remain elusive. "The difficulty is that we don't have a boat and we don't have survivors," Murray says.

Could the *Miss Ally* be salvaged to aid the investigation? The TSB has done it in the past. In January 2004, the *Lo-Da-Kash*, a small fishing boat based out of Maces Bay, New Brunswick, sank as it was steaming back from Campobello Island. All four people aboard died. Four months after the sinking it was raised and towed to shore. The *Miss Ally*, however, is not just off the coast—it's offshore. "It's a bit different from going out there in the open sea and trying to recover a boat," Murray says reluctantly.

At JRCC, Major Martell Thompson explains to reporters that boarding the hull wasn't an option during the search because the conditions were too rough. Now it's up to the RCMP. The Mounties are caught in having to weigh the raw emotions of the families against the dangers of launching a salvage operation. "Everything is on the table. That's certainly one avenue, but no decision has been made," RCMP Corporal Scott MacRae tells reporters. "We understand the emotions with the tragic loss of family members—the human aspect of wanting to retrieve your loved one." The Mounties are sympathetic, but they lack the resources for an offshore salvage. Their biggest boats—no longer than the *Miss Ally*—can only go 18 kilometres from land. The Mounties require assistance from the military and Coast Guard.

On Wednesday morning, the Mounties make an official request to have a remotely operated underwater vehicle investigate the hull for bodies. That will involve sending a ship back to the flipped hull. That evening, the Mounties gather the families of the missing men for a meeting at the community centre in Woods Harbour. Sylvie Bourassa-Muise, the RCMP's district policing officer for southwest Nova Scotia, is trying to address the families' many questions and concerns, but she's in an odd position. The RCMP was not officially alerted to the *Miss Ally* search by JRCC; RCMP officers only learned of the search on Monday through Facebook and questions from reporters. Yet now they are in charge.

Bourassa-Muise arrived in Woods Harbour this morning. She's now addressing the fifty or so grieving and angry people in the community centre, providing all the information she has. It's clearly not sufficient. She doesn't know why the hull wasn't tracked or searched. The families asked on Tuesday for a remotely operated vehicle to inspect the hull, but Bourassa-Muise can't say if one will be provided. "There were a lot of questions that couldn't be answered," she recalls. "That certainly didn't help our credibility."

Jimmy Newell, again acting informally as a bridge between the Coast Guard and the families, can see this meeting is not going well. There's little information and, apparently, no plan. If there's no next step, why have the families been called together? They had been expecting some plan of action, some groundwork to bring their boys back home. Jimmy can sense the grief-stricken frustration.

Near the end of the already tense meeting, Bourassa-Muise leaves the room to take a phone call from her commanding officer. Angry family members follow her out—they think she's leaving. It's a short call. Bourassa-Muise returns and announces that the military has agreed to assist the RCMP. It's still unclear, however, what that assistance will entail.

The mood in the room improves slightly, but the RCMP's response proves insufficient for George Hopkins, Joel's father. George, fed up with what he sees as excessive bureaucratic delays and stalling, starts to mull other options for securing the answers and closure the families so desperately want.

He'll go it alone if that's what's required.

CHAPTER 11

BELOW THE SURFACE

DONNIE MAHANEY'S PHONE RINGS ON THURSDAY MORNING, FEBRUARY 21. On the other end is George Hopkins. Joel's father wants to know how much it would cost to organize a recovery expedition to the *Miss Ally*. Donnie, a commercial diver for the past forty years, thinks it over and estimates the cost at a couple thousand dollars.

"Well, okay. That's fair enough. That sounds good," George responds. "I'll get back to you."

Donnie hangs up and thinks it over further. Has he misunderstood the request? Confused, he calls George back. Sure enough, George isn't organizing a salvage trip—he wants divers to venture below the surface to see what remains inside the *Miss Ally*'s overturned hull. Could the crew, somehow, still be alive, perhaps surviving in an air pocket in the cabin? Are their bodies inside? At the very least there could be clues to help determine why the boat flipped. No longer confused, Donnie alters his quote.

"There's no money involved in this, George. It's *au gratis*."

"That's awfully good of ya."

George has one diver already signed on, but he's looking for more. Donnie expects it would be no trouble to nab his diving partner, Gary Thurber. Donnie is correct—Gary is keen to help. Though he recently sold his boat and has taken to diving with Donnie full-time, Gary is a long-time fisherman. He lives in nearby Doctors Cove and fished for lobster out of Woods Harbour for more than thirty years. "They always treated me like gold, everybody up there," Gary says. "One thing about Woods Harbour: when someone gets in a bit of a scrape, it's hard to help out because there's such a line-up of people ahead of ya." In this situation, however, Gary's diving skills mean he's uniquely positioned to assist.

Donnie and Gary are not alone in offering to help. It doesn't take long for a flotilla of local boats to form, all piloted by fishermen willing to help search for the *Miss Ally* and, hopefully, bring its five crewmen back to shore.

Though the five families were told Wednesday evening that the military would help, it's still unclear what exactly they're offering. Officials at JRCC are also curious. Shortly before midnight on Wednesday, Captain Kristin MacDonald, a search and rescue air coordinator at JRCC, sent an email asking if an Aurora long-range patrol aircraft would be sent from Greenwood. "I assume some consideration is being given to a CP140 [Aurora] re-establishing visual with hull of *Miss Ally*?" MacDonald wrote. A few hours later, at 2:52 A.M. Thursday, Rear-Admiral Dave Gardam, the regional search and rescue commander, noted in an email sent to JRCC that there's "no need for a MPA [maritime patrol aircraft]…At least not yet."

In the absence of a firm plan from the military, the private flotilla has formed and is making preparations for a quick departure. Jimmy Newell isn't surprised. He isn't formally connected with the military's planning,

Donnie Mahaney and Gary Thurber outside Donnie's dive shop in Barrington Passage.

but as the commanding officer of the Clark's Harbour Coast Guard station—
and a conduit between the families and JRCC during the search—he's still
being sought out for information. There's confusion about what's being done
to find the hull. The RCMP has set up a mobile command post outside the
Woods Harbour community centre, with two chaplains and volunteers from
victims' services, but the amount of available information has proven insufficient for locals. "It's the nature of fishermen to want to help one another,"
Jimmy explains. "And you're seeing these five grief-stricken families and
it doesn't look like there's anything being done or any concrete plans, so
fishermen start to organize to do something on their own."

The first boats leave port Thursday morning. Tim Nickerson is preparing
to leave after lunch. Like many, he's angry that the military and Coast Guard
have pulled away. "Somebody's got to do something," he says at the dock.
"These are local boys and the boat is there—do something."

Justin Nickerson, one of Cole's uncles, has been running through the likely scenarios for days. It's unlikely Cole or the other men were on deck when the wave hit. They were most likely in the wheelhouse, with the door shut and the windows secured, trying to weather the storm. When the boat overturned, they were inside. Justin is sure of it. And that means they're still in there. "We're going to do what we need to do—as a community, as fellow fishermen," he says with a sniffle at the Falls Point wharf. "We know what's right."

Sixty-five-year-old Davis Nickerson is standing on the wharf watching as more boats load up and pull away from shore. "I've seen three boats leave in an hour. I've just seen two more go. There's three more getting ready to leave," he says, looking around the bustling wharf.

Davis is a life-long resident of Woods Harbour. He's fished for lobster and halibut most of his life, and knew all five of the missing men. He watched them grow up, saw them progress in the fishery. "I hope we can bring these guys home," he tells a *Chronicle Herald* reporter.

Davis has never seen his community rally the way it is now. Locals are arriving with groceries for the fishermen heading out to search. Fathers and brothers of some of the missing crew have stopped at the wharf to see the searchers off. Friends of the missing five stand on the dock and call out to the departing boats: "Bring our boys home!"

"It's hugs all over the wharf, everywhere," Davis says. "Pretty heart-wrenching." He watches as diving gear is loaded into one of the boats. "They took diving tanks, so they mean business," he says proudly. "If we can't find these boys alive, we need to bring the bodies home. [We] see no other option."

Vessels are not only departing from Woods Harbour. The fishing vessel *No Pain, No Gain,* with divers aboard, also leaves Thursday from Ecum Secum on the other side of Halifax. The growing private flotilla is putting the RCMP in an awkward position: the Mounties are in charge, but civilians are displaying the most initiative. From a public relations standpoint it looks awful—parents of possibly drowned men relying on friends to recover the bodies. Where's the Navy? Where's Canada's proud and noble Coast Guard?

Sandy Stoddard, back from Cape Breton where he talked to Katlin during the storm, is pleading with the local RCMP to push the military and Coast Guard to continue the search for the bodies. He knows well that his fellow fishermen aren't going to sit on the wharf and wait for someone in Ottawa to offer help. "We are men of little patience," he declares. "We don't wait for protocol to do things. When you're a fisherman on the ocean you don't follow protocol, you follow knowledge."

The Mounties, who lack the resources to go offshore, can only watch as the boats leave port—and hope another boat is not wrecked by the wicked winter weather. "Certainly we didn't encourage it, but we can't do anything to stop it," acknowledges RCMP Superintendent Sylvie Bourassa-Muise.

George Hopkins is not one to cause trouble, but what other options do the families have? It's clear to him that the military and Coast Guard won't help. "We've decided we don't want to wait any longer," he explains. "This boat could sink. There's nothing guaranteed and it's [still] afloat now, so we're going to search for it."

The crew of the *Earl Grey* last spotted the *Miss Ally*'s overturned hull just before 3:30 P.M. on Tuesday. The hull was drifting east–southeast at 3 kilometres an hour. Its current location can only be estimated. Spotting an overturned, partially submerged hull from the deck of a Cape Islander would be a challenge even if its exact location were known. Without coordinates it's a near impossible task. An air search offers the best chance of relocating the boat.

The Defence Department—bombarded by the angry demands for a recovery effort—eventually agrees on Thursday to return to the waters off the southwest coast of Nova Scotia and again hunt for the *Miss Ally*. According to Jay Paxton, a spokesperson for Peter MacKay, the defence minister has instructed the Canadian Forces to "do everything they can reasonably do, maintaining safety, to assist the situation."

George Hopkins is elated. Finally something is being done. "The military wouldn't have done nothing if we wouldn't have sent these boats," he recalls. "We kind of showed them up."

Cole's mom, Marlene Nickerson, cries as she thanks all those who helped pressure the government to launch a recovery operation. "Hopefully we can bring 'em home," she sobs. "I won't be pleased until I see him again."

Three aircraft patrol the air on Thursday, searching above the location of the *Miss Ally*'s last known position. Though the RCMP is in charge, the military has sent a Hercules. And there's concern about the bureaucratic wording of their mission. JRCC wants to be clear: this is not a reopening of the search and rescue mission. This is a post-search mission. "This is not SAR [search and rescue] tasking," writes Major Ali Laaouan, the officer in charge at JRCC Halifax, in an email sent Thursday to Captain Kristin MacDonald, one of the search and rescue air coordinators at JRCC.

Also sent to sea Thursday is a Bombardier Dash 8 surveillance plane from Transport Canada (usually used to catch vessels dumping oil and other environmental pollutants at sea) and, again, Provincial Aerospace's King Air plane. The airborne crews survey an area of more than 1,700 square kilometres. Small items of debris are spotted roughly 20 kilometres east of the boat's last known position. The hull, however, is nowhere to be seen.

The crew of the Hercules drops a self-locating datum marker buoy near the debris field, a move that prompts confusion at JRCC. The buoy was supposed to be dropped to mark the hull, if it is again found. The mix-up is a result of the odd organization of the mission. "There is an issue with three aircraft going to the same position and tasked by three different agencies," reads the JRCC log. "One agency needs to be coordinating and the RCMP is the lead."

Just past 5 P.M. on Thursday, personnel at the Canadian Mission Control Centre at CFB Trenton contact their colleagues at JRCC: Katlin's EPIRB has not transmitted a signal in more than five hours. It's dead.

On Thursday evening, the RCMP provides the five families with the latest, albeit scant, information, as well as photos from the afternoon's surveillance flights. The RCMP says the debris spotted from the air is likely from the missing vessel. The families interpret this information with suspicion. They believe the RCMP is implying the hull has sunk and the debris on the surface was released when the hull went down. And, in fact, that's what the military believes. In an email sent that evening, Jeff Hamilton, a military commander, concludes: "We are led to believe the [*Miss Ally*] has sunk based on cumulative evidence from three air sorties today."

George Hopkins, meanwhile, argues the debris could have been on the *Miss Ally*'s deck. "You're going to have some debris, I mean, you've got lots of things on deck," he reasons. "If they've seen parts of the hull, well, that would be different."

Meanwhile, in Halifax, the Coast Guard vessel *Sir William Alexander*—with a fresh crew and a new commanding officer to replace Captain Rob Gray—begins steaming back toward the debris field around 6:30 P.M. Two members of the RCMP, the agency technically in charge of the operation, are aboard. Some family members have asked if Jimmy Newell, the commanding officer of the Clark's Harbour Coast Guard station, could board the ship, to serve as a representative for the families. The idea is dismissed. There's also been confusion about whether a Coast Guard ship would be sent at all. The RCMP told the families a vessel would be on-site, but Major Martell Thompson, a spokesperson for JRCC, is initially unaware of any plans to send a ship. Earlier in the day, officials at the Transportation Safety Board heard rumours a ship was headed out to recover the bodies. If so, TSB investigators should be aboard.

Although now away from the dock and steaming in the dark from Halifax, the *Sir William Alexander*'s exact purpose remains vague. "The vessel is being deployed to provide safety and security on the water and is prepared to stand-by until further plans are developed," the RCMP notes in a press release on Thursday night. The mission appears to lack a clear goal.

Despite the general vagueness, the RCMP press release does make one thing clear: this is a search for an overturned boat and, possibly, bodies—not for five fishermen clinging to life in survival suits or a life raft. "This is devastating to the families and to the entire community," notes a statement attributed to RCMP Superintendent Sylvie Bourassa-Muise. "These men were deeply loved and the loss of young lives will impact the hearts and souls of the fishers and their community for many years to come."

In other words: they are gone.

At 9:40 P.M., Bourassa-Muise sends an email up the RCMP chain of command. It includes "intelligence" from "one of the veteran fishers"—likely Sandy Stoddard—about the probable position of the hull. She hopes the rough coordinates, determined through "years of experience" at sea, will aid the search. Attached to the email are sections of a chart, marked up with a potential search quadrant. "I am requesting that the coast guard consider initiating patrols in this area," Bourassa-Muise writes.

Later Thursday night, Captain Kristin MacDonald, a search and rescue air coordinator at JRCC, sends a similar email to Major Martell Thompson and other military officers. MacDonald notes that JRCC received a call earlier in the evening from a family in Woods Harbour. The family heard a plane is scheduled to search Friday morning and has provided coordinates where they want the search to resume. This information is likely from George Hopkins. George has a large nautical chart laid out on his family's dining room table. He has attempted to estimate where the hull has drifted from its last known position. Using a pencil, he's drawn a box around a large patch of offshore water. The hull is in there, he reckons. "The family has stated that they will be content if this area is searched," MacDonald notes in his email. "This is a great opportunity to 'build a bridge' with the family."

Réal Brisson, a captain with Maritime Forces Atlantic, agrees. "Absolutely we are going to do that," he responds. He'll ensure the crew of Provincial Aerospace's King Air takes a photo of the starting point in the morning, stamped with latitude and longitude coordinates.

By 4 A.M. Friday the *Sir William Alexander* reaches the area where debris was spotted on Thursday, more than 100 kilometres from Halifax. The ship proceeds to search a grid pattern for any sign of the *Miss Ally*. Shortly after, Gary Thurber, Donnie Mahaney, and two other divers—Thomas Nickerson and Tommy Hennigar—depart from Port Mouton aboard the *Slave Driver*, to join the rest of the private search flotilla. Bobby Hines is at the wheel of the *Slave Driver*. Bobby, who fishes out of nearby Pubnico, is familiar with all the missing men. He fished with Joel and watched as Katlin jumped into the captain's seat of his own boat. Bobby also went to school with many of the missing men's parents. George Hopkins initially planned to lead this search party himself, but Bobby told George to stay on shore. Let others take care of it. George will stay in regular contact with Bobby, updating him on what the military and Mounties are doing. Why is Bobby helping? The families need answers. Without some certainty, a lot of good people will be left in a rough state for a long time. For Bobby, it's simple: a job needs doing; someone has to do it. "In a small place, everybody knows everybody," he explains. "When something like this happens, it's like one big family."

The rescue flotilla is comprised of colourful boats with equally colourful names. In addition to *Slave Driver*, the fleet includes *Lady Faith*, *Crustacean Frustration*, *Rachel Elizabeth*, *Vicious Fisher*, and the *3 Generations*. The weather, however, forces some of them to turn back.

The *Slave Driver*, loaded with diving gear, a Zodiac inflatable, and body bags, continues pounding forward. At the wheel, Bobby adjusts the throttle to match the 5-metre seas. As a large wave approaches, he slows down to lessen the impact. Then he accelerates until the next large wave emerges. The wind is blowing up to 40 knots (75 kilometres an hour) but the conditions don't deter Bobby.

Donnie Mahaney is less confident. "What we went out in that day, most people would have been terrified," he recalls. It's not until three or four hours into the trip that Donnie realizes that the actual location of the *Miss Ally* is unknown. He figured they were heading directly for it. He asks if it's possible they might not even get a chance to dive on the boat.

"That's right," someone responds. "We gotta find it first."

The short days of February mean daylight disappears early, leaving only darkness and the waves. Unlike the men on the *Miss Ally*, the men aboard the *Slave Driver* have a working crab light, so they can see the waves coming at them.

The search at sea is combined with a second day of air coverage. Two five-hour patrols, covering the morning and afternoon, are launched. The starting point for the initial patrol is the position requested by the families, believed to be the likely location of the *Miss Ally*. But searchers find nothing.

On Friday afternoon, Captain Kristin MacDonald, the search and rescue air coordinator at JRCC, sends another email, this time to see if anyone from the military or the RCMP has told the families that the day's air search began at the coordinates supplied by George Hopkins. The night before, MacDonald emphasized that acting on the families' suggested starting point would serve to "build a bridge." "It is important that families are aware that 'DND' [Department of National Defence] acted swiftly on their request," he writes.

"Negative," replies Major Martell Thompson shortly after. The information was not relayed to the families.

Captain MacDonald does not appear impressed with the lack of communication. "JRCC worked all night to provide this assist to [the military] to try and establish a good relation with the family. Will the families be briefed of the search today and the search area they requested?"

Major Thompson insists it will be done, but the exchange reveals that communication between search officials and the families is not ideal. The RCMP is on the front line, dealing with angry family members at the mobile command post in Woods Harbour, but the Mounties must get their information from other sources. It's like a child's game of telephone and clearly there's been some miscommunication. "What's the first thing to go wrong during an operation? It's always communications," admits the RCMP's Sylvie Bourassa-Muise.

For a second day the *Miss Ally*—a yellow speck in a massive grey sea— has eluded searchers. The empty search and wasting hours are causing anxiety to grow back in Woods Harbour.

Throughout Friday, family members, friends, and neighbours are checking in regularly at the mobile RCMP command post to see if the hull has been located. Bourassa-Muise senses some family members want to strangle her; others are so angry she wouldn't be surprised if the command post is set on fire. Still others remain seated in their cars nearby, quietly waiting for updates. Jimmy Newell, representing the Coast Guard at the command station, does his best to explain drift patterns and the area being searched. But he can't answer the ultimate question: where is the *Miss Ally*?

Among those visiting the command station are Sandy and Chrisjon Stoddard, both now back from Cape Breton, where they escaped the storm that swallowed the *Miss Ally*. Sandy, like many others, is dismayed that the boat must again be hunted for. "Why they left it is a million-dollar question that these people need answers for," he tells reporters outside the command post. "Why would they leave the boat when there was a high probability that [the crew] were still inside?"

Katlin's sister, Falon, whimpers and wipes away tears while answering questions from reporters. "He'd do anything for anyone," she says of her brother. Her voice is trembling and her blonde hair is whipping around in a swirling breeze outside the command post.

"They feel very let down and disappointed," Sandy adds of his discussions with the families. "They feel that they weren't treated fairly. In all honesty, I feel the same way."

Even among the most hopeful, the cold reality of the situation is setting in. The initial denial is turning to anger. Todd Nickerson says his son's boat should have been marked after it was first found. George Hopkins goes further: the Coast Guard should never have abandoned the boat, certainly not without stabilizing it. It may have been too rough to inspect the hull, but it should not have been left to drift off, unmarked and untracked. "They should have stayed there," George argues on Friday. "That was a big mistake, right there. You don't leave it, you leave someone by it."

The decision to leave the hull unattended is defended by Major Martell Thompson at JRCC. When the search for survivors ended at 6 P.M. Tuesday, so did JRCC's direct involvement. "We don't do recovery, we do search and rescue," Thompson explains. "We focus on saving lives, not assets."

For JRCC, the overturned boat was always a dead end. Ships and sailors can't be tied up dealing with a bobbing hull. Their only focus is trying to find and recover survivors. The same cold logic applies to the floating survival suits. Some family members are upset the suits weren't recovered. But again: JRCC can't commit resources to the collection of debris. It hunts only for survivors.

When the military and Coast Guard pulled away, so did the ability to track and possibly salvage the *Miss Ally*. The Mounties, now in charge of the case, fully admit they had no ability to track the boat. A salvage effort at this point would require the RCMP to hire a private company. An open-ocean salvage operation is an expensive and risky task, and at this point it doesn't appear to be under serious consideration. Instead, RCMP Corporal Scott MacRae says the Mounties are trying to get a submersible, remotely operated vehicle "to come up with answers."

But George Hopkins's displeasure extends beyond the lack of focus on the hull. He also thinks there has been too much emphasis placed on finding the life raft spotted Monday morning by the American Coast Guard. George insists the object in the infrared photo taken by the Americans is actually the overturned hull, not a life raft. "There was no raft, there never was," George tells the CBC. "They wasted a lot of time looking for a raft that wasn't there."

The complaints have been steady at JRCC. "The days following the Search Reduction for the *Miss Ally* has seen numerous phone calls from concerned citizens questioning JRCC Halifax's handling of the case," notes Captain Kristin MacDonald in an email. "As an emergency operations room we are not here to justify our actions to the general public."

The criticism, whether valid or not, has made its way far up into the government, and across the Atlantic. Defence Minister Peter MacKay, speaking to reporters on Friday from Brussels via conference call, promises a review of the Canadian Forces response to the case. "I know, having grown up in Atlantic Canada, that these tragedies are devastating for the families and for the entire community," he says.

MacKay's call for a review, however, comes as a complete surprise to some high-ranking military and search and rescue officers. Kevin Grieve, an Air Force major and search and rescue officer, hears about the review through media reports.

"Still have not heard exactly what they are looking for on this," he writes in a string of emails Friday afternoon. "The public perception of a 'review' is that something was wrong...Would like to say I know what is next with this but still in the dark."

Major Ali Laaouan, the officer in charge at JRCC Halifax, is also puzzled. "Review of what? The Case and how it was handled?"

Chris Denko, a lieutenant colonel with the Canadian Joint Operations Command (CJOC)—which conducts Canadian Armed Forces operations at home and abroad—addresses their concerns: "JRCC Halifax did an outstanding job with this case," Denko assures them in an email. However, he believes CJOC and the Air Force should review the case. For instance, why was an Aurora without anti-icing capability on standby in Greenwood during a winter storm instead of a Hercules? He also notes that CJOC didn't know the Hercules was out of action. "Why not??" he writes. The Aurora and Hercules should have been redeployed to another location—one free of storm conditions. "This is a broad-level review, not a review of JRCC Halifax," he adds. "Again, they will be shown to have done great work."

The internal military review is of little interest in Woods Harbour. At the Calvary United Baptist Church, Pastor Phil Williams is concerned. There will be immense anger if the *Miss Ally* is not relocated. The men aboard deserve more than an anonymous burial at sea. "There will be a great disappointment, a great letdown," he tells a Canadian Press reporter. "A lot of hope will have been dashed and we will go into a very dark time of despair."

By Saturday morning, Bobby Hines has steamed the *Slave Driver* for more than twenty hours to reach the general search area. Bobby is coordinating with the captains of the two other remaining search boats: the *Lady Faith*, out of Woods Harbour, and *No Pain, No Gain*, out of Ecum Secum. The three boats move within the search grid offshore. Lurking somewhere in the messy sea and breaking waves is the *Miss Ally*. But the vessel is not giving up its location easily.

Shortly after 9:30 A.M. the news comes in over Bobby's radio on the *Slave Driver*: a surveillance crew aboard Provincial Aerospace's King Air has finally spotted the *Miss Ally*. The overturned boat is floating 240 kilometres southeast of Halifax, in an area where the water is nearly a kilometre deep. The yellow hull is roughly 100 kilometres to the east and slightly south of the crew's last known position, drifting quietly on a dark and lonely stretch of ocean. The King Air crew takes photos and records video before returning to land.

A nautical chart still covers most of George and Mary Hopkins's dining room table. For days George has been trying to calculate where the hull has drifted. Using a pencil, he's drawn a box marking the area where he believes the hull is floating. His calculations were correct: the overturned hull is near the middle of his pencilled box.

Della, meanwhile, ignoring the water temperature, the opinion of rescue officials, and common sense, continues to believe her son and his crew could still be alive under the waves, surviving in a pocket of air. Todd knows she's in denial. He's spent his life at sea. He knows their son is dead. Todd and Della have been separated since 2010, but on Saturday Todd visits Della on Cape Sable Island. He wants to lessen the impact of the news he knows is coming later today.

"Della, you gotta stop," he tells her. "You've got to understand, it's impossible."

"Todd, I can't give up," Della responds. "I can't."

The coordinates of the hull, relayed to Bobby Hines on the *Slave Driver*, prove discouraging. Of the three search boats, his is the furthest away. He and his crew will need another seven or eight hours to reach the wreck. As Bobby pushes on the throttle and points the *Slave Driver* toward the horizon, Donnie Mahaney begins to wonder if they'll even be able to dive. The conditions are poor: strong wind and 3-metre seas. And what will they find below the water? When upright, the contents of a well-kept Cape Islander are stowed tightly and orderly; upside down it's a mess of debris. For a diver, it'll be a dangerous maze of hanging trawl lines, tubs, buckets, anchors, electronics, clothes, food, and anything else that was aboard—all of it tangled and floating within a boat being pitched around in the waves.

And then there's the crew. The chances of finding the men miraculously alive inside the crippled boat are miniscule. More likely, the *Miss Ally* is now a makeshift coffin. The divers will likely find bodies in some stage of decomposition. This fact is particularly troubling for Gary Thurber, one of the other divers aboard the *Slave Driver*. Donnie didn't know the *Miss Ally* crew but Gary was familiar with all of them. He'd seen Katlin around the wharf and knew Joel, like everyone else, to be a local joker. Years earlier, Gary coached Tyson's junior high soccer team. Though only in grade seven, Tyson made the team, beating out boys in the two grades above him. Gary remembers him as a quiet but competitive leader. "He was only a little fella. He put his whole heart into it," Gary recalls. "You don't pick every grade-seven boy—only the ones that show the most promise. He had some spirit about him. He was still pretty young but you could see something in him."

Sitting inside the *Slave Driver*, Gary is troubled by the thought of finding Tyson inside. "I wasn't looking forward to going and retrieving Tyson's little body with his face all contorted out of shape. That was the hardest part for me," he recalls.

Donnie's stress level, meanwhile, rises as the *Slave Driver* finally motors within sight of the *Miss Ally*. A month or two earlier he'd repaired the rudder on a yellow-hulled Cape Islander. He hadn't noticed the name of the boat but remembered seeing a bunch of young guys on board before he dove to replace and tighten some bolts on the rudder. This was the boat.

Oh my jeez, suppose something's happened to that rudder and that's the cause? he thinks to himself.

Though Bobby is the captain of the *Slave Driver*, he's assigned Donnie to lead the four-man dive team.

"What do you want to do?" Bobby asks as they linger nearby.

"I want to make a tight circle around the boat," Donnie replies.

The hull is floating with the stern sticking out of the water, exposing its rudder and propeller. The bow is just below the surface. A quick inspection from the side of the *Slave Driver* quickly alleviates Donnie's concern: the rudder is fine. But determining anything else will require getting in the water. Though the wind has suddenly dropped, the sea is still rough. Should they risk it? Gary makes his thoughts clear: "We steamed all this long way to stand and look at it and not dive? I don't think so."

The three fishing vessels aren't alone near the *Miss Ally*. Lingering in the distance is the *Sir William Alexander*, with the two RCMP officers onboard. At 4 P.M., a Coast Guard officer on the *Sir William Alexander* sends a bulletin to update the six government departments and agencies concerned with marine security (the Coast Guard, Defence Department, Transport Canada, Border Services, Fisheries and Oceans Canada, and RCMP): "Fishermen on scene are discussing diving operations and may not wait until the Naval dive unit arrives."

The HMCS *Glace Bay*, with a diving unit and a Transportation Safety Board investigator aboard, is not expected to arrive until midnight. That means the Navy won't be diving until the morning—if it dives at all. By Saturday afternoon it still hasn't been decided if military divers will enter the water to investigate the hull.

From aboard the *Sir William Alexander*, the RCMP informs the fishing boats that there is to be no diving on the flipped boat. Bobby, hearing the warning on the *Slave Driver*, reaches up and flips off his radio.

On shore, Sandy Stoddard is taken aside by the RCMP and asked if he can convince the divers to stand down, until the Navy arrives.

"No," he replies, "they would hang me and you're not stopping them anyway."

When Donnie Mahaney sees an inflatable rescue craft lowered from the *Sir William Alexander*, he knows it's time to get wet.

"They're soon going to be over here and be on our case," he announces. "They can't stop us from swimming. Boys, put your suits on."

Around mid-afternoon on Saturday, the RCMP issues a press release stressing that "sea and weather conditions [...] further complicate efforts to investigate the submerged portion of the hull." At about that exact time,

Donnie Mahaney, Gary Thurber, and Tommy Hennigar are pulling on their dry suits and adjusting their masks and snorkels. The trio, displaying less trepidation than the RCMP and Coast Guard, enters the water. They've decided to take a quick look below the surface before donning their bulky dive gear. Thomas Nickerson, the fourth diver, will provide support from the deck of the *Slave Driver*.

Dipping his head under the cold water, Gary reaches an instant conclusion: *There's no fucking wheelhouse on this thing!*

"You could see the house was gone," Donnie recalls. "She was clean right to the gunwales, just as if somebody had cut it off with a knife or a saw. And the bolts that had held the house on were bent to the starboard side and broken off."

Their findings are not surprising. In most cases involving flipped Cape Islanders the wheelhouse eventually shears off. In fact, they come off relatively easily, unable to withstand the weight of the water inside as the boat heaves up and down in the waves.

Donnie had planned to find a safe entrance into the cabin and then slowly work his way inside by pulling out loose gear piece by piece. The retrieval plan is now completely unnecessary. Some wires, torn away from the electrical instruments in the wheelhouse, are hanging down like tentacles. Everything else is gone.

"There was nothing," Donnie says. "The inside of her looked like somebody had moved everything out to clean it, like they were getting ready to scrub it down. There was nothing left. No air pockets. And there was no sign of life of any kind, either dead or living."

The only task left involves checking inside the hull. Donnie and Gary return to the *Slave Driver* and suit up: tanks, regulators, weight belts. Only two divers are needed for this task, so Tommy Hennigar stays with Thomas Nickerson on the boat. At the wheel, Bobby makes another close pass and Donnie and Gary jump back into the water. The Coast Guard inflatable continues to linger near the mother ship, its operators apparently content to let the dive operation continue.

Before he goes under again, a member of the *Slave Driver* crew gives Donnie a warning: "Watch it because she could go down at any second." Gary, meanwhile, is wearing a new dry suit and is unsure how much weight he should attach to it. He's in the water checking all the belts and buckles when he looks up and realizes the *Miss Ally* is above him and disappearing from view. He's attached too much weight. He's sinking, and quickly. *Jesus!* he thinks before scrambling to the surface.

Back at the surface, he finds Donnie. Both men have lights in hand but they aren't necessary—the water is perfectly clear. The main objective is to avoid being struck by the heaving boat. "You can imagine it's kind of eerie," Gary says. "You've got a boat going up and down…and you're not really sure what you're going to see."

Gary is again struck by the position of the bolts and screws that once attached the wheelhouse to the hull: they are all sheared off in the same direction—to starboard. He then sticks his head up through the skylight on the *Miss Ally*'s bow. A boat with five men aboard should be full of clothes, sleeping gear, and other personal items. "All the crap that should have been in there and I saw nothing," he says.

Donnie, meanwhile, moves carefully through the companionway door. Inside he sees only a cupboard door. Gary examines the engine room. There should be tools and batteries and spare oil. There's nothing. "The whole boat, the inside of it, looked like someone had taken a pressure washer and cleaned it," Gary says. "It was pretty much immaculate."

The two men don't take any photos. Donnie can't imagine anyone wanting a memory of this. "Whatever was in her was gone," Donnie adds. "It had a spirit about it that was kind of lonely and empty."

"It was a lonesome sight," Gary concurs.

In all, the crew of the *Slave Driver* spends only an hour at the boat they spent thirty hours steaming to. There is simply very little to examine. Donnie and Gary, back aboard the *Slave Driver*, peel off their suits and stow their tanks. A moment of silence is held for the *Miss Ally*'s crew, wherever they might be. A little before 6 P.M., Bobby Hines radios the *Sir William Alexander* and reports the findings from the dive: no wheelhouse or sleeping quarters. No bodies.

That evening the RCMP, Department of National Defence, and the Coast Guard issue another joint press release, outlining what the divers discovered below the waves. They also note the *Sir William Alexander*, with the two RCMP officers onboard, "remains on scene to provide safety and security in the vicinity of the vessel." At this point, however, it's unclear whose safety and security is at risk. The military also continues to provide air coverage to maintain a visual fix on the hull, though by now such attention is no longer being called for. (The ultimate fate of the hull remains unknown. JRCC could not confirm whether it was left to drift or intentionally sunk to prevent it from being a navigational hazard.)

The long-awaited answers gleaned at sea are relayed back to shore, to the families and neighbours and friends waiting for updates at the Woods Harbour community centre. A dozen cars are parked outside the Hopkins's house. It's dark outside but the house is brightly lit and a stream of friends and family is constantly coming and going. They offer condolences. They cry. They struggle with the news from the search vessels. "It wasn't the result we wanted," George tells The Canadian Press. "But for me there's closure knowing the search is over and there's no hope now of anybody being alive."

For George, the critical and crushing fact is the missing wheelhouse. It sunk to the bottom, perhaps with the life rafts still secured to the top. "With the wheelhouse gone, I think things happened so fast, they didn't have a chance to get in the life raft," he says. "It would be false hope to continue."

The news brings George some relief. It's been a week since he first began to worry, calling Katlin by satellite phone to warn him that the weather was worsening. Since then, George's mornings have been awful, the worst part of already terrible days. Each day he has awoken, laid in bed, and pictured the bodies of Joel and his fellow crew members down in the sleeping area at the front of the boat. They were surviving in an air pocket and needed to be rescued. "Realistically, we knew in our minds it wasn't so, but it was hard to go from my mind to my heart," he says. "Now we know. At least we know we did all we could."

George's use of "we" is specific. He's referring to the community: the fishermen and divers who ventured out in rough conditions, at no charge, seeking answers on behalf of the families. George is convinced that if local boats and divers hadn't led the operation, the Navy and Coast Guard wouldn't have gone back out. "If we wouldn't have sent our divers and men, we don't feel that the Coast Guard or the Navy would have ever left [shore]," he says. "We wouldn't have even had a plane."

Katlin's father, Todd, agrees. "I don't think it was handled right. I think the only reason the Navy stepped back in was because the boats from home had left to go out," he says. "They should never have left the boat to start with. It probably cost millions of dollars to find that boat again."

Sandy Stoddard, meanwhile, initially critical of aspects of the search effort, praises local RCMP officers for passing the concerns of the community onto the Defence Department and Coast Guard. "They went to bat for us," he tells a Canadian Press reporter. Approaching sixty, Sandy can still remember the disappearance of the *Colville Bay* four decades earlier. In fact, the captain of the *Colville Bay,* Victor Brannen, had asked if Sandy—then seventeen—was interested in joining the crew for that trip. Fortunately, Sandy's father told Victor his son wouldn't be interested. Sandy had just returned from a fishing trip and likely wanted a break. In the end, seven men were lost, including Cole's great-uncle, Andrew Nickerson. "There was never any closure to that accident," Sandy explains. That's why the community pleaded so hard for the hull to be examined. "We can't live through this for another thirty or forty years."

Despite the effort of the local fishermen and divers, the result this time is similar: there are no bodies to bury. Family and friends of Katlin, Joel, Billy Jack, Tyson, and Cole will likely never find complete closure.

Crew from the HMCS Glace Bay *investigating the* Miss Ally's
overturned hull.

As Bobby Hines pilots the *Slave Driver* back to Port Mouton, the HMCS *Glace Bay*—with a Navy diving unit aboard—is headed toward the wreck site. The Naval vessel arrives overnight. At 8:30 A.M. Sunday morning— nearly a week after contact with the *Miss Ally* was lost—a remotely operated vehicle (ROV) is lowered into the water to examine the crippled hull. The images sent back lead the crew to an easy conclusion: "additional diving operations were not required." The ROV is used to confirm what a group of fishermen on a Cape Islander determined the previous day.

"The assessment confirmed the *Miss Ally* sustained significant damage. The wheelhouse and sleeping quarters were not attached to the vessel," notes the final joint press release issued by the RCMP, National Defence, and the Coast Guard. "No bodies were located."

The final release, issued around noon Sunday, also includes a photo of military personnel in a dark inflatable near the overturned yellow hull.

The HMCS *Glace Bay* is in the background. On shore, some see it as public relations staging.

"They done nothing," George Hopkins concludes. "They didn't even put a diver in the water. We put our divers in the water. Military divers and they didn't dare go in the water?"

CHAPTER 12

ALL THE UNKNOWNS

DONNIE MAHANEY'S DIVE SHOP IS LOCATED AT THE END OF A QUAINT lane that runs behind the No Frills grocery store in Barrington Passage. Despite the odd entrance, the view from the property is picturesque: morning sunshine is sparkling on the ocean and, in the foreground, an old Cape Islander rests in retirement on the shore.

Donnie owned a boat once. That was back when he thought he should try his hand at "this fishing thing." He bought an old Cape Islander and went handlining for a year or two. "I never made any money at it," he says. "It was just one of those things you thought you should do it. Anyway, that was the end of my fishing career."

He's been diving commercially ever since. Fishermen strive to stay on top of the waves; Donnie gets paid to go below them. His yard is cluttered with odds and ends of the dive trade, including an old oxygen tank and a Suzuki outboard engine.

Donnie is sitting on the tailgate of his copper Dodge pickup. The rear window of the cab has two *Miss Ally* memorial stickers, one in each corner. It's been more than two years since Donnie dove below the *Miss Ally*. His opinion of what happened to the boat has not changed since he went under the waves to examine it. The position of the bolts that once fastened the wheelhouse to the hull—sheared off toward the starboard side—lead to only one conclusion: the wheelhouse was smashed off in a major blow.

"Whatever happened, it happened viciously. It was not a succession of pounding, pounding, pounding," Donnie says. The *Miss Ally* was obviously hit by at least a few big waves, evidenced by the broken stern board, destroyed bait shack, and lost anchors. The final wave, Donnie says, likely flipped the boat entirely and tore the wheelhouse right off. "Water has a tremendous, tremendous power behind it. It was [probably] just like crushing an egg."

Huddled in the wheelhouse and without their exterior light, the five men could not have seen the killer wave lurking in the darkness. Based on what he saw, Donnie believes Katlin, Joel, Tyson, Cole, and Billy Jack were either killed instantly or knocked unconscious. "My personal view is that nobody suffered an agonizing drowning," he concludes. "When that wave hit—that smash—it was just like somebody put a stick of dynamite in it. It just— BANG—it was over. And I'm thinking they went to the bottom with it."

Donnie eventually makes his way into a large cluttered garage where his father once built boats. A few minutes later Gary Thurber pulls into the driveway and ambles into the garage. Donnie and Gary aren't scheduled to dive today, but that doesn't mean they won't. You never know when a rope will become tangled in a propeller, when an underwater pipe will break, or when a fisherman will drop something off a wharf. Diving is a line of work that is rarely scheduled far in advance. The pair laugh while listing off the items they've been paid to help recover for errant owners: wallets, cellphones, false teeth, a shotgun, an excavator. The two men have been diving together for three years. Donnie asked Gary to join him after learning Gary had sold his lobster boat. Bigger contracts usually require two-man dive teams. Gary expected to dive once a week. In 2014, he dove 240 times. Many of the trips are mundane. Their trip to inspect the *Miss Ally* was not: Donnie had never dived offshore before.

The trip led Gary to draw a similar conclusion about the final minutes of the *Miss Ally*'s crew. "If I was betting on what happened, I would say it was one diabolical, violent smash, and I don't think they knew when they got whacked. I think they were dead before they even realized it. I think it was like being in a train wreck or an airplane crash or something." The wheelhouse bolts were not worked back and forth, Gary notes. They were ripped clean off. "It took some force to do that. It was dark and they were wet and it was blowing. I think they didn't know what hit 'em," he says. "We figured at the very least we could go back and tell the families that their nightmares were unfounded."

As for the theory that one or more of the men might have survived in an air pocket inside the hull, Donnie dismisses it. "That wasn't the case. And I know it hadn't been the case right from the get-go," he says.

Their findings were not what the families were hoping for, but Donnie says the operation itself went as well as could be desired. "I don't think the Coast Guard or the Navy or anybody else could've or would've done any better."

And they didn't.

On November 20, 2013, nine months after the sinking, Donnie and Gary—along with Tommy Hennigar and Thomas Nickerson—travelled to Province House in Halifax and each received a Nova Scotia Medal of Bravery from Premier Stephen McNeil. The Barrington Municipal Council nominated the men for the award.

George Hopkins, who originally called Donnie for help, was overwhelmed after the four men received their awards. "It's hard to keep the tears out of my eyes," George said at the time. "I'm just proud of them. They know that. I've gone up to every one individually so they know that by now. I've thanked them a thousand times and that's probably not enough."

Neither Donnie nor Gary believes the awards were necessary—they'd done far more dangerous jobs in the past. Donnie initially thought the bravery awards were part of a "great joke." And why were Bobby Hines and the rest of the volunteers not included? "The only difference was that we jumped in the water," Gary says. "None of us were feeling especially brave," he explained after getting his award, "but if the situation had been reversed I would have appreciated someone doing the same for me."

Gary insists going to Province House was more harrowing than diving on the *Miss Ally*: "Everybody all dressed up in shirts and ties, and this pomp and ceremony," he recalls. "You had to do this and act this way and sit with your legs crossed and all this kinda stuff."

"You're right," Donnie adds with a nod.

Donnie pinned his bravery medal on his Legion uniform, although he admits it's odd to stand next to veterans with rows of medals and bars on their uniforms.

"I have one little medal," he says. "It's the only medal I've ever had."

Gary says he last saw his award certificate, nicely framed, on the floor leaning up against the wall of his hutch. He's not sure where his medal is. "It's home somewhere," he says. "I don't get it out and polish it and parade it around or anything like that."

The two men, standing in Donnie's garage, are visibly awkward talking about the awards. Awards don't bring back drowned fishermen. "The world is full of assholes," Gary offers. "For the most part they were good young men. They were men that you wanted to have in your community. It was a fright that it had to happen to anybody and it was worse that it had to happen to them."

Donnie is puttering in the garage as Gary talks, but soon returns to the conversation. "I think they bit off a little more than they could chew," he offers. "It goes along with being young: you think you're ten feet tall and bulletproof…A more seasoned, older crew or captain probably would have turned her to long before they did."

Gary, however, is less willing to render a judgment.

"I went fishing for thirty-odd years and I got caught in storms before," he says. "Eventually you get caught. There have been different times when I've looked and I've seen that big wave probably a quarter of a mile away and think, 'Phew, I'm glad that one didn't hit me.'" Gary's great-grandfather drowned when a wave broke over top of his boat, sinking it. "It's not a new phenomenon for people to drown around here. A lot of it comes down to luck. You get caught in the wrong place at the wrong time," he says.

Gary pauses and thinks it over a bit. "It requires luck," he says again, though with slightly less certainty. "Sometimes, anyhow."

Snow is falling again, blowing in off the ocean, on Sunday, February 24. It's been a week since the *Miss Ally* was caught in the winter vice of hurricane-force winds and massive waves, and just over twelve hours since word was relayed from the divers that nothing remains under the flipped hull. As they have been doing all week, many Woods Harbour residents have their porch lights turned on—even through the day—as a show of community support.

About five hundred people are crammed into the pews at the Calvary United Baptist Church. Families of the men—now confirmed gone—are sitting near the front of the church, crying and hugging one another as the other members of the congregation sing and pray. Sandy Stoddard is among them. He's not family. But he's hurting nonetheless. "I've lost a piece of me," he says in a hushed voice to one of the crying relatives.

At the front, Pastor Phil Williams says the sinking of the *Miss Ally* is now a defining moment in the community's history. "That which we have feared the most has come upon us." Pastor Williams tells the churchgoers that he recently talked with an elderly grandfather who insisted Woods Harbour would cope with the loss as it has with past disasters. With tears tumbling down his cheeks the man told the pastor: "We shall get through this together."

The previous week—filled with uncertainty, evaporating hope, and criticism of both the search and recovery efforts—has left the families ragged and emotionally raw. Anger still lingers over the decision to abandon the *Miss Ally* after it was first discovered earlier in the week. Sandy, who beat the storm into Cape Breton, is among those calling for an investigation to examine why the Coast Guard left the vessel and why locals were forced to compel the RCMP and the Defence Department to relocate the hull. The divers aboard the *Slave Driver* are expected to arrive home from sea on Sunday evening. Sandy calls them heroes and urges the community to greet them at the wharf when they pull in. "The fishermen had to take matters in their own hands to try to bring our loved ones home," he says on Sunday. "I pray the government will look at this incident and realize they have to do a better job."

In his sermon, Pastor Williams urges the crowd to focus on supporting one another. "I would like to beg with you this morning to suspend judgment and contempt," he implores.

Billy Jack's uncle, Kenny Hatfield, is standing in the parking lot in the snow shortly after the service ends. "I had a nephew aboard who was like one of my own sons, and I've been crying ever since it happened. There's nothing I can do about it. I loved him and he loved me too," he tells a Canadian Press reporter.

Lost vessels and drowned fishermen cause other fishermen to pause briefly and reflect on their own decisions and the risks involved with their line of work. But it won't keep them from leaving the wharf. Fishermen in Woods Harbour will still steer their boats to the freezing fishing grounds in the middle of February—that's simply how the business works. "We've got to go back to work on this ocean. This is the work God gave us," Sandy offers on Sunday. He'll be fishing for halibut again soon on the cold North Atlantic, though he'll no longer be offering advice to Katlin and the other men. "I'll look across that ocean and I'll always wonder, 'Why didn't you just take me, God?' Those children still had their lives to live."

Shortly after the service, George Hopkins is standing at the wharf answering questions from a CBC reporter. With the search over and all hope gone, the reporter asks George what he'll do now.

"That's a good question. I've been asking myself that," George says. He's got work to do to prepare for the next fishing season, but he doesn't feel like doing it. "I don't know what to do," he says. "I'm walking around in circles a lot of the time. Going nowheres."

緣

Joel's funeral is scheduled to begin at 2 P.M. on Saturday, March 2, but people are arriving two hours early. Anyone familiar with the twenty-seven-year-old daredevil knows this service will be completely full.

The funeral—the first of five over the next two weeks—is held at the Calvary United Baptist Church, but it's also broadcast live to a crowd in the church basement, as well as to mourners gathered at the nearby Wesleyan Church. In all, about six hundred people are crammed into the two churches, and five hundred people are watching the broadcast through an online feed.

Joel's parents, George and Mary Hopkins, are in the first row. Behind them are Joel's biological parents. Joel's girlfriend, Elaine, encouraged Joel to find his birth parents after their first son, Julius, was diagnosed with meningitis. Shouldn't he learn about his genetic background? Elaine tracked the birth parents down on Facebook and immediately recognized Joel's birth mother: she had Julius's eyes. Joel eventually visited his birth parents. They've now travelled from Toronto for the funeral, while a biological grandfather has come from Antigonish, where Joel was born. He looks much like Joel. He's obviously the genetic source of the smile Joel so often wore.

Also in the church are the families of Tyson, Cole, Billy Jack, and Katlin. Both the Coast Guard and RCMP have sent representatives. Nova Scotia's premier, Darrell Dexter, and local MLA Sterling Belliveau are also in attendance. (Flags at Province House in Halifax and all provincial buildings in Shelburne County are lowered to half-mast to honour the men.) Joel's dirt bike and a favourite camouflage jacket are both on display at the front of the church as Pastor Rod Guptill officiates. Hanging from the dirt bike is part of a pink dinosaur costume Joel wore as a child. Mary couldn't resist adding it. Joel's obituary, handed to those in the church, emphasizes his love for all types of fishing, from lobstering to longlining to "sticking for tuna and swords. Joel also loved sport fishing, hunting, dirt biking, wheelering, and speed!"

Prayers, readings, and a poem, "All Ye Fishers," are read. There's also a video summarizing Joel's life. Three speakers deliver tributes, including Bobby Hines, who led the private search for the *Miss Ally* after the military and Coast Guard retreated.

Bobby has known Joel since Joel was a boy. They'd sometimes go on day trips fishing for mackerel during the summer. Bobby steps to the front with a written speech but doesn't end up reading a word of it. Instead, he tells the crowd a story he heard from Arden Townsend, Tyson's grandfather.

One day Joel arrived abruptly at Arden's house in Woods Harbour. Joel parked his dirt bike behind the house and hurried inside. Arden thought the visit a bit unusual, but took it as a compliment. The two men sat down and Joel immediately starting gabbing about his favourite topic: fishing. Arden, a career fisherman, was enjoying Joel's "yarns" but noticed he seemed distracted. As he spoke, Joel was regularly looking out the front window at the main road. Eventually an RCMP car whizzed past the house in the direction of Barrington Passage.

"Okay, good talking to ya," Joel said suddenly. "I gotta go."

Arden then understood the purpose of the visit: Joel had been hiding. With the cops gone, Joel hopped on his dirt bike and roared off in the opposite direction, toward home.

The story captures much about Joel—his love of fishing, his ability to talk to anyone, and his habit of getting into trouble. It draws laughter throughout the church, even from Mary. She hadn't heard it before.

The arrangement for Cole's funeral, on Tuesday afternoon, is almost identical: service at Calvary United with overflow seating at the Wesleyan Church. Again, hundreds of people also stream the service online. At the front of the church are photos of Cole with his family, a lobster trap, and some of his hunting gear, including his bow. The twenty-eight-year-old is recalled as kind and thoughtful, with an infectious smile. "He made his living by the sea," his obituary reads. "He later broadened his work experience in the oil field, but his heart was always back home."

Pastor Wayne Crowell, a family friend, struggles to explain the disaster. "I wish I could explain why," he offers. He can only quote from the hymn "Farther Along": "Farther along we'll know all about it. Farther along we'll understand why."

Tyson's memorial, fittingly for a natural athlete, is held on the ice in the Barrington Arena on Sunday, March 10. Four years earlier, Tyson was captain of the Barrington Ice Dogs team that won the Junior C Maritime Championship in this building.

"He will be remembered in the arena, on the golf course, and at all the places he loved to be," the family notes in his obituary. Memorial donations, they add, can be made in honour of Tyson's seven-month-old daughter, Lilly. "His new-found passion was being a dad," the family notes. More than one thousand people attend the service, during which Tyson's hockey jersey is retired to the arena rafters.

Dustin Goreham, Tyson's friend since childhood, steps forward to speak with three pages of notes in his hand. Dustin recounts a story from when he and Tyson were both about fifteen. They had travelled to the Dominican Republic for a week with Dustin's grandparents. The boys had recently started smoking and quickly hatched a plan to bring a dozen cartons of cheap cigarettes home with them. Dustin somehow convinced Tyson that it would be better for Tyson to carry the full load of cigarettes in his suitcase. On the way home, while passing through Customs, Tyson was pulled into a side room. Looking back at Dustin over his shoulder, Tyson flashed a look that Dustin easily translated: *I will get you back for this.* Tyson, after claiming the cigarettes were for his father, was allowed to keep two cartons. He then tore into Dustin.

"If words could kill he would have killed me that day," Dustin recalls.

Four days later, on Thursday, March 14, Sarah McLachlan's "I Will Remember You" is playing in Huskilson's Funeral Home in Barrington as a slide show of photos summarizes Billy Jack's life—from his childhood to his years as a father of three. Roughly one hundred mourners are forced to stand at the packed service for the oldest of the five men.

Billy Jack's childhood friend, B. J. Sears, tells the overflowing crowd about life growing up with Billy Jack in Clam Point on Cape Sable Island. There was the Halloween night when the two boys knocked on the door of an elderly woman's house: "Trick or treat, but we'd prefer a cigarette," the pair told the woman as she opened the door. The woman didn't smoke, but she returned with a bottle of Captain Morgan rum. Billy Jack and B. J. were stunned. "Of course we weren't old enough, but she didn't ask for ID," B. J. tells the crowd.

The woman had clearly been drinking and proceeded to pour each boy a couple generous glasses of rum. In return they spent a good portion of the evening talking with her, before helping her across the street to a friend's house. "She loved our company," B. J. recalls. "Billy enjoyed it. He was that kind of guy...he had that kind of soft heart to spend time with anybody. Especially somebody older."

The two men, friends from boyhood, always discussed their plans with one another. Even during his darker years, when you couldn't be sure what Billy Jack might do or say, he always had plans. And he always discussed them with B. J. Shortly before the sinking, Billy Jack and B. J. met to do some carpentry work together. "It gave us quality time to talk about the past and talk about things that were on our minds and mostly it gave us time to stay close," B. J. tells the crowd.

B. J. still has two of the wooden knives he and Billy Jack whittled as kids. One is very unique: the handle is made of deer antler. B. J. can't remember if Billy Jack gave it to him, or if he swiped it. It doesn't matter now. He plans to give it to Billy Jack's children when they're all old enough to appreciate it.

Family friend Wayne Smith, who gave Billy Jack his first job as a deckhand, is officiating. He reads letters from Billy Jack's sister, Natasha, his mom, Janet Reynolds, and his fiancée, Cheryl Brannen. Why did Billy Jack not don the survival suit he brought for the trip? Cheryl believes he wouldn't have used his if the other men were all without.

Life for Billy Jack seemed to have stabilized in the years before the sinking. He and Cheryl were engaged and had plans to build a house in Ingomar. At their rented cottage, they were raising Icelandic sheep. Wayne tells the crowd that some of the sheep will soon give birth. "Billy was anxiously looking forward to new little lambs. He cut posts and formed a fence and he and Cheryl put the wire around to keep the lambs safe," Wayne says. "It's kind of sad to think that Bill won't be here to see them born," he adds. "But Jesus, the lamb of God, will be shepherding Billy now, and that is far more glorious than anything this world could have offered Bill."

The funeral for Katlin, on Saturday, March 16, concludes two weeks of mourning. Five funerals in fifteen days. A day earlier—March 15—Katlin would have celebrated his twenty-second birthday.

A steady montage of photos is being projected on a screen as mourners file into the Calvary United Baptist Church. There are baby photos, graduation photos, pictures of family gatherings, and plenty of fishing photos: the *Miss Ally* fully loaded with high flyers and buoys, Katlin posing with friends beside a large swordfish, Katlin and a friend wrestling on deck in their rain slickers, and one of Katlin lying on deck surrounded by freshly caught halibut. A short video shows Katlin tossing high flyers over the stern of a boat. At the front of the church is a framed picture of him crouched next to a huge fish.

A cousin steps forward and reads a letter written by Todd, who is too overwhelmed to read it himself. "You are the best son I could have asked for," Todd writes. He recalls the first time he took his son fishing: Katlin was terribly seasick and Todd was relieved to think that his son wouldn't spend his life at sea. But when Katlin did end up following his father and grandfather to sea, Todd was proud. When Katlin was young, Todd was often away. As Katlin grew older, fishing helped them bond. And just as Todd tried to best the catches of his father, Captain Wayne, Katlin wanted to outhaul Todd. (Ailing in the Yarmouth hospital with health problems including diabetes, Big Wayne cannot attend his grandson's funeral.) "You gave me the desire to be competitive again," Todd notes in his letter. "You wanted to beat me at every chance out there on the water."

Despite their competitions, Todd enjoyed chatting with his son at sea, sharing the best spots to fish. "I miss those calls from you so much," he writes. "You had drive and worked so hard at your dream. You were building your empire so fast...a true entrepreneur."

A number of Katlin's friends give short speeches. Common descriptions emerge in their recollections: Katlin's crooked grin, his ease with the opposite sex, his love of speed, and his impressive ability to lose bank cards, iPhones, and other important items. One Sunday morning, around 6 A.M., Katlin—frazzled, his hair sticking up—was spotted in a ditch, scouring frantically for his latest lost possession: a $5,000 cheque. It had disappeared the night before and Katlin thought it might have blown out of his truck.

As Katlin hunted along the side of the road, his cheque was resting on the bathroom floor at the Dooly's pool hall.

And then there was his tendency to break things. If Katlin touched something, it broke. One speaker notes that that is why John Symonds—who took Katlin fishing right out of high school—nicknamed him Cletus. One day, while scalloping with John, Katlin asked if he could use the winch to haul in the drag. "No, Cletus, that's a negative," John responded. "I can't afford another winch."

Sitting nearby in a pew, John Symonds has never cried as hard as he is right now—not even at his own parents' funerals. His son, Nolan, is hugging him. The tighter Nolan hugs his burly father, the more he cries. "It was like they ripped a part of my heart out," John says. "I don't know what it was about that boy."

Eventually, Sandy Stoddard steps to the front of the church. Sandy reads from *Genesis*. God, he notes, told man to have dominion over the fish in the sea. "Katlin was a fisherman," he says. "I truly believe Katlin was following God's plan for his life."

Yet Sandy also feels compelled to address questions about Katlin's experience and ability to handle a boat. "Many people will stand here today and say how young he was," Sandy acknowledges. "Yeah, it's true in years Katlin was young, but Katlin did more in his life than most people accomplish in a lifetime. Many people will say, 'Was he too young? Did he have the experience?' Well I want to tell you: he had the experience."

Working on the ocean at a young age is a tradition in this community, Sandy says, pointing to himself as an example. "Katlin didn't want to be a crew member; he was going to the head of the boat. He was going to be the captain. And a good captain he was," Sandy tells the crowd. "Good captains get all kinds of opportunities. Courageous young men get opportunities." In a bold comparison, Sandy calls Katlin the Sidney Crosby of the fishery. The comparison startles and angers many in the church. Crosby is a Stanley Cup winner and Olympic gold medallist; Katlin helmed a boat that sank with his crew aboard. The comparison seems unwarranted.

Some want to walk out immediately, but don't. To support his claim, Sandy recalls that Katlin returned home from the Grand Banks the previous summer with a full hold.

"Katlin was becoming known as one of the best at this industry. Many people looked up to him, even older people, because of his abilities and his courage and his faith. It was unreal."

Sandy returns to his seat and Pastor Phil Williams concludes by stressing that Jesus was with Katlin and the other men on the night of February 17.

"God doesn't promise us no storms. He doesn't promise the wind will never blow," Pastor Williams says. "But he does promise that we shall get to the other side."

It's been just over two weeks since a massive wave flipped the *Miss Ally* and again the North Atlantic fishing grounds are being stirred up by winter winds. On this evening Sandy Stoddard and his crew are back aboard the *Logan & Morgan*, roughly 120 kilometres off Canso, Nova Scotia, and the breeze is whipping over their boat at 45 knots (85 kilometres an hour). Sandy is again out in this mess in search of valuable halibut. His son, Chrisjon, is nearby on the *Benji & Sisters*. It's their first trip since the *Miss Ally* crew was lost.

Sandy is in the wheelhouse as his four-man crew—including Greg Nickerson and Gordie Rhyno—are working on deck, with the wind at their backs, pulling in a string of trawl. It's cold, blustery, dark, and the boat is rolling, but jokes are being told and there's laughter on deck. Suddenly, there's a smash and the *Logan & Morgan* is lifted fully onto its starboard side, plunging the gunwale under water. The boat has been rocked by a rogue wave and is nearly flipped over. The men—mixed with gear—are hurled to the low side of the boat. Greg and Gordie are both launched overboard, into the two-degree water. Under the surface, Greg immediately thinks of the *Miss Ally*. He disappears into the froth and smashes into the cage that protects the propeller. Gordie, meanwhile, is able to quickly clamour back into the boat and immediately starts hollering: "He's gone! He's gone! He's gone!"

"Who's gone?" Sandy yells in the commotion.

"Greg is gone!"

Sandy takes the boat out of gear and quickly kills the engine. Gordie, meanwhile, struggles to the stern. The deck is a mess of trawl tubs, balloons, high flyers, and other gear. Gordie screams Greg's name into the darkness, but no one answers.

"Greg!"

Greg had surfaced but is now under water again. The boat is on top of him. Shocked by the near-zero-degree water, he thinks of Joel Hopkins. Then everything goes black. His muffled voice eventually emerges at that stern. He's clinging to an aluminum bracket. He manages to yell once and then goes silent.

"He's here under the stern!" Gordie hollers to the others.

Gordie grabs a life ring and lowers it into the water. It takes four agonizing attempts before Greg reaches out and latches on.

"I got him!" Gordie yells.

Pulling on the line, Gordie manoeuvres Greg to the side of the boat, but the difficult task remains: getting him out of the water. It's a couple metres from the water to the top of the rail. With all the gear strewn around, the other men can't get near Gordie to help him lift.

"You gotta get him out of the water or he's going to die!" Sandy hollers, his voice largely silenced by the wind.

Gordie leans over the side as far as possible and slowly lifts Greg—weighing close to three hundred pounds in his soaked work clothes—out of the water and up to the rail. Gordie is fuelled by adrenalin and breaks a rib in the process, but is able to pull Greg up over the rail. Greg, now unconscious, lands in a clump on the deck and starts spewing water. The other men drag him into the wheelhouse and put him by a heater.

"Get his clothes off!" Sandy barks.

Greg is stripped to his underwear and quickly taken forward to the men's bunks. Sandy snatches Greg's sleeping bag and wraps him in it. Dishtowels are heated and shoved under his armpits and between his legs. It takes an hour before his eyes start to flutter.

"Greg can you hear me?" Sandy asks.

Greg looks up at Sandy but says nothing.

"Are you all right?"

There's a pause before Greg speaks.

"I lost my boots."

Sandy smiles, relieved. He lost three men overboard in the 1980s and got them all back. Two more overboard, two more back aboard and alive.

"Don't worry about your boots," Sandy says. "I'll get you another pair of boots."

Sandy, Gordie, and the other men pray in a circle, thankful Greg was spared.

They eventually pull in the string of gear they were handling when the wave struck. Then Sandy lets the *Logan & Morgan* lay-to for the night, pushed only by the wind. The plan is to haul up the rest of the gear in the morning.

Lying in his bunk later that night, Sandy is unsure how to proceed. At the beginning of the trip, he and his crew lowered five wreaths into the water and he read passages from the Bible to honour the lost men of the *Miss Ally*. Back on February 16, Sandy told the men on the *Miss Ally* to abandon their gear and head for shore before the storm worsened. There is more bad weather on the way. Why is he not obeying his own advice? Tonight he nearly lost two men and his boat was a matter of degrees from flipping. Sandy gets little sleep and at 5 A.M. calls his son, Chrisjon, who is nearby on the *Benji & Sisters*.

"We're going home. We're gettin' outta here," Sandy tells his son.

Sandy has gear in the water but he doesn't care. The weather is awful and it's not worth the risk.

Three weeks later Sandy returns to sea and retrieves his gear.

Every piece of it.

In March 2013, a month after the sinking, the Transportation Safety Board of Canada (TSB) calls off its investigation of the *Miss Ally* case. The TSB does not assess blame; the agency simply tries to determine if an accident holds lessons that could help prevent similar incidents. There were no such lessons gleaned from the *Miss Ally* case. The investigators interviewed many people, reviewed the boat's history and previous inspections, and observed the flipped hull at sea with the Navy's remote underwater vehicle. In the end, there were no safety recommendations to be made for other fishermen. The boat was in good working order and no additional equipment would have changed the outcome.

Captain Pierre Murray, the TSB's regional manager for the Maritimes and Newfoundland, uses the analogy of teaching someone to safely cross a busy street; you can instruct the person to carefully look both ways before crossing, but what if that person then looks both ways, sees traffic approaching, and decides to cross anyway? "There's nothing we can do to prevent that," he says in an interview from Dartmouth, Nova Scotia. "All the information was there for the crew to decide what to do, right? And they chose to stay there and retrieve their gear. All the information they had available was available to all the other boats, and all the other boats came back before the storm."

On May 20, the families of the lost men gather in Yarmouth for a briefing on the search and rescue operation. Coast Guard officer Ray McFadgen, the JRCC maritime coordinator who was the first to work on the case on the evening of February 17, leads the briefing. He explains the search timeline and plays the three audio recordings of Katlin's conversations with McFadgen and other JRCC operators. It's clear to McFadgen that family members still harbour misgivings and frustrations about how the search was handled. One lingering issue: why were the survival suits not picked up by searchers? McFadgen again explains that searchers only search—they don't recover debris. The survival suits were spotted during an active search. It would be a waste of precious time to recover objects when men could still have been in the water.

The lingering misunderstandings about how searchers do their jobs are later addressed in the final assessment of the *Miss Ally* search and rescue operation. The report notes that search and rescue agencies must better explain that search missions end when there is no further possibility of finding survivors, not simply when searchers feel like stopping. "It is clear to those of us who work in search and rescue that we need to make the resources ready for the next incident," notes Stephen Waller, a maritime coordinator at JRCC Halifax, in the report. "That is not clear to the general public as evidenced by the comments of numerous callers to local radio phone shows who felt search and rescue should have continued beyond the point at which we reduced the search."

The report authors conclude that communication between search officials and the families was "very good," though they admit "later issues developed with the families." They recommend a change for similar cases in the future: families should be allowed to give feedback on a search reduction before the search is actually called off. "Answering their concerns before the search ends may reduce/prevent blowback," the report notes.

In the case of the *Miss Ally*, they also note the need to better explain why the hull was not recovered. "As a result of leaving the overturned hull, the Coast Guard received a great deal of negativity from the media and general public," writes Waller's colleague, Harvey Vardy. "The Coast Guard does not have the expertise or the equipment to salvage overturned vessels."

Adds Major Ali Laaouan, the officer in charge at JRCC Halifax: "It is evident from this case that the majority of people removed from search and rescue do not understand the roles, processes, responsibilities, and capabilities the system is able to offer. Our organization needs to engage in a proactive campaign to educate the public, media, and partners about search and rescue."

Rear-Admiral Dave Gardam, the Halifax search and rescue region commander, concurs. "The Department of Fisheries and Department of National Defence need to proactively continue to educate the public, media and partners about search and rescue to demystify the process," he notes.

The report also addresses the handoff of the case from searchers to the RCMP as a missing persons case. As the report notes, there were "misunderstandings with the next of kin" that could have been avoided. "The issue of transfer from search and rescue authorities to RCMP [...] is one that requires attention and improved coordination," Major Laaouan notes, pledging a review of the handover process and improved cooperation between JRCC Halifax and the RCMP.

Despite the lingering questions and frustrations of the families, Stephen Waller notes that one positive element did emerge from the sinking: proof of the effectiveness of Emergency Position-Indicating Radio Beacons. Waller argues that every effort should be made to encourage fishermen to register their EPIRBs. Katlin's was registered, so JRCC was notified as soon as the distress beacon was activated. "Although no lives were saved in this incident it did provide the earliest possible notification to search and recue authorities and clearly demonstrates how essential that is when lives are at risk in the North Atlantic Ocean," Waller notes.

After the sinking, Katlin's father, Todd, obtained phone records that appear to show his son took a final call via satellite phone at exactly 11 P.M. Todd insists he was on the other end of the five-minute conversation. He also says the call ended abruptly at 11:05 P.M. Todd assumes his son's boat flipped while the two were talking. The EPIRB was activated at 11:06 P.M., one minute later. The phone records appear to dispute JRCC's conclusion that Katlin's final call via satellite phone occurred at 10:52 P.M. "They were wrong," Todd says flatly.

The exact timeline remains foggy, as does the question of what actually happened to Katlin, Cole, Joel, Tyson, and Billy Jack on February 17. In the final JRCC report, Stephen Waller can only say the boat met with a "catastrophic event" between 10:52 P.M. and 11:08 P.M.:

It is unlikely we will even know for certain what happened, but most likely the vessel broached and was capsized in heavy seas. It is unlikely that the crew were able to launch a life raft given the weather conditions at the time. The crew did not appear aware that they had immersion suits aboard and in any event did not don them as immersion suits were found in the debris field still in their bags. It is extremely unlikely that any of the crew could have survived in the water without an immersion suit long enough for a vessel or helicopter to arrive on scene.

Another nagging question remains: why was the life raft sighted by the American Coast Guard, and later chased by searchers, never found? Again, Waller cannot say for sure. "It is likely that it sank. It is also possible that the object sighted was not a life raft."

In all, JRCC's work on the *Miss Ally* case involved 1,637 phone calls over nearly forty-four hours. And it was not the centre's only concern at the time; nine other cases were active at the same time, two deemed urgent.

The report's conclusion: "This case was well handled by JRCC."

CHAPTER 13

ECHOES

CAPTAIN WAYNE'S CAFÉ IS BUSY. A COUPLE DOZEN PEOPLE ARE EATING or waiting for their meals around noon. It's a Sunday in June and the two waitresses are trying to ensure food and bills get out quickly.

"Are you going to the service?" an older waitress asks as she seats a party at their table.

It's Woods Harbour Days, an annual week-long celebration that includes lots of food and community events, including a dance and a frog-hopping competition. It's the final day of the festival and the annual Fishermen's Memorial Service is being held down the road at 2 P.M. If these customers are going, they'll probably be served a bit quicker, to ensure they're not late. It turns out they won't be attending the service, so it's likely they'll wait a couple minutes longer for their clams and chips and lobster platters.

Among those seated in the restaurant are George Hopkins and his grand-daughter, Brooklyn. She's finishing her nachos, picking the last bits of cheese off the plate, while George has pushed aside his almost-finished plate of turkey, potatoes, and cranberry sauce. George checks his watch and says they should get going. Brooklyn agrees. She has to brush her hair before the service and that sometimes takes an hour, she says. George doesn't dispute it. On school days she's up at 6 A.M. and spends most of the time before the arrival of her bus, at 7:10 A.M., getting her hair just right. She'll make it look extra special for the memorial.

The night's scheduled sail parade has been cancelled. It's already raining lightly and more rain and heavy wind is expected by evening. The weather has also forced the memorial service from the actual Woods Harbour Fisherman's Memorial near the cenotaph to the Calvary United Baptist Church. The white building is within view of the water and its back parking lot is just metres from a large stack of lobster traps. Inside, Pastor Rod Guptill walks up the aisle, passing out boxes of Kleenex.

The service begins sharply at 2 P.M. with a moment of silence and a prayer. A folksong, "Sea People," is played over the speakers. It's the type of song that's sung in bars, celebrating working-class fishermen and the communities they live in:

They go down with their nets to the shore,
They go down like their fathers before;
And the sea seems to say, "If you ride me today,
I will grant you the wealth of my store."

The crux of the ceremony involves reading a list of names: local fishermen lost at sea, some from as far back as the 1800s. Shortly after, wreaths are laid, one by one, at the front of the church. Wreaths are placed in memory of fishermen lost long before the *Miss Ally*'s crew, though tears no longer fall for those men. Those lost men are still honoured at ceremonies, but not grieved during breakfast or when a song plays on the radio.

The Fishermen's Memorial Service feels very much like a *Miss Ally* memorial: family members of the lost men lay the vast majority of wreaths. Multiple wreaths are placed for each man, by various relatives, including grandparents, mothers, fathers, uncles, sons, and daughters. Two Coast Guard employees, in their blue uniforms, take a wreath to the front. Janet Reynolds sobs as she lays a wreath down for her son, Billy Jack. In all, nearly twenty wreaths are laid for the men of the *Miss Ally*.

"Father, we've remembered all good men here today," Pastor Guptill concludes. When the rain breaks, all the wreaths will be moved to the cenotaph.

There's little mingling afterward. Tyson's mom, Lori, leaves immediately, hurrying off into a car with Tyson's girlfriend, Ashley, and his daughter, Lilly. "They're still very mad," notes one Woods Harbour resident of the Townsend family. "Mad at the world. Their grieving process is not over. They're not over it. Well, they'll never be over it. But the point is, they went into a silent mode. It's the way they're treating it—very privately."

Cole's father, Stephen Nickerson, also makes his way out of the church and into the parking lot. Stephen appears matter of fact about his loss. He loved his son. His son is gone. He misses his son dearly. But there's no point in showing much emotion about it. Tears won't bring Cole back.

Stephen still goes to sea—mainly for lobster and some swordfish harpooning in summer—but it's been difficult since Cole died. Standing at the back of the boat, Stephen starts to think about what happened aboard the *Miss Ally*, especially when the wind begins to pick up. "I think of it a lot. It's on my mind the whole time," he admits. Stephen can easily mull twenty different scenarios where the *Miss Ally* ends up safely back at the wharf instead of flipped at sea. If only they'd used a sea anchor to steady the boat. If only they'd steamed with the wind behind them, instead of with it on their side.

If only.

If only.

When he's busy on deck, such thoughts disappear, but when the work slows, they resurface. There are also times when Stephen thinks about his Uncle Andrew, lost on the *Colville Bay* in 1974. "It seems to never go away," he admits. "I don't think it will ever go away."

But Cole's loss is different. Stephen believes it was preventable. "It all could have all been avoided if they'd just come in when they should've," Stephen says. "He [Katlin] just made the mistake of staying. He should have left the gear and come in. They'd all still been here if they'd done that."

For Shelby Peters, Cole's girlfriend, an envisioned future evaporated when the *Miss Ally* was found floating hull-up. Cole and Shelby had only been together for ten months, but they were looking at buying a house and had talked about marriage and having kids. "That was my future and then my entire reality was just blown to pieces. I had to stop and figure out how I was going to start a new reality all by myself," she says. "I miss Cole and I loved Cole. And that was what my life was supposed to be, but I've had to realize that life goes on."

Shelby still wears the ring Cole left her as a Valentine's gift before leaving. Her own grief aside, Shelby is saddened that Cole wasn't able to fully rehabilitate his reputation. During high school and his early twenties, Cole was seen as a rough-and-tumble jock and a partier. Shelby believed he'd changed, matured, softened. But his reputation hadn't fully changed among his friends.

"I knew him in the end and I knew his most personal and deepest thoughts, and he wouldn't want to be known for that," she says. "I think he'd be really upset to think that people still saw him how they saw him in high school. It's really heartbreaking to know that that was one of his biggest goals—to show people he had changed."

Shortly after the Fishermen's Memorial Service, Sandy Stoddard is back at his home in Charlesville, just past Woods Harbour, seated in a recliner, feet in the air. These remembrance events always reopen the emotional wounds still nursed by the families. On the other hand, Sandy notes, the gatherings show that many in the community are still thinking about Katlin, Billy Jack, Joel, Cole, and Tyson.

After the sinking, Sandy emerged as something of a spokesman for the community—quoted often in print, featured on CBC's *The National*—as well as a defender against those who question the decisions that led to five men struggling through hurricane winds and 10-metre seas. Sandy and his son, Chrisjon, escaped the storm; Sandy alerted the Coast Guard to Katlin's struggles that night; Sandy later spoke at Katlin's funeral. He's a key figure in the story of the *Miss Ally*. Sandy is outspoken, quick with a quote, and not one to shy away from a microphone or TV camera.

On this rainy June day, Sandy notes that a woman is considering writing a book about him and the history of the Nova Scotia longlining industry, which has employed him since he was fifteen. "Our breed is dying and our industry is dying and our way of life is dying in the longline industry," he says. And no decent longline captain has succeeded in the industry without making risky—and sometimes very bad—decisions, he argues.

At nineteen, Sandy was skippering his first Cape Islander. One day he and his two-man crew were out lobstering during a March gale. They were the only boat out that day. "We shouldn't have been there," he says. But he was young and "full of piss and vinegar." On the way home, a plank came loose, causing a major leak. They were 40 kilometres from shore on a leaking boat with no life raft and no life jackets. The crew bailed frantically with a bucket as Sandy steamed for shore. If the plank came off completely, they would sink. By the time they reached shore, Sandy's crewmen were both flaked out on the deck, exhausted. He rammed the boat up on a beach.

"Why the plank stayed on there, only God knows. God had a plan for my life I guess," he says.

Another of Sandy's boats, the *Debbie & Jamie*, was once rolled so far over by a wave that he had to climb up the boat to the reach the throttle. The rail was under water and men on deck were tossed into the ocean. "How she didn't just go over I don't know."

Similarly, there was the rogue wave that sent two of his men into the water just two weeks after the *Miss Ally* foundered. Then there are the hurricanes Sandy survived—at least three—including one he steamed directly into. That was in 1995 when Sandy was swordfishing on the Grand Banks. Hurricane Felix was coming up from the US, sending most of the fleet to Newfoundland for shelter. Sandy decided to stay at sea with one other boat. He was cocky and figured he knew where the storm was headed. A member of the crew claimed Sandy was crazy and would drown them all. The wind topped 160 kilometres an hour, but by the next night Sandy and the crew were back fishing. The decision paid off. "I don't know why God saved me. I don't know. I intentionally went into a hurricane."

It sounds like every boat Sandy has skippered nearly sank.

"Yeah!" he says excitedly. "I've had a lot of close calls. A lot."

Sandy's point: Katlin's decision to stay out and retrieve his gear was no worse than many of his own previous decisions. "Don't let people go around saying, 'He shouldn't have been there,'" Sandy says. "Katlin didn't do anything different than all the rest of us have ever done. We've all done it—every skipper. He just didn't make it. Simple as that."

What about Katlin's age? Was he too young, at twenty-one, to be skippering the boat? "Did he have the experience? No, because he was too young to have the experience. But how do you get experience?" Sandy points to Billy Tyne, captain of the *Andrea Gail*, from Sebastian Junger's *The Perfect Storm*. Tyne was very experienced, but that wasn't enough against 10-storey waves and 200-kilometre-an-hour winds. "It happens. You make mistakes. You make bad decisions," Sandy says. "Was Katlin capable of taking a boat? Yes sir, he was. He was aggressive. He was fierce. He wanted to make a name for himself, like all the young skippers do. You want to be talked about. You want to catch the most. It's an ego thing. Not in a bad way. Not a bad ego."

It's cold and raining outside as Sandy speaks. His dog is nearby, sleeping on a small bed under the living room window. Relaxed in his recliner, Sandy continues his defence. As he did at Katlin's funeral—to the great frustration of some in attendance—Sandy compares Katlin to Sidney Crosby. Katlin was a top fishing prospect. Eventually he would have been one of the best: a high liner like his father, Todd, and grandfather, Wayne, the Cod Father. "Katlin was up in that crowd. He was up with the big boys. Even though he was young, he was still considered up with us," Sandy insists. "He was energetic and he was going to do all he could do. That's what made you a high liner."

Sandy then takes his hockey analogy even further: "Katlin was no different than Wayne Gretzky. Gretzky wanted to be the best at what he did. Katlin wanted to be the best at what he did," he says. "People will say '[Katlin] was greedy.' No. No. Got nothing to do with greed. It's got to do with being on top of your game. People would say, 'If he wasn't so greedy he wouldn't have been there.' Well, if Gretzky wasn't so greedy he wouldn't have been there [at the top] either."

Sandy sits up slightly and leans forward to emphasize his point. "People will call it greed and people will call it all kinds of things. But no, he was just aggressive—doing what he loved to do. And he wanted to be the best that he could be at it," he says. "In your story, portray him that way. Portray him in a good, honourable way. Don't portray him to be some young, inexperienced kid out there not knowing nothing, not listening. I'd be disappointed if you ever portrayed him that way. Because that's not true. He was a young individual trying to be his own man, wanting to beat his father, wanting to beat the top guns. That's all. And that's what [fishing] is all about—the prestige and trying to be competitive. We're very competitive in this fishery about who can catch the most. That's just the way it is."

Lobster season is over so John Symonds is at home, wearing a T-shirt and shorts. No longer consumed by the thought of what he'll find in his next trap, he's happy to talk about Katlin, his little buddy.

"I could have adopted him so easily. I knew his parents didn't want to get rid of him, but I still wanted him," John says. He laughs at the idea: adopting a twenty-one-year-old "boy." John only knew Katlin for four years, "but he touched my world so much," he says. "It feels like it was forty years."

John thought of Katlin as a son. Not a day goes by when John doesn't think about his friend and former deckhand. And he often dreams about him.

John is also often haunted by a question he can't answer: did Katlin delay his retreat from the storm because he didn't want to abandon John's longlining gear? John admits that as a young man he would have worried about losing another man's gear. "When I lay down at night I think he stayed there because he had my gear in the water," John says. It's a painful thought.

John also dismisses the criticism that Katlin's actions were directly to blame for his boat and crew being swallowed by the storm. "Everybody said he put himself in that situation. I don't think he did."

Sure Katlin could have benefited from more experience in rough weather. Perhaps then Katlin would have considered turning his boat to the southeast, allowing the storm to push him along, instead of continuing to plow north to Sambro, which put the storm on his port side. Sometimes going away from land is safer than making directly for shore. "Did he do anything wrong? I don't think he did everything right. None of us do," John says.

As John sees it, the real problem was a lack of visibility, not a lack of good judgment. If Katlin's overhead light hadn't failed, Billy Jack, Tyson, Cole, and Joel could have hauled the gear during the night. Then the five men would have steamed to safety in Sambro and been tied up at a wharf as the storm raged. They would have eventually landed at home with twenty thousand pounds of halibut aboard. That catch, in February, would have netted a solid profit and further boosted Katlin's reputation as a top young fisherman.

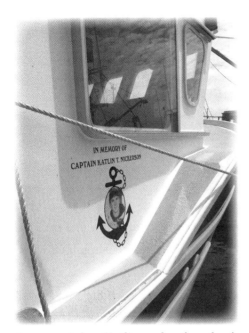

A memorial to Katlin under the wheel-house window of John Symonds's boat, the Hit N' Miss I.

"He would have been following in his grandfather Wayne's footsteps—one of the best fishermen that ever walked in a pair of boots here in Woods Harbour," John says. "Katlin was going down the same road. He was gonna be the best fisherman. Katlin didn't want to be second-best. He wanted to be number one. And he would stay longer and he would fish harder."

John, like Sandy, insists Katlin wasn't trying to be a "big shot," and his youth—a common refrain—isn't to blame. Katlin was more than 160 kilometres offshore for one reason: he had to make money. "I want people to know the truth about Katlin: he was [just] trying to pay his bills," John says. "He had some big bills. Three quarters of a million is what he paid for that piece of machinery. He had bills and he had everyone—myself included—rooting for him…and I don't think he wanted to disappoint any of us. That's why he was there doing this. That's why he pushed things to the limit."

John admits, though, that he worried Katlin was pushing beyond the limit. "There's a fine line between being aggressive and being stupid. And you have to make sure you don't cross it," he says. "Katlin was still learning."

When local fishermen launched the second search, John considered joining. He went to the wharf, intending to add his boat to the fleet, but he had to turn back. He couldn't bear the thought of actually finding something from the *Miss Ally*, even a trawl tub or a high flyer. He stayed home and cried every night while watching the news. He'd retreat to his barn to mend traps, but couldn't shake the search from his mind. Normally an enthusiastic worker and keen to be on the water, John couldn't muster the energy or desire to even leave his house. Losing Katlin tore the good out of fishing.

"It was a hard old go," he says, his voice heaving. "It really was."

When John did eventually return to his boat he noticed his book of contacts was open to the page with Katlin's satellite phone number. John couldn't even turn on his VHF radio, not wanting to see the channel he and Katlin used for their private conversations.

Since Katlin's death John has bought a new boat, the *Hit n Miss I*. His daughter, Paige, christened the boat by smashing a bottle of wine over the bow. On the bottle was a picture of Katlin. In the wheelhouse, John has two framed pictures: one of his mother and one of Katlin. In it, Katlin is grinning and holding a lobster. On the exterior of John's boat, below the wheelhouse window, is what he calls "the memorial." There's a photo of Katlin's face on top of an anchor and the words "IN MEMORY OF CAPTAIN KATLIN T. NICKERSON." Whenever John hauls a good string of traps, he reaches out and touches Katlin's head.

"Old boy, thanks for putting lobsters in Johnny's pot," he says each time.

John recently bought another lobster licence. He wishes he had it 2013. He would have given it to Katlin. Perhaps having more lobster to catch would have kept him out of the halibut fishery and he'd be here today.

In the years since the sinking, John has noticed one positive trend emerge among local fishermen: an increased attention to safety. "I see people wearing PFDs [personal floatation devices] today who never ever wore them in their life," he says. On his boat, PFDs are now mandatory. "If they don't do it, they don't get paid."

A PFD couldn't save you from an offshore storm of the calibre experienced by Katlin, Joel, Billy Jack, Tyson, and Cole, but at least it provides a good chance your family can bury a body. A body provides closure. John wishes he could have at least held Katlin's hand at the funeral.

"No one ever touched my heart like that kid, ever," John finally says. "Nobody."

Della Sears has just returned from work and hasn't yet changed out of her uniform: black leotards and a matching top with a Lobster Shack logo on it. She only recently started waitressing at the Barrington Passage restaurant and it's already a big improvement over her previous job at a local fish plant. Her shifts at the plant provided too much time to sit and think. It's been two years since Katlin's death, but he's still a near-constant presence in her mind. A boring eight-hour shift quickly becomes mentally torturous. The Lobster Shack, on the other hand, is often full of people and is only a three-minute drive from her home on Cape Sable Island. She's saving gas and her sanity.

It's a grey April day and the spring potholes were particularly bad on her drive home across the causeway, causing her to swerve often. But at least the long winter is finally over. The four-month span from December to March is full of hellish reminders that Katlin is gone: first there's Christmas and then the February anniversary of the sinking. Each year, on February 12, Della drives to the West Head wharf, following the same route she took when she dropped Katlin, Tyson, Joel, and Billy Jack off for the trip. Katlin's birthday then arrives on March 15. The long, dark days only add to the gloom. "I always have a bad winter," she says. "When the weather changes [I] start to feel better."

Della is sitting at the kitchen table in the house she shares with her boy-friend, Adam, her daughter, Falon, her son-in-law, Chris, and her grandson, Easton. One of the chairs is broken but there are no plans to fix it. Katlin broke it. "That's his fork," Della says pointing to the framed utensil on the wall. "He always had to have that fork."

Della is wearing a ring with five birthstones, one for each of the lost crew members. She also has a tattoo that includes the date of the sinking, the time the EPIRB was activated, the boat's last known coordinates, Katlin's signature, and five doves. She doesn't recall when she got the tattoo; the weeks and months since Katlin's death are blurred.

For months after the sinking Della was in denial. She clung to visions of Katlin and the crew being picked up by a passing tanker. No longer. "Nobody got in the life raft," she says matter-of-factly.

Then the severe depression arrived. For months she couldn't even go out for groceries. She didn't want to see anybody. One day, she finally made her way to Sobeys. Walking out of the store, a woman stopped her.

"How are you doing?" the woman asked.

"I want to die," Della responded.

She regrets saying it aloud, but it was true. "I did. I really wanted to die. For two years. Every day." She pined for her son and spent hours imagining what happened that night, playing over different scenarios in a form of self-inflicted mental torture. She was also guilt-ridden over her part in it all. "He was the captain. I feel responsible for five lives, not just one," she says, her voice shaking. "I think about it from the time I get up 'til the time I go to bed. I've been dealt it and I have to figure out a way to live with it."

It's only in the past month—more than two years later—that she's noticed an improvement in her mood and outlook. "It's still hard to talk about it sometimes. But I'm better now," she offers. "I've changed my way of [thinking]. Instead of questioning, 'Why did you take him and why didn't you give me enough time?' I say, 'Thank you for the time you did give me.'"

Part of her recovery started after reading *When Bad Things Happen to Good People*, Harold Kushner's 1981 bestseller. Della now believes she has a choice in how she feels. "If I am depressed, if I'm bitter, if I'm hating the world, then he's died a devil's martyr. If I choose to be kind and loving and to show my faith, then I keep him alive in a good way, right?" she says. "Of course I miss him and I hurt, but Katlin wouldn't want me to be miserable and in bed. He was so happy-go-lucky. He would be so upset with me if he knew I was dwelling on things and being mean."

Katlin's white Dodge pickup is parked behind the house. Della drives it now.

"Sometimes I feel weird. But then I have people tell me 'just drive it if it makes you feel good.'"

Last night she dreamt about Katlin for the first time in a while. She's usually a mess for a day after seeing him in a dream. Today, though, it makes her laugh. In the dream, Katlin asked about his truck. She explained that it's in her name now, and assured him that it is insured.

"I can still hear him," she says.

There are photos of Katlin throughout the house, even along the side of Della's bathroom mirror. The home screen on her phone is a photo of Katlin. She points at the patch of living room floor where he'd often lay and watch TV after a day of lobstering. He preferred the floor because he could get close to the warm air blowing from the heater.

Della exhales deeply.

"I can still smell him in his pillow. I don't smell it every day because I'm scared I'll take all the smell of it out. But when I do smell it, and it's there, it's like, 'Ahhh. This is awesome.'"

Della misses simple things like getting her son something to eat and folding his clothes. Her thoughts are no longer completely hijacked by grief, but she still has many sudden moments. Just the other day she started sobbing while driving across the causeway. "You get a pain in your heart, you really do. And it hurts. But I don't get that all the time anymore. I did."

Della is still haunted by the JRCC audio recordings, which were played for the families at the meeting three months after the sinking. She had talked to Katlin throughout the day of the storm. By the time he was talking with coordinators at JRCC Halifax, his voice revealed concern. "I could hear his voice change—as a mother, probably. I could tell that he was probably thinking…." She can't finish the sentence. "And that's the part that gets stuck in my head."

Eventually Easton, her grandson, waddles into the room and calls for his nanny. He's wearing nautical-themed pyjamas with images of boats and a compass rose. Della picks him up.

"Who's this boy? Who is this?" she says pointing to a photo of Katlin on the table. "Who's that? Who is this boy?"

Easton doesn't seem to know, but his father, standing nearby, insists Easton identified the photo as Katlin earlier that day.

Della is familiar with the questions and criticisms that were raised in the days and weeks after the *Miss Ally*'s crew disappeared. Was Katlin qualified to be out there? How could a twenty-one-year-old captain possibly have the skills to manage such a situation? She still feels the need to respond, even without being asked to.

"They'll say 'inexperienced, young.' Yes, he was young. Inexperienced? Not so much," she says. "He probably spent more time on the water than most people." She notes that Sandy Stoddard was hit by a huge wave in the weeks after the *Miss Ally* sank. Even a skipper with four decades of experience encounters trouble.

"It happens to everybody," she offers.

Della also passionately disputes the charge that Katlin's recklessness put his boat and crew at the bottom of the ocean. "It makes for a great story, right? [That] he's reckless," she says. "I don't believe it to be reckless at all. I think he was just trying to do his job, get his gear back, and head in. That's what he did."

She quickly acknowledges her bias. Della knows her opinion won't alter the conclusions of others. "I'm his mother, of course I'm going to stand up for him, right?" she says. "So, yes, I will defend Katlin right 'til the day I die."

※

It's a perfect August day for softball: 25 degrees and sunny. Della is lugging a cooler across the grass and puffing on a cigarette shortly before noon. It's the final day of the Katlin Nickerson Memorial Tournament. The softball tournament, started in 2013, culminates with a championship game at noon. The first pitch will be lobbed soon and Della is making final preparations for the pig roast and auction that will follow.

The tournament raises money for students in the Options and Opportunities (O2) program that Katlin participated in during high school. Each team (there are eighteen this year) puts up $250 to take part. Combined with the auction and food sales, Della expects to raise close to $8,000 this year. Each year she reviews applications and then awards two $500 bursaries for students in the O2 program. She tries to pick students involved in carpentry, as Katlin was, or students who are in great need of financial support. Her goal is to bank enough money to supply bursaries for twenty-one years (the number of years Katlin was alive).

Della is wearing one of the shirts sported by the members of her team: Kat's Meow. The shirts pay homage to Katlin's favourite show: *The Dukes of Hazzard*. The shirts are orange and have 01, the number of the General Lee, on the back. On Della's shirt, MOMMA is printed in bold letters above the number. Della's team isn't usually competitive but this year Kat's Meow made it to the semifinals.

A couple hours later the championship game has concluded. The Running Rapids have defeated the Got the Runs. Della hands out medals, then asks everyone to gather inside the dirt infield. About one hundred helium-filled balloons—black, white, gold, and orange—are handed out.

"I can't believe we're in our third year," Della says, speaking into a microphone while standing near the pitching mound. "It still seems like yesterday that I seen that silly crooked grin. This is a bittersweet weekend for all of us, but he would be so proud of his family and friends coming together, remembering him and his crew, sharing memories and making new ones. Nine-hundred and ten days have passed," she notes. "Katlin and his crew will never be forgotten. The joy that they brought us continues on, especially on a weekend like this."

Now crying, Della thanks all the players for participating and all the volunteers who helped out. Among those she thanks: Reg LeBlanc and Terry Zinck, the two men Katlin fished for. They've sponsored the whole tournament, so that all the money raised can go to the O2 program. Della apologizes if she forgot to thank anyone.

"My mind is a little bit crazy this weekend," she says.

Della reads a poem and then the balloons are released, floating higher and higher, blown by a decent breeze until they become specks and finally disappear.

Katlin's annual tournament raises money and also brings together many of the friends and relatives affected by the sinking. This marks the first year that Billy Jack's family entered a team: Billy's Jack Hammers. Katlin's best friend, Sherman Crowell, is helping with the auction. Another friend, Devin Smith, now a DJ in Halifax, is providing a steady stream of music.

Colby Smith, who likely would have been aboard the *Miss Ally* had he returned a month earlier from school, is leaning up against his pickup truck. On the back window is a sticker that says, "Ah. That ain't nothin'"—Katlin's common response to tough situations. Colby had the sticker made in the days after the search was called off. This year Colby played on Della's team. Even three years later he finds it difficult to comprehend that his friend is gone. "I still don't really believe it," he says. "It's never easy, but you learn to live with it. It's good to be around family and friends, having a good time—instead of sitting around crying. It's good to celebrate it, rather than mourn it."

Tyrone Nickerson, Cole's uncle, is leaning against one of the dugouts, nursing a Budweiser. His family went through all this before, after the *Colville Bay* disappeared in 1974. Around his neck is a medallion. One side is engraved with the name of his uncle, Andrew, and *Colville Bay*. On the other side, Cole's name is engraved along with *Miss Ally*.

"It's hard," Tyrone says. "I miss him a lot." Tyrone knows, though, that every passing year makes it all easier to take. "It eases over time," he says. "You never think it will but it does."

George and Mary Hopkins are sitting in their living room in Woods Harbour. George is in a brown leather chair by the window, occasionally glancing out at the harbour. Mary, in a T-shirt and jeans, is seated on the other side of the room on a large sectional couch. On the walls are various paintings of fishing vessels, including one of the 65-footer George used to take to the

Grand Banks. Outside, the lawn is finally visible after a long winter, one of the worst in memory. It's lobster season but George says the crustaceans aren't crawling much yet. The water is still too cold.

If they were both still alive, Joel might be lobstering with Katlin again this year on the *Miss Ally*, as he was during the fall before the sinking. And no doubt Joel would be thrilled doing so. "He loved everything about fishing," George says. "And if it was windy, blowing a gale, he would always say, 'Stay Dad, stay.' He didn't want to come in."

George assumes Joel, during the onset of rough weather, likely told Katlin they could get all the gear onboard before retreating. "In the storm I always figured he was probably one of the ones that said 'stay' to Katlin."

It's been just over two years since the sinking and only now can George and Mary talk about Joel without immediately crumbling into tears. "He was a little guy but he had a big presence," Mary offers. "Did he ever shut up?"

"Not from the time he was three," George immediately answers.

On this night George and Mary are happy to tell stories about their third child, like the time George took all three of his boys harpooning for swordfish. Joel had no problem climbing the rigging to get a good view of potential targets. They had a simple arrangement: when a swordfish was spotted near the boat, one person was designated to throw the first harpoon. If the dart missed the fish, a second person would throw their harpoon. But Joel always hurled the second harpoon regardless of whether the first one connected or not. "Every time I threw, he threw. It didn't matter. He'd still throw and put an extra dart in it," George says, laughing. "That was one of the most fun things we done together. He loved it and I loved it, too."

Then there was the time Joel, who enjoyed cooking, prepared stew using rabbits he caught with his friend Ryan Malone. Sitting at the table, George put a spoon into his bowl of stew.

"Joel, what is this?!" George asked. He fished out a rabbit turd. Joel's rabbit-hunting skills clearly exceeded his rabbit-cleaning skills.

"Um, I'm done," George said.

"Yep, me too," Ryan added.

"Bah! A little turd ain't gonna bother ya!" Joel insisted. He kept eating.

Mary and George are both laughing hard. Slowly, the laughter falls into silence. George was only eighteen when his mother died. He missed her dearly but says the pain doesn't compare to losing a child. "Your children are supposed to bury you," he says. "You're not supposed to bury them."

A week before, George was talking to a friend who lost his brother the year previous.

"I hardly go a week without thinking of my brother," the friend told George.

"Hardly go a week? I hardly go an hour without thinking of Joel," George replied.

"If I hear a wheeler or if I hear a motorcycle go by, if I see someone dressed in camouflage, I think of him," George adds, "Trouting season starts on Monday. Joel would have been there." Hockey, geese in the harbour during hunting season, Joel's house, his young sons, Julius and Tate—the reminders are everywhere.

"It's the first thing you think about in the morning, and the last thing you think about at night," Mary says. Even now, the sound of a police siren can prompt Mary to momentarily think: *Oh no, what did he do?*

Even sleep isn't a barrier to remembrance.

"I have woken up dreaming about him," George says.

Mary leaves the room to find a photo of Joel as a child. George points to a concrete wall at the front of the house. "He'd take his dirt bike and he would drive it right off that wall," he says. "I thought, 'Ah jeez, if he don't kill himself.'"

Mary eventually returns with a Reebok shoebox full of photos.

"I can bore you to death with a thousand pictures of him," she says.

There are photos of all four of their children and plenty of Joel, including one of him in pink hand-me-downs from his sister. "We didn't have to lie. He was really cute," Mary says, smiling.

At last, Mary finds the photo she has been searching for: Joel, wearing little boots, next to a big fish.

"Anything with fishing you'd see a sparkle in his eye," George says.

The sun is setting over the harbour as George pulls out his phone and starts flipping through more recent photos. There's one of Joel climbing the rigging of the *Miss Ally*. He's 10 metres in the air and there's absolutely no reason for him to be up there.

"That's what he'd do, stuff like that. It would drive you crazy," George says. "He's doing it for foolishness—because it's a challenge to get up there." George then flips to a photo of Joel popping a wheelie on his dirt bike.

"He could go from here to Lockeport," George says.

"And if he couldn't, he'd try," adds Mary.

George pauses, suddenly realizing that he and Mary are using the past tense to describe Joel.

"It's hard to say 'was,'" George finally says.

It's early on a Saturday morning in October 2015 and a consistent stream of four-wheelers is motoring out of the parking lot of the community centre in Woods Harbour. The riders head up the road to the former rail bed that runs through Shelburne County, down to Yarmouth. They turn left onto the trail and, in most cases, hit the accelerator—just as Joel would have. Before the *Miss Ally* sank, the sound of a four-wheeler blasting wide-open down the trail could often be attributed to him.

This year, more than two hundred people are registered for the second-annual Joel Hopkins ATV Poker Rally. The riders motor down to Argyle and then return back to the community centre in Woods Harbour, a three- or four-hour round trip. Along the route are five stops. At each stop the riders draw from a deck of playing cards. Secure a Royal Flush with your five cards and you win the top prize: a new four-wheeler.

Graydon and Jessica Mood are manning one of the stations, set up in the parking lot of a golf course along the trail. Jessica was Joel's cousin. Graydon, her husband, knew all five of the guys aboard the *Miss Ally*. Katlin used to dock the *Miss Ally* next to Graydon's boat, and Graydon and Joel were in the same grade. They hung out in the same group—riding wheelers, making camps, playing sports. Jessica and Graydon are part of a small group of friends that developed the idea for the ATV rally to honour Joel. The money from registration and an auction is put toward local causes. The first event, in 2014, helped fund four $500 bursaries for local community college students taking fishery-related courses.

Back at the hall, there's food being served—including chowder made from Joel's recipe—and the auction is underway. Items include a barbecue, a lobster trap, and a bluefin tuna fishing trip. Todd Nickerson, Katlin's dad, is raising his hand for a number of items and is being generous with his bids. Della is also there, helping clear tables.

Out back, a group of Joel's friends is standing near dozens of mud-splattered wheelers. Among them are brothers Sandy and Tyler Goreham. Tyler, with an ear to the proceedings inside, starts to laugh. A fisherman he knows—a man apparently without any interest in art—is bidding on a painting. He's definitely drunk.

Sandy Goreman, meanwhile, recalls the camping trips he and Joel went on. There were often up to fifteen guys, all riding wheelers. Joel was often the organizer, and he always bagged a deer. They would play cards and eat deer steaks. "We always had a drink and we always had a good time," Sandy says. He pauses. "We don't do that much no more. It ain't been the same since they've been gone."

The sinking, he continues, took the "sap" out of things. "It's different now around here."

Joel's two sons, Julius and Tate, are inside the hall, running amongst the tables and chairs. Elaine, Joel's long-time girlfriend, says Tate, who was only four months old when the *Miss Ally* sunk, is doing "okay." Julius, meanwhile, has had "a rough go." He was six when Joel died. "He was daddy's boy," Elaine says. "If Julius wanted something, Joel got it for him. He wanted a wheeler and Joel went and bought him a wheeler."

Elaine and the boys live in Clark's Harbour, close to her parents, where she and Joel were planning to move. Jada, the dog Joel bought to stand guard while he was at sea, still watches over the family. "My outlook on life now is: wake up and be happy," Elaine says. "I try to."

At the end of the day, as the tables and chairs are being packed away, Joel's mom is sitting in the corner.

"I'm really pleased," Mary says.

Despite some thunder and a brief spitting of hail, it was a nice day to be on the trail. She's also relieved. Nobody secured a Royal Flush to win the grand prize—the wheeler. They didn't buy insurance and one rider came within a card of a Royal Flush. "That was a little scary," she says. It was a risk Joel likely would have appreciated.

Mary is happy. The day brought all of Joel's friends and family together. But the event is also a reminder of what is gone and what has changed. That includes the dynamic within her family. The sinking was particularly difficult for her son Jesse. Jesse lost a brother *and* his best friend, Tyson.

Of her four children, Joel was the most outgoing, the most social, and most vocal.

"Joel was the glue that held the family together," Mary says finally. "I didn't realize it, but his personality kind of kept us all together."

Janet Reynolds steers her van into the parking lot of Drinking Brook Park. She steps out, unloads her two old, slow-moving dogs and looks around.

Drinking Brook Park, in Clam Point on Cape Sable Island, overlooks Barrington Bay. The land was originally given to local settlers in 1784. In the days before the causeway, residents often stopped to rest here and drink from the freshwater brook on their way to the ferry. Today, the park includes a memorial to Janet's son, Billy Jack. At one end of the park is the wooden gazebo Billy Jack built for the municipality, one of his many carpentry projects in the area. At the other end, on a patch of grass near the brook, is a headstone and a small stone bench. The bench is engraved with an image of Jesus holding a lamb and watching over three sheep—the actual sheep Billy Jack owned before he died. The headstone is engraved with images of a saw and a hammer and a short description: *During his life, Billy Jack wanted to be a shepherd like Jesus, who was also a carpenter, a fisherman and who died at the age of 33.*

Janet visits the memorial often, ensuring everything is tidy, replacing flower arrangements, and maintaining a steady supply of small solar-powered lights and battery-powered candles. "I don't think he was scared of the dark. But he always wanted a nightlight," she says. At home, Janet has burned a candle in a window every night since Billy Jack disappeared.

Janet frowns. She forgot to bring a rag today and there's some dirt on the monument. "I'm not impressed with that mess," she says. She walks over and scrapes it away with her hand.

Billy Jack grew up close to this park. He and his friend B. J. Sears made their log cabin in the woods nearby. B. J. recently built a log cabin in the same style, in memory of his lost friend, on a piece of land where the two men used to chop wood together.

"Billy Jack always went clamming out here," Janet says looking out across the exposed shoreline.

Billy Jack's family does not run an annual memorial sports tournament like the other four families connected to the *Miss Ally*. (In addition to Katlin's softball tournament and Joel's four-wheeler rally, there's a hockey tournament for Cole and a golf tournament for Tyson.) Janet isn't sure what type of event would be suitable to honour Billy Jack. Perhaps a bunch of his friends could build a house for a homeless person. "That's what Billy would like to do. He had his own sawmill. Made his own lumber and everything."

Janet still struggles most days with Billy Jack's death. "People that say it gets easier as time goes by—they're lying to you. It's a lie. It never, never gets easier," she says.

Janet often scans the island shoreline for debris. When something washes up, she hustles down to inspect it, hoping it might be something of Billy Jack's—a jacket, anything. "I'm still looking," she says. "I haven't got any closure yet."

Billy Jack, she admits, was, for a time, on the wrong road. "He was a bad boy right from age eleven," she says. "And he was mine and I loved him. It don't matter how bad he was." She is comforted by her belief that Billy Jack was improving his behaviour and righting the direction of his life. "And he got back in his Bible," she says. "He was a believer. Always was."

Toward the end of Billy Jack's life, Janet drove to Yarmouth to fetch him a couple sheets of leather. He wanted to start working with leather again, in addition to all the other things he could do with his hands. "He wasn't just a bad boy," she says. "He had a lot of talents."

Janet eventually finishes tidying and inspecting her son's memorial. She snaps on a couple electric candles, lifts her dogs back into the van, and closes the door. Janet has always believed that if anyone could survive the sinking, it would be her son. Billy Jack was self-sufficient and knew how to survive the elements.

Before pulling herself back into the van she takes a final glance around. "I'm hoping he's coming home."

Todd Nickerson is nearly ready for the upcoming 2016–17 lobster season. Dumping Day is three weeks away—the last Monday in November—and Todd has just finished preparing his traps for the six-month season. But he isn't looking forward to it. For Todd, lobstering and fishing no longer hold much appeal. "I've seen so much in the last three or four years," he says soberly.

First, Katlin died. Then, on November 30, 2015, Todd was at the wheel when a friend and crewman died aboard his boat, the *Cock-a-Wit Lady*. It was Dumping Day 2015 and Todd and his four-man crew were setting the season's first string of traps in the early morning light. Around 9 A.M., they were more than 40 kilometres from Clark's Harbour; the wind was moderate from the north, and the seas were about 1 metre high. The crew only had two traps in the water when one snagged on the port-side guardrail. An experienced crewman, Keith Stubbert, jumped quickly to free the lodged trap. It went over the side and so did Keith—a coil of line had wrapped around his leg. When the line went taut, the coil became snug around Keith's leg. "It pulled him right off the stern," Todd recalls, his voice flat.

Keith, despite wearing a PFD, was dragged under the water by the weight and momentum of the other traps. In an effort to save time, the crew attempted to pull Keith back up with the trap hauler, but the line was pulled at an extreme angle and snapped under the strain of Keith and the traps. Using an overhead block, which had been stowed, they desperately hauled the other end of the line. Three traps came up, then Keith. He'd been under the frigid water for ten minutes, likely kicking frantically to free himself as the rest of the crew struggled to retrieve him. "We got him back but he'd been in the water too long," Todd says.

Todd and the crew worked to resuscitate Keith—who was now without a pulse—and issued a distress call. The call was quickly detected by the crew of a nearby JRCC Hercules, which was already in the air in anticipation of Dumping Day drama. Two search and rescue technicians aboard the Hercules jumped into the water to help. Unfortunately they parachuted near the wrong vessel. The Hercules crew had been unable to determine the *Cock-a-Wit Lady*'s exact location, in part, because there were forty similar-looking lobster boats within a 5-kilometre radius. There was also extensive, confusing emergency-related chatter on channel sixteen, the VHF distress channel. The search and rescue technicians, floating in the water, were given a thumbs-up by the captain of the nearest boat, who then turned and continued fishing; the technicians were forced to launch a smoke flare to secure the assistance of nearby vessels. The Coast Guard cutter *Clark's Harbour* eventually dropped them at the *Cock-a-Wit Lady*, 4 kilometres away. Keith was later airlifted by helicopter to hospital in Yarmouth. He was pronounced dead shortly thereafter. The fifty-three-year-old man was the son of a fisherman. His father also died while lobstering.

According to the Transportation Safety Board (TSB), there were fifty-five deaths on Canadian fishing vessels due to people falling overboard between 1999 and August 2015.

A TSB investigation of Keith's death highlighted three safety deficiencies: the crew did not participate in emergency drills on board the *Cock-a-Wit Lady* before the beginning of the season; although the risk of falling overboard when setting traps was well known, no safety/toolbox meetings were held; and Todd did not address the increased level of risk associated with the opening day of the lobster season, which, according to the TSB, is "one of the most dangerous days of the year for lobster fishermen due to the high volume of traps carried on board and the desire to set those traps quickly." Among the report's conclusions: "despite many safety initiatives, unsafe practices continue in the fishing industry."

Keith had fished with Todd on and off for a decade. He had recovered from cancer and was back on the water. Though he was from Cape Breton, Keith often stayed with Todd in Woods Harbour. "He was part of the family," Todd says. "It's still tough. It's hard to believe."

As a young man Todd followed his father, Big Wayne, to sea, and fished for years with vigor and a competitive spirit. Now he just wants to be done. "I don't enjoy the fishing part no more," he says with little emotion.

Todd no longer pursues swordfish in summer, other than a little harpooning, or "sticking" as it's colloquially called. He continues to go lobstering strictly for the money. He just wants to bank enough to retire. When will he quit? "As soon as I can get a couple good years, I guess," he explains. "We'll see how this season goes."

Up and down the road, many of Todd's fellow Woods Harbour captains are itching for the new season. They'll load their boats with hundreds of traps and race to set them in the best spots—just as Katlin would have on the *Miss Ally.*

Todd will join them, but his will be a pursuit without passion.

EPILOGUE

ON THE EVENING OF FEBRUARY 11, 2013—THE NIGHT BEFORE HE departed on his final fishing trip—Katlin talked to Reg LeBlanc, the owner of Wedgeport Lobsters. The pair discussed potential long-term fishing arrangements. One plan involved Katlin leasing the *Miss Ally* to another fisherman and using Reg's *Row Row* year-round—for lobster in the fall and winter, and swordfish and tuna in summer. Reg had proposed calling the venture 50/50 Fisheries.

Terry Zinck, the owner of Xsealent Seafood, was also interested in entering an arrangement with Reg and Katlin, and suggested adding his halibut quota to the deal. There was talk of building a new, bigger boat for Katlin to fish throughout the year on behalf of the two men. Reg and Terry would get their fish, and Katlin would have all the quota necessary to keep his fishing business humming along and growing. Katlin was excited, and Terry felt it had the potential to be a serious money-maker. Nothing was finalized, though. They all agreed to discuss the ideas further when Katlin returned.

After the *Miss Ally* sank, Terry retreated. He sold off his remaining 2013 halibut quota—which Katlin was fishing—and backed away from the 50/50 Fisheries proposal. Katlin was a family friend—the same age as Terry's son Brock. "I was a little bit shell-shocked," he admits. "I felt somewhat responsible for what happened. I know I wasn't responsible. There's nothing I did that caused any of this to happen, but regardless...." He trails off.

As for the 50/50 Fisheries plan, Terry was no longer interested. "When we lost Katlin it all stopped. He was the key to the whole thing."

Terry is sitting in the Lobster Shack, the Barrington Passage seafood restaurant he recently bought. In an odd twist, Terry has partnered in the business with Katlin's mom, Della. At Terry's suggestion, they renamed it Capt. Kat's Lobster Shack.

Della had been working at the Lobster Shack since 2015. When, in early 2016, the restaurant closed suddenly, fourteen people were out of work. Della and a few of the other workers approached Terry. Despite never owning a restaurant, Terry agreed to buy the Lobster Shack, with Della as his operations partner. He suggested the new name, and Della was honoured. So far, the venture has been an experiment for both.

"I've never run a restaurant," Della admits. "I've never run anything before."

Little has changed in the takeover. There are, however, pictures of Katlin and his crew scattered throughout the dining area. The restaurant—specifically the name and the direct connection to the men lost on the *Miss Ally*—has unearthed some of the tensions that linger in the wake of the sinking. One family member notes there is a "general paranoia" that some people are profiting from the incident and the memory of the lost men, including myself with this book and Della with the restaurant. The restaurant has "offended a lot of people," the relative notes in an off-the-record conversation. "It will be a while before I can go there," they say.

There's also still "a lot of blaming about what happened on the boat." Many see it as being all Katlin's fault. Some hold him responsible for four deaths and cannot understand why there is now a restaurant named in his honour.

I mention Capt. Kat's to another *Miss Ally* family member, and am immediately cut off: "I won't be attending that," they say. "Della can do what she wants but I see that as borderline distasteful." (Six months later, however, after visiting the restaurant, they'd changed their mind—the restaurant was not offensive: "I gave it a chance [and] it's not poorly done. It's not too much. There's not any big shrine.")

Della and Terry are aware of at least some of this lingering sentiment. It's unavoidable, especially in such a small community. Della maintains that the local reception has been mainly positive. "We're super busy and if people thought anything bad of it, I would think they wouldn't come," she offers. "You can't please everybody."

"This is more than just a restaurant," Terry says, sitting beside her in the dining room.

"Yes, I agree with you on that," Della adds.

"Some people will get it and some people won't," Terry continues. He notes that diners often ask who Captain Kat is. "That's an important story," he says. "We as a society tend to forget way too quick about things that happened in the past."

Still, Terry is quick to clarify that the restaurant isn't a shrine: "This is not all about Katlin. The place is not overrun with Katlin. It has a great name and he's here, just exactly the way he should be," he says. "It's just one more good thing that has managed to come out of something so terrible."

Recently, a couple from Ontario asked about the restaurant's name.

"This story doesn't have a good ending, right?" the woman said.

"No," Della replied, "but we're feeding off positive vibes instead of the negative."

"I'm trying to be positive," she adds, "so people can see that we can survive as grieving parents." Della says she struggled when considering how to incorporate Katlin's crew in the restaurant. She believes he would have wanted them to be included. "It was my son's crew. I respect them and I think they should all be here. Not just Katlin," she says. "I'm just trying to keep him alive. The more people speak of him, it keeps him alive."

Della's recollections sometimes run in contradiction to the facts. She maintains the storm hit earlier than expected—it didn't—and she is puzzled by claims that Katlin failed to listen to those who told him to head for shore.

One night, a man entered Capt. Kat's and, like many people do, mentioned the sinking. The man concluded by saying: "Well, if he [Katlin] would have listened...."

Della, standing in the packed restaurant, was stunned.

"And exactly who did you want him to listen to?" she demanded. Overwhelmed by the offhand comment, she walked out and hurried home.

"Katlin would have listened if there would have been anyone to tell him," she insists.

Della is, understandably, guilty of some fuzzy memories and revisionist history. As for the accusation of profiteering, it seems a low blow. Della is clearly guilt-ridden. The sinking, she says, continues to be "a complete nightmare."

"I, as the mother of the captain of the boat, feel responsible. That was my child. That was his boat," she says, crying. "It was a bad accident, and that's what it was—an accident. Katlin did not go out to try to kill anybody. He lost his life, too."

Chrisjon Stoddard backs his red pickup truck quickly down one of the many fingers of the Falls Point wharf. The mix of coloured hulls and decks crammed with orange, yellow, red, and pink buoys provide a splash of colour on an otherwise grey Sunday in June. Chrisjon hops from his truck to the wharf and then down to his boat, the *Double Mischief*.

After Katlin died, Terry Zinck stepped away from the plan he and Reg LeBlanc hatched but never cemented for combining their quota and getting Katlin to fish for it. Reg, meanwhile, went ahead, partnering with Chrisjon. The two are now equal partners in 50/50 Fisheries Ltd., incorporated in 2014. The *Double Mischief* was also built in 2014 and is, essentially, the new boat that Reg and Terry proposed building for Katlin. Chrisjon helped design the *Double Mischief*: it's longer and wider than the *Miss Ally* and, according to Reg, likely would have been even bigger had Katlin been involved in its design. He would have insisted on a larger vessel to hold all the fish he planned to catch.

Chrisjon was skippering the *Benji & Sisters* when the massive storm that killed Katlin and his crew approached from Cape Hatteras in February 2013. Chrisjon saw the coming weather and—along with his father, Sandy—retreated. Put one way: he lived to fish another day. He then secured the fishing partnership and new boat Reg first offered to Katlin. (Chrisjon says Reg initially approached him about a partnership in the winter of 2012, but he turned it down.) Regardless, Chrisjon and Reg now co-own the company and the *Double Mischief*. The boat loan is for $600,000.

"She's brand new," Chrisjon says proudly. "We owe every cent on this boat. I gotta hope that Mother Nature lets me catch enough fish to pay for her."

Today Chrisjon is making final preparations for his first trip of the current longlining season. Tomorrow he and his four-man crew will head more than 300 kilometres offshore in search of tuna and perhaps swordfish. The priorities are straightforward: load enough bait, ice, diesel, and "grub" for a two-week trip.

First a forklift arrives at the edge of the finger and sets down stacks of boxes filled with whole frozen squid from Argentina. This is their bait—seven thousand pounds of the stuff—and it must all be loaded into the *Double Mischief*'s hold. There's also more than $2,000 worth of groceries in the back of Chrisjon's truck. The dangers at sea are numerous, but this crew will certainly not perish from starvation. The crewmen—at least two of them nursing hangovers—load the food with far more enthusiasm than they do the frozen bait. Even Chrisjon's seven-year-old identical twin sons, Cruz and Conner, lend a hand. Cruz and Conner are the inspiration for the name *Double Mischief*, but other than pinching a couple cans of pop from the provision pile, they're fairly well behaved. It's Father's Day and they're clearly happy being with Dad on his boat.

Do they plan on being fishermen?

"Probably," Cruz says before scurrying off with his brother.

As ice is loaded in the hold, Chrisjon is standing in the wheelhouse making a few final adjustments. Before leaving the wharf he'll have loaded the *Double Mischief* with roughly $25,000 worth of bait, ice, fuel, food, and other supplies. He'll stay at sea until he fills his hold, runs out of bait, ice, or food, or is pushed in by weather or injury. "We're going to fish until we're forced in," he says. He can only hope for good prices when he returns, and decent weather while he's at sea. "I might go out this time and get caught in a storm and beat my windows out. I don't know. Nobody's perfect, and it's Mother Nature. It's like driving a car: there's a high-percentage chance you could have a car accident, whether a fender-bender or a serious one. Fishing is a high-risk job," he adds. "You have to make an educated assessment and hope that it works out."

Chrisjon's description of the industry is interrupted by a bellowing voice on the wharf.

"Who's the frog race champion?" asks a man sporting a black leather jacket and a thick goatee.

Chrisjon's twins stare at the man hovering above them on the wharf. Chrisjon explains to the man that, yes, both boys were in the previous day's frog race, part of the annual Woods Harbour Days festivities, but that neither won.

"You all set?" the man asks Chrisjon, stepping aboard the *Double Mischief.*

"No, I'm going to need another half pallet of bait," Chrisjon replies.

The two men walk into the wheelhouse. Chrisjon introduces the visitor as Almond Mood. He's vice-president of James L. Mood Fisheries Ltd.

Established in 1970 by Almond's father, James, Mood Fisheries now exports an array of seafood including live lobsters, halibut, tuna, and swordfish; the company has shipped its seafood as far as Europe and Japan. Almond now runs the business with his brother Corey. Chrisjon begins to say that Almond owns 50 percent of the company.

"Now Chrisjon, don't say that," Almond says, interrupting.

Pointing to the stranger in the wheelhouse, Chrisjon tells Almond there's a book being written about the *Miss Ally.*

"Which story you writin'?" Almond asks me.

"The good side. The truth!" Chrisjon says quickly.

"No. No. He ain't writing the truth. The truth ain't going to be told," Almond snorts. "When I get on my deathbed I'll tell you the truth, okay?"

"Don't listen to him," Chrisjon tells me. "Forget I introduced ya." Turning back to Almond, he says: "See? No wonder people don't like ya, when you talk like that!"

Almond has driven the short distance from the Mood Fisheries building to the wharf in a black pickup. He clearly has some affection for Chrisjon and wants to check on his preparations for the first fishing trip of the season. They chat for a minute or so before Chrisjon announces that he has to leave to get more food from the local general store. Before Chrisjon leaves, I ask Almond to elaborate on his claim about the "truth." He laughs.

"Nobody knows the story of the story. Nobody survived to tell the story, right? In today's world, with the communications and electronics that we have, and when…experienced seamen are going to shore, don't you think you should?"

Almond is picking up momentum. He complains about the "basic fact" that many skippers lack the necessary skill or experience. He says his son, Graydon—a friend of Katlin, Joel, Cole, and Tyson's—spent $3,600 on a course that certified him as a captain. Almond describes the course as a joke, alleging it was taught by a teacher with limited experience.

"They don't know if [the student] knows which end is the front of that boat or the back of the boat. He never docked a boat. He ain't been out on the water.

They don't know what he'd do. If he opens the engine room and it's full of smoke, they don't know if he'll freeze. And they're certifying people to go fishing," he says. "Anyway, you don't want my version of anything."

Chrisjon is clearly growing restless with Almond's rant. He checks the time on his phone and says he must go get his final groceries.

"In today's world you don't have to stay out in weather. You come home. All right? That's the decision that they made," Almond continues.

Standing in the wheelhouse, he calls in Chrisjon's request for additional bait. It will soon be brought to the wharf. Almond puts his phone back in his pocket.

"That's the crime of it all," he adds before walking out of the wheelhouse and back to his truck. "That's the crime of it all."

ACKNOWLEDGMENTS

IN THE SPRING OF 2015 I NERVOUSLY DIALLED MARY AND GEORGE Hopkins's home phone number. I wanted to talk to them about their son Joel. Mary answered the call and was immediately receptive to my questions. Within days I was sitting in the Hopkins's living room in Woods Harbour, looking at photos and learning about Joel and his fellow *Miss Ally* crewmen.

This book could not have been written without the willingness of the families to discuss the sinking and the resulting loss of their loved ones. I spoke with members from four of the five families involved (Tyson's family declined). The family members I interviewed were all open and generous with their time, sitting for long stretches to discuss a topic of great personal pain. They shared memories, photos, and answered my many follow-up questions. Thank you. I am particularly indebted to Mary and George, my initial contacts in the community, as well as to Della Sears, whom I interviewed more than half a dozen times. I sincerely hope no one regrets the decision to speak with me.

In all, more than fifty people were interviewed for this book, most of them on multiple occasions. They told me about Katlin, Joel, Cole, Tyson, and Billy Jack, about the community, about fishing, and about how life has changed since the sinking. Thank you to everyone who spoke to me. No one was obligated to take my calls or answer my questions but most people did, and with little hesitation. I must give particular thanks to Sandy Stoddard and John Symonds, who answered my many questions about the *Miss Ally* and fishing in general.

I'd also like to thank the entire team at Nimbus Publishing, including Whitney Moran and especially Emily MacKinnon, my main editor, for all her excellent suggestions and changes.

A NOTE ON SOURCES

MUCH OF THE INFORMATION IN THIS BOOK WAS GLEANED FROM INTER-
views I conducted with the family members, friends, and relatives of the
Miss Ally's crew, as well as with other key people connected to the sinking,
including at the JRCC, Coast Guard, RCMP, and so on. Interviews with family members were most often conducted in person, typically in the person's
home. Follow-up interviews were done in person and by telephone. All interviews were digitally recorded to ensure the accuracy of the information and
quotes used. I also received some information via email and text message.
A number of news reports were also consulted, mainly from The Canadian
Press and the Halifax *Chronicle Herald.*

The official JRCC case log was secured through an Access to Information
request, as were the official JRCC case review, internal emails related to the
case, and the audio clips of Katlin and others speaking with JRCC officers
on February 17, 2013.

Information about the 1974 sinking of the *Colville Bay* was found in
long-sealed government documents, including the case log, which were also
secured through an Access to Information request.

Information about the sinking of the *Sir Echo* in 1950 was taken largely
from *A Sea Tragedy: Wood's Harbour, 1950*, a limited-run local publication
by Theodora Amiro, Marilyn MacDonald-MacKenzie, and JoAnne (Cline)
Newell. (Sentinel Printing Limited, 1977.)

Much of the historical information concerning past fishing losses was drawn from the three volumes of *Lost Mariners of Shelburne County*:

Robertson Smith, Eleanor, ed. *Lost Mariners of Shelburne County: As Inscribed on the Fishermen's Memorial Unveiled 1990 Shelburne, Nova Scotia.* Stoneycroft Publishing, 1991.

Stoddart Terry, Patricia, ed. *Lost Mariners of Shelburne County, Volume II: Commemorated on Memorials at Woods Harbour, Shag Harbour, Cape Sable Island, Nova Scotia or in Accounts of Marine Disasters from 1789–1990.* Stoneycroft Publishing, 1991.

Wray Nickerson, Debbie. *Lost Mariners of Shelburne County, Volume III: Those Who Were Lost or Died at Sea from Barrington Passage, Port LaTour, Baccaro and Other Areas of Shelburne County, 1767–2003,* ed. Kimberley Robertson Walker. Stoneycroft Publishing, 2009.

Other works requiring mention include:

Bruce, Peter. *Adlard Coles' Heavy Weather Sailing: Thirtieth Anniversary Edition.* Camden, Maine: Ragged Mountain Press, 1999.

Hamilton, William B. *Place Names of Atlantic Canada.* Toronto: University of Toronto Press, 1996.

Junger, Sebastian. *The Perfect Storm: A True Story of Men Against the Sea.* New York: W. W. Norton & Company, 1997.

Woods Harbour Women's Auxiliary. *Then and Now: Community Change.* Woods Harbour, 2008.

Many photos in this book were generously provided by family members (on pages 15, 21, 25, 55, 66, 69, 73, 81, 83, 87, 105). Others are from The Canadian Press (109, 164, 237), Facebook (41, 43, 51, 91), and the Department of National Defence (151, 169, 189, 191). I took three of the photos myself (19, 171, 219).

Callen Singer

ABOUT THE AUTHOR

QUENTIN CASEY IS A JOURNALIST WHO CONTRIBUTES REGULARLY TO the *Financial Post*, *Atlantic Business*, and *Saltscapes* magazine. Based in Mahone Bay, Nova Scotia, he is also the author of *Joshua Slocum: The Captain Who Sailed Around the World*.

A portion of royalties from the sale of this book are being donated to causes connected with the *Miss Ally* sinking, including: the Katlin Nickerson Memorial Bursary, the Joel Hopkins Memorial ATV Poker Rally, the Kid's Fair Play FUNd (a sports, recreation, and culture program in Shelburne County), and the Cole Nickerson Memorial Hockey Tournament bursary.